The Reach of Criticism

THE REACH
OF CRITICISM

Method and Perception in Literary Theory

PAUL H. FRY

Yale University Press
New Haven and London

Published with assistance from the Louis Effingham deForest Memorial Fund.

Designed by Nancy Ovedovitz and set in VIP Bembo type.
Printed in the United States of America by Murray Printing Company, Westford, Massachusetts.

Library of Congress Cataloging in Publication Data
Fry, Paul H.
    The reach of criticism.
    Bibliography: p.
    Includes index.
    1. Criticism. I. Title.
PN81.F73   1983   801'.95   83-3535
ISBN 0-300-02924-1

10   9   8   7   6   5   4   3   2   1

To my parents

Like the elements of which we are composed, the action of these forces extends beyond us; it rusts iron and ripens corn. Far out on every side of us those elements are broadcast, driven by many forces; and birth and gesture and death and the springing of violets from the grave are but a few out of ten thousand resultant combinations. That clear, perpetual outline of face and limb is but an image of ours, under which we group them—a design in a web, the actual threads of which pass out beyond it.

Walter Pater, "Conclusion," in *The Renaissance*

Persona: that through which sound passes.

Walter Benjamin, "Karl Kraus"

CONTENTS

ACKNOWLEDGMENTS

I should like to thank the following persons most especially for their advice and criticism: Hans Frei, Harris Friedberg, Ellen Graham, Geoffrey Hartman, John Hollander, Ronald Paulson, Brigitte Peucker, Richard Poirier, and Thomas Whitaker. An article by Jerrold E. Hogle, "Shelley's Poetics: The Power as Metaphor" (*K-SJ* 31 [1982], 159–97) has anticipated my treatment of Shelley in many ways, and I regret that I came to know it too late to make use of it in my argument. I am grateful for permission to reprint a substantial portion of my last chapter from "The Image of Walter Benjamin," in *Raritan* (Spring 1983).

INTRODUCTION

Method in Interpretation

To write a critique of method, which is the aim of this book, one does not need to suppose that the ways of critical understanding—of one's own critique, for example—are in themselves immethodical. Being "against method," I share with Paul Feyerabend an emphasis on the irreducible preselectivity of perception, but I disagree with his assumption that this emphasis perforce entails an "anarchistic theory of knowledge."[1] That there is method in our inadvertencies is such an old and clearly established paradox in nearly all fields of cognitive inquiry that it scarcely bears repeating. Preselectivity, whether it be unconscious, ideological, or simply, in general, what Hans-Georg Gadamer calls "prejudiced,"[2] is of course methodical—so intensely so, indeed, that it makes the firmest efforts at formal thinking seem absentminded by comparison. I shall finally argue, in fact, that the doggedness of preselectivity is itself what makes method in interpretation necessarily absentminded in proportion to its rigor.

But however relentless the forces of error may be, we cannot study their effects as though they were structurally constant. In a book whose main informing principle in some ways anticipates mine, *Blindness and Insight*, Paul de Man argues compellingly that the findings of critics "about the structure of texts contradict the general conception they use as their model," and that furthermore "they seem to thrive on" this discrepancy "and owe their best insights to the assumptions those insights disprove."[3] We find de Man at an opposite extreme, then, from that of Feyerabend among cognitive skeptics; whereas Feyerabend presupposes the anarchy of knowledge, de Man presupposes the dialectically obverse patterning of knowledge by repression. But to discern any definite symmetry between method and result (within the canon of what de Man would call "authentic" critical discourse), one must first suppose that "insight" is always an insight concerning structure that is itself structurally constituted. To be sure, the term *structure* could easily be invoked to cover all cases, but in my view the structural properties of knowledge and of its objects are just what will always remain, to one indeterminate degree or another, obscured by the activity of knowing. To contend that a second and more answerable structure is what subverts an interpretive model is simply to invert, without qualification, the contention of E. D. Hirsch, among others, that a second and more answerable "corrigible schema" is what corrects an interpretive model.[4] I shall argue, in contrast with both these latter views, that the connection between error and insight is a necessary one yet cannot be characterized with consistency.

My own view of method is perhaps closest in spirit to that of Gadamer, who derives his sense of the "fore-structure" of understanding from Heidegger's analysis of the hermeneutic circle.[5] Gadamer's enabling assertion, that we are "always already" (*immer schon*) implicated within the history toward which our methodologies would claim a detached perspective, is indispensable to any critique of method. Nevertheless, my disagreement with Gadamer's way of rehabilitating "prejudice" (*Vorurteil*) is if anything deeper and more surely founded than my disagreement with Feyerabend or with de Man. Following Heidegger's distinction between the "fore-having" (*Vorhabe*) of unfounded prejudice and the "fore-conception" (*Vorgriff*) of knowledge that corresponds to actuality, Gadamer rescues truth from the jaws of doubt by arguing that there are salutary prejudices as well as crippling ones. The former we are said to derive not from caprice but from tradition (*Überlieferung*), a category that is also hallowed by Heidegger. Thus if our way into the hermeneutic circle is "Traditionell"—if, that is, in the case of texts, it is graced by historical empathy—then, subject to correction by our experience of anomaly in specific matters, our way toward the truth at the center of the circle can be safely assured (*Truth and Method*, pp. 251–53).

Gadamer's faith in tradition reflects a much happier view of temporality ("historicity") than most persons can hope to share. Temporality, he writes, "is not a yawning abyss, but is filled with the continuity of custom and tradition" (ibid., p. 264). Although this is a cheerful view, it is not unfair to notice the implicit politics that Gadamer here inherits from Heidegger, a politics more clearly present in (to cite a well-known example) the advocacy of cultural and racial homogeneity in T. S. Eliot's late writings. From my own standpoint it is indeed not unfair to broadcast this very serious criticism once again, not because I think it necessary to apologize time and again for an interest in politically liable writers, but because it is just those who themselves most blithely invoke tradition who have most frequently complained that any qualified attitude—like my own—toward the fruits of historical understanding harbors what is politically the most dangerous stance of all. But to all progressive axioms one can oppose a rival phrase, "The Ruins of Time," which has itself ebbed and flowed with the tide of history. It appears as the title of a poem by Spenser which questions the archaeological optimism of the Humanists; it appears in Blake's letter to William Hayley of 6 May 1800 as a law of apocalyptic compensation ("The ruins of Time build mansions in Eternity"); and it recurs, albeit feebly, skeptically, throughout the work of Walter Benjamin, whose witness to the return of barbarism will in part occupy the final pages of this book.

In the force-field of "methodology," every theorist will reduce all rival terms to trivial synonymity while proclaiming the irreducibility of his own. Thus the most breathtaking turn of a recent history-oriented review of modern criticism by Frank Lentricchia is his conclusion that the old formalists and the newer poststructuralists are, as he puts it, "flipsides of the same coin."[6] Taken in a reductive spirit, this is a justifiable observation, but it can be achieved only by disregarding, of necessity, the critique of form itself, as a concept, which led, for some critics, "beyond formalism." There remains a sense in which the metaformalist is not, or at least not essentially, a formalist manqué, and it is that sense that I wish to arrive at and develop in the present book. Because method is itself, as method, formalistic, including the historical method that Lentricchia prefers, I shall choose to play down the current and very lively methodological conflict that interests him, the conflict between the ontology of art as form and the historical nature of art as production, in order to concentrate instead on the tension, in the history of criticism and at present, between the objective of form in interpretation and its more radical alternatives—the sublime, the "grace" beyond the reach of art, and the modes of recognition that are themselves dislocations of form.

At the end of the book I shall return to consider the fallacy of misplaced concreteness that in many cases characterizes the currently resurgent emphasis on the priority of history in interpretation. The cry of "history" seems mistaken only partly because, for the purposes of interpretation, historical discourse tends to be abstract and concrete in just the wrong places; it is also possible to suppose—and admittedly one can do no more than suppose—that the representation of being rather than the representation of social conditions is the primary motivation of all writing. In this view, lyric would invoke being openly, while narrative and drama would solicit being indirectly from the domains of existence and praxis, respectively. The belief is at least tenable that written texts are not to be understood most radically as modes of production but as modes of substitution, as ways of recovering the experience of being. Writing, even pamphleteering, pursues an intensity in the activity of thought that is almost a sensation and is *not* the thought itself. The desire to write is not itself, therefore, the desire to represent, evade, or reform "objective existing conditions," even though very probably it cannot appear in isolation from what Aristotle called the instinct for imitation. This qualifier would not seem surprising if mimesis itself were once seen as a displacement of the urge to reproduce being. Here in any case, if not before, the lines must be drawn, as I take it, between interpretation that is historical and interpretation that neither resists nor overdetermines the evidences of history.

It is misleading to say that, with our fractured memories, we fully or systematically "forget" the past. Rather we know it invariably as a ruin, even if it is no further away than the previous instant. I hope to recover this caveat from the useless gloom of Pyrrhonism. Borrowing the term *distraction (Zerstreuung)* from Benjamin, I shall attempt to show that the forehaving of error is itself a way of knowing, our only way of knowing, indeed, but still a fortunate one. Although in the long run I shall attempt an obliquely theoretical defense of this idea, I remain so chary of method that I prefer to let my position take shape through examples. Thus I have chosen first to show how method goes wrong in an actual text, one that is famous as a model of method, and then to illustrate the virtues of texts in which method is, in various ways, disregarded. Having begun with the formalism of Aristotle's *Poetics,* I shall then offer Longinus's *On the Sublime* as a model of the sort of criticism that does what will not, perhaps cannot, be done by the Aristotelian reader. After that I shall take a favorable view of opposite extremes, not in "the Longinian heritage" (there certainly is no such thing) but within what could be called, for reasons that will appear, Longinian thinking. These extremes are represented by Dryden's "Preface to *Fables*" and by Shelley's *Defence of Poetry.* In a fifth chapter I develop a personal view of method, one that is mediated especially by the work and example of Walter Benjamin.

Any method entails two fundamental disadvantages. The first has already been mentioned: within the constraint of method the necessarily incommensurable implication of the interpreter in the interpreted is denied, with the result that the effects of that implication are unheeded rather than foreseen, even if some definite ratio of prejudice has been taken into account. The second disadvantage is that method, which is always configuration, is precisely that aspect of thought which falsifies the representation of experience in its temporality.

The first of these propositions can be illustrated with a series of methodologically conditioned but widely differing passages. Here, for example, is the response of Georg Lukács to the Modernist novel: "Joyce uses Dublin, Kafka and Musil the Hapsburg Monarchy, as the locus of their masterpieces. But the locus they lovingly depict is little more than a backcloth; it is not basic to their artistic intention."[7] A nicely modulated view is struggling to emerge in these sentences: with "lovingly" and "little more than," Lukács concedes that the historical engagement of these writers is more than perfunctory. But in its main thrust his assertion remains tenable only as long as it is considered abstractly. While it is true enough that all three novelists render society for consciousness rather than vice versa, the poverty of the critic's response appears in his refusal to do justice to their rendering regardless of what it is "for," and in his omitting to mention that each of the three is subjective in a differing degree. What is most pertinent to mention here, though, is the implication of Lukács himself in his critique. His criticism of Modernist narrative for its inwardness is itself no less an analysis of consciousness—and no more disapproving of the inwardness of consciousness—than the fictive analyses of Joyce, Kafka, and perhaps even Musil themselves. The irony of this observation deepens when one recalls how much Lukács himself disliked "mythology," which for him was the tendency to impose sameness, through reification, on diverse materials. It was Lukács who wrote what could stand as a motto for the present argument: "Mythology inevitably adopts the structure of the problem whose opacity had been the cause of its own birth."[8]

Another interesting implication of criticism in its object may have been written tongue in cheek, but if so, it is Northrop Frye's clandestine way of casting doubt on the otherwise continuous claim of his *Anatomy of Criticism* to be a science. He must certainly have noticed how easily his own name could have appeared in the following list, and that that would have made him the exemplar of an epoch—or "mode"—and not its dispassionate anatomist: "We have Nietzsche proclaiming the advent of a new divine power in man, a proclamation which is somewhat confused by including a theory of identical recurrence. We have Yeats telling us that the Western cycle is nearly over and that a new Classical one, with Leda and the swan taking the place of the dove and the virgin, is about to begin. We have Joyce and his Viconian theory of history which sees our own age as a frustrated apocalypse followed instantly by a return to the period before Tristram."[9] And we have Frye, a skilled ironist, hoping to begin a revolution of myth from irony back to romance by declaring from time to time that the revolution is now taking place.

When more machinery is brought in, with a more authoritarian tone and fewer practical results, the implication of method in its field of study is less admirably exuberant than it is in Frye. Here is Hans Robert Jauss's critique of Gadamer's ontologically based notion of the literary "classic" that is accessible for all eras: "This concept of art may hold true for the humanistic period, but not for the preceding medieval period and definitely not for the succeeding period of modernity, in which the aesthetics of mimesis has lost its authority like the metaphysics of substance . . . which founded it."[10] The flaw in this statement is the fact that the classic is no longer held to be permanent primarily because critics like Jauss have inverted Gadamer's perspective and made novelty the only permanence and indeed the only means of becoming visible in literary history, thus pre-shaping, like Gadamer (and in accordance with Gadamer's own formula for all interpretation), the history of which they purport to be detached observers.

The temptation to suppose that we can hypostasize our subjectivity in order to transcend or at least bracket it is incomparably great, of course, but it must be remembered in reproof of this hope that the subject itself becomes an object in proportion as it is reflected upon, paradoxically ceasing to be aware of its self-identical nature in becoming conscious of itself, while the object takes the shape of the subject in proportion as the subject remains unself-conscious. We know these things well enough in everyday life: some objects are inward, like the Freudian id ("it") and superego, while some subjects can be objectified only in their projections as doubles, epigones, children, and so on. What method supposes is that these and other perceptual imbalances can be factored out of objectivity. But it should be clear—and not at all shocking or depressing—that even where one's purpose is to decide whether Hamlet said "solid" or "sullied" the preselectivity of the interpreter cannot be eliminated with certainty from the methods of, for example, philology. Even within the scientific method, as Thomas Kuhn has influentially argued, the context of experimental research consists of the categories that are pedagogically or socially predestined to appear.[11] In denying the possibility of estrangement between subject and object, finally, one may also doubt its value supposing that it were possible; for estrangement, alienation, and not "detachment," is what it would be. A safer and, as I will show, potentially more accurate critical stance emerges at the moment when subject and object are not only commingled but seem also to be, each in itself, unstable and fluid.

My second complaint against method will require more diverse illustration and comment, although it can begin succinctly enough with the observation that method as such is what constitutes the necessary error of any given representation. It is here that the largely tacit analogy that informs much of this book will be clearest, the analogy, that is, between methodology in criticism and form taken as the object of criticism. The value of method and the significance of form alike can be affirmed only insofar as one accepts the metaphorization of time as space. Formal thought decreases in fidelity to experience as its formal properties increase. It is prone to distort, misapply, or misunderstand the relationship between space and time that is actually available to experience. What needs to be reconsidered in order for this to be apparent is what Joseph Frank called "spatial form" in his well-known study of modern fiction.[12] Frank's concept has often been criticized, I think with justice, for minimizing the processual aspect of writing and reading. Even when his concept is reaffirmed in modified form, it is still not quite satisfactory. *Static* spatiality, says W. J. T. Mitchell, for instance, is indeed outmoded and Newtonian, but all experience is still saturated and determined by "relative" spatiality. Thus spatial experience has an element of time, and vice versa, so that each dimension is symmetrical with respect to the other.[13] What makes this compromise attractive is its implication that if the world itself is thus formal, it may be possible to approximate it closely in formal categories.

Surely, however, space and time cannot be balanced in representation in the same way that they are balanced in experience. In representation, space—the space of the universe, for example—cannot be imagined other than spatially; it cannot even be grasped as "space-time" unless one resorts to such visual aids as the Möbius strip. Experience moves toward the opposite extreme: even a very small picture-plane is not a "spatial form" but reveals itself to us, as we "read" it, predominantly in time. It is and is known to be in space-time, but it is experienced primarily in time. As for the representation of time, it too takes place, like the representation of space only not as exclusively, primarily in space. We refer ourselves to the duration of an experience necessarily in freeze-frames. But in experience we know time solely *as* time, in its nonsuspension. We can feel it slow down and speed up, as it were, probably in accordance with the frequency of repetition of which we are conscious at a given moment, but no spatialization is involved. Time does not "unfold" except when we represent it to ourselves as it happens.

There can be no formal liaison, then, neither an analogy or a completely mirrored opposition, between representation and experience in spatiotemporal terms. There can be no spatial equivalent for time because space is not symmetrical with respect to time in any accessible framework of knowledge. If there can never be a form of representation that corresponds to an interval of time, the spatialization by which all formalism pursues its course is not only not valid for all cases but is not wholly valid for any. Category fosters recognition metonymically, by the successive appearances of a family resemblance, and not synecdochically, by the inclusion of parts in a whole.

Thus, what results from method is the oversimplification of criticism by oversophistication. Methodical criticism fails in responsiveness and subtlety while fairly bristling with untenable distinctions. I have already mentioned the misplacement of abstraction and concreteness alike in much historical interpretation. An exaggerated instance is the one derisively offered as a travesty of his own method by the Marxist critic Umberto Barbaro. He cites "a young Italian critic" who declared "that impressionism and the *plein-air* pictorial style derived from the use of tin, which made possible the creation of tubes of prepared paint" for carrying into the field.[14] I find even this explanation fascinating, in fact, not as an instance of method but as a suggestively imaginative exercise in the alignment of information. In my view even the most sophisticated sociohistorical accounts of art differ from this one in degree but not in kind, more often than not sacrificing the interest of this one to the duty of plausible comprehensiveness.

The blunting of interpretation by method is more intricately reflected in an alleged crux offered by E. D. Hirsch to illustrate "the decisive function of generic expectations." In a discussion of "A Valediction Forbidding Mourning," says Hirsch, one of his classes insisted that the poem was not about the parting of lovers but about dying—and could not be dissuaded except by the teacher's appeal to the correct "intrinsic genre," after which everything was cleared up. The class made "not only a subtle [!] mistake in identifying a particular type of simile but also a genre mistake in confusing one type of farewell with another."[15] The students then proceeded, phrase by phrase, to put the wrong coloring on everything, with nothing in the poem, Hirsch says in their defense (see *Validity in Interpretation,* p. 74), to stop them from continuing to go wrong. This is a surprising report. The mistake about the simile—"As . . . so"—is by no means "subtle," unless these students had encountered other similes in which the term of comparison is compared with itself. (Or if "As" means "during the time when," then we must suppose the poem to be about a pair of intimates who plan to synchronize their death with that of virtuous men.) The misreading performed by this class, and misreading in general for Hirsch, too closely resembles the overstrain of prolonged misunderstanding in comic dialogue.

In one respect, anyone who is not trying very hard to misconstrue can see that this poem is not about dying. Hirsch is needlessly complicating matters with his insistence on the need for proper expectations. For practical purposes, choosing between expectations of this broad, "generic" kind only becomes a crucial matter with trick newspaper headlines or more truly controversial literary cruces. And in any case, if it were really a matter of making an informed choice between "types of farewell," many readers who understand the poem tolerably well would not even have known how to proceed with it. These are the overcomplications, in this instance, of method. But their net effect is to oversimplify. Although the problem as stated is slight or nonexistent, the solution as stated is ultimately invalid. Donne's "Valediction" *is,* after all, arguably as much about, and as much occasioned by, the intimation of death as it is about the parting of lovers. Concerned with the trepidation of all spheres, it is a love-poem inching toward the more openly Christian-moralist framework of the later poems, with the first two stanzas its minatory death's-head. We recognize the topic of death as a preoccupation, the burden of a mood, for which it would be hard to imagine a sufficiently distinct schema or "intrinsic genre." Another turn of the screw and this would be a penitential and renunciatory poem. And yet, decidedly, it is not; it would be soberly sad only if mourning were not expressly forbidden in its title. Thus it is not solely about love or death, and finally it is not about love *as* death, despite the suggestion of *petit mort* in the compass image.

There is no need for a machine to arrive at the plain sense of a text—and any machine, once it is in place, constrains us within the plain sense. Hirsch is an experienced reader with a subtle and elegant mind. He has no doubt noticed everything mentioned above, and much more, but rejected it from the sphere of "meaning," consigning it instead to the areas of "symptom" or "significance"—or perhaps to what he calls "the dim penumbra of meaning" (ibid., pp. 61–62). So imperious is his method, though, that it overcomplicates by oversimplification not just occasionally but regularly. Of the first ten lines of *Paradise Lost* Hirsch says: "To understand these lines an immense amount of relevant knowledge is required" (ibid., p. 83). This is disputable: a normal amount should suffice, or perhaps less (the story is a familiar one), simply to get at the plain sense. Total understanding is another matter, and Hirsch presumes it too quickly in supposing that "happy seat" can be substituted for "blissful seat" (1.5) without changing the intrinsic genre of Milton's proemium. The word *happy* alone would have prompted the reader to expect, not *Paradise Lost,* but a Calvinist poem on the theme of predestination. No more crucial change of intrinsic genre could be imagined. Or could it? Some readers of "the Devil's party" might insist, after all, despite God's disclaimer of book 3, not precisely that *blissful* is synonymous with *happy* but rather that *blissful* is a tellingly forced substitute for *happy,* a word which would have more candidly anticipated the poet's resentment of God. Just as Donne's "Valediction" is and is not about dying, then, so Milton's adjective and Hirsch's substitute are and are not synonymous.

Hirsch's examples thus tend to undermine themselves in such a way that the refuted error proves more fruitful—and neither more nor less valid—than its correction. This suggests, among other things, that in actuality there are no fewer intrinsic genres than there are utterances to put in them. Although in the present remarks I will not discuss the problem here touched upon, namely, the linguistic character of all thinking and the consequent unavailability of the saving distinction between discourse and the generic idea *(signifié)* to which it refers, that issue will recur everywhere in this book. I would maintain for the moment, in any case, that interpretation, as it continues beyond the simple parsing for which common usage is in most cases a sufficient guide, must outdistance the generic subdivisions made available by any method.

All critical methods honor the norm of consistent explanation, consistency being itself the "spatial form" of knowledge, "our basis for making history and temporality intelligible."[16] Of course, then, consistency is in some measure necessary, even unavoidable; in our rush to profess bafflement we forget how little there is in our experience that is altogether unintelligible. But among the attributes of critical intelligence the function of consistency, like that of form, has been overvalued. We are too much inclined to suppose, without compelling reason, that because thinking necessarily begins with the perception of some difference—and in this rudimentary sense method is indeed the ground of knowledge—it must also necessarily end by promoting that difference to a law of nonidentity, a law which is self-identical and serves to suppress or reject the differences that continue to present themselves. Most critics believe that they have achieved consistency only when they have reduced their working terms to two, or at least to pairs. And perhaps, in the interest of consistency, they are right. But what I shall attempt more than once to show, alternatively, is that the best moments in theory and practice occur when the two sides of a system nearly collapse into one, or many, resisting rather than hurrying toward the inevitable closure of category.

As I shall argue in my final chapter, it is only the inspired category-*mistake* that can narrow the distance between representation and experience. I shall be defending what Vico called "imaginative metaphysics," which "shows that man becomes all things by *not* understanding them"[17]—that is, by giving up the attempt to shelter the objects of perception from the formless flow of time in which perceiver and perceived are alike immersed. The commonplace objection to formalism in literature may be directed at least as appropriately against method in interpretation: as it becomes more consistent and thus more sophisticated in the use of its operative terms, method finally becomes internally rather than referentially consistent. It becomes self-reflexive, that is, and has less and less to do with experience. Method is meant to secure exactitude, yet commitment to method is probably the main cause of strife in interpretation. The following pages are written not least in the hope that what some call the "discipline" of letters is best served as a persistent grasp upon the diversity that marks experience, not as a struggle for the unnatural stillness of consensus.

ONE

Aristotle as Oedipus: Form and Recognition in the *Poetics*

The reputation of the *Poetics* at present is not easy to characterize. Aristotle has not been given much careful attention by the critical schools that have flourished in recent years, yet most students of criticism continue to agree that the *Poetics* is a document of unparalleled importance.[1] Few can agree even in part, however, when it comes to defining its importance. There has never been a consensus interpretation of Aristotle; the eccentric yet superbly consistent polymath of Gerald Else is only the most recent of the great Aristotles who would scarcely recognize one another. In this chapter, emboldened by this lack of consensus, I shall hazard still another view of the *Poetics,* one that questions Aristotle's authority, to some extent, by stressing the drawbacks of his attitude toward literature for the practice of contemporary criticism.[2]

Aristotle is the parent, not of criticism, but of a major critical tradition, one that can be said largely to have determined the nature and function of academic criticism in this century. This tradition passes from the several stages of neoclassicism to the "organicism" of Coleridge (tempered, of course, by a great deal else) and on to the climate of aestheticism that fostered the translation and commentary of S. H. Butcher. In our century Aristotle is invoked by some as a prophet of realism, I think wrongly, and by others on account of his formal values—rightly, I think, but to the detriment of criticism. So defined, this tradition obviously casts a broad net, but it does not include everything. In my view the authority of Aristotle should be supplemented, and in some respects superseded, by that of Longinus. Aristotle's formalism not only averts the attention of criticism from much that is valuable in literature but also hinders a just estimate of what remains. In defense of this assertion, and on the supposition that an inductive argument is no stronger than its understanding of the data it uses to build its case,[3] I shall extend my attention to include not only Aristotle's literary principles but also his performance as a reader, especially as a reader of the *Odyssey* and the *Oedipus.*

There is a simple and also a rather complex way of summarizing my view of the *Poetics* in advance. The simple way is to say that Aristotle dislikes both unenclosed and overly contracted spaces. His formalism modifies the shape of the universe in order to avoid its vertigo and its perilous straits.[4] To what is implied here it will be objected very properly that the clinical character of an idea—or rather, say its instinctual character—need have little or nothing to do with its value, especially if the idea remains a flexible one. I think, though, that in his preoccupation with form Aristotle is not altogether flexible, except in the hands of friendly interpreters whose formalism (thanks to him, of course) is in fact subtler than his. It must be admitted, on the other hand, that his position seems modest when contrasted with later and more controversially extreme views of the purpose of art. The great Modernists very openly thought of form as a kind of protection and also as a mainstay: "These things I have shored against my ruins," wrote the author of a poem that fences off the waste land. Much more firmly shored up in later years, Eliot was able to quiz his contemporary I. A. Richards for wanting the modern critic constantly to bear in mind "the inconceivable immensity of the universe."[5] T. E. Hulme was appalled as a young man by the flat prairies of Canada and later associated his preference for "geometric" art with "space-shyness," "the fear that makes certain people unable to cross open spaces."[6]

It is only when the idea of formal order becomes definitely totalitarian, then, as in Wyndham Lewis's *Time and Western Man,* that the defiance of time by form clearly betrays a hysterical basis, and the space-shyness of the *Poetics* is not like that, of course. It is not even noticeable unless it is seen to have set going a drift toward bottlenecks of every kind. Which brings me to the complex way of summarizing what follows: Aristotle's rage for order, the "narrower" and more "concentrated" the better (ch. 26), leads to moments, primarily though not entirely at the level of the tragic plot, in which characters who are too intimate overcrowd one another and threaten to break out of their confines with violence.[7] The *pathos,* or "tragic incident," that occurs in such close quarters is brought on by the recognition of what could have been kept hidden in a less constricting situation, the recognition, that is, of the kinship or intimacy *(philia)* of antagonists. The irony of Aristotle's critical predicament is that his formalism, with its bringing to the fore of likenesses and affinities and its praise of the craftsman who has "an eye for resemblances" (ch. 22; concerning the making of metaphors), tends to ensure the coming to light of just the sort of unruliness that the observance of proportion is meant to suppress. Thus the *Poetics* itself imitates the kind of poetry with which it is chiefly concerned. For all its serenely decisive, authoritative appearance, the *Poetics* reflects a "tragic" reversal of theoretical intention whereby its innermost defenses turn against it and threaten its composure. One might call the *Poetics* Aristotle's Recognition Scene (for certainly it does harbor implications for every aspect of his philosophy) except that he does not seem to have recognized his recognition. What we can recognize in his predicament, though, is the dilemma of his favorite hero, Oedipus.

I

Both in Plato's *Republic* and in the *Poetics* one finds the first avatars of Wordsworth's "Child" in the "Intimations Ode," who passes through a period at the age of about six when it seems "As if his whole vocation / Were endless imitation." "The instinct of imitation," writes Aristotle, "is implanted in man from childhood" (ch. 4; see bk. 3 of the *Republic*). In Aristotle's view, we can infer, the child is not yet a mature "maker" of plays, for whom action would take precedence over character; like Wordsworth's "little actor," he "cons another part," because "novices in the art" are best at "precision of portraiture" (ch. 6). Presumably Aristotle's child, then, like Wordsworth's, spends time comparing pictures of people with their originals and saying " 'Ah, that is he' " (ch. 4. Bywater's translation: "gathering the meaning of things").[8]

All agree, in short, that the dramatist who imitates *praxis,* or action, began as a child by imitating *ethos,* or character. Evidently so, because neither the Aristotelian nor the Wordsworthian child has yet learned the practical arts and maxims of maturity: that the end of knowledge is virtuous action *(Nicomachean Ethics)* or that it is best to serve Duty "strictly" ("Ode to Duty"). The child is a primitive whose "rude improvisations" (*Poetics,* ch. 4; concerning the earliest poets) will not submit to the forms of art or life. Aristotle subdues that tendency by enjoining the dramatist to give up his youthful love of characterization. Wordsworth's child-mimic too must suffer anxiety concerning the order of things as a result of his attention to character. He is beamed on by his father, the sun (l. 91), and "fretted by sallies of his mother's kisses" (l. 90). His first impressions, which must strike him with preternatural force, are impressions of his parents' characters. Almost of necessity, drama for the male child envisioned by both Aristotle and Wordsworth is oedipal drama in its first stages of displacement; it presents an ideal father and a mother who seems interfering and frivolous, like the Jocasta who shoos Oedipus offstage as if he were a little boy and later tells him not to bother with oracles.

Thus the wrong kind of curiosity—concerning the foundations rather than the practical masks of personality—places the forms and restraints of civilization in danger. In fact, the very concept of man is threatened by immaturity. More than once Aristotle is at pains to distinguish children from animals, but it is not easy for him to do so. Children are not different in kind from animals but only in degree, being "the most imitative of living creatures" (ch. 4; Wordsworth's Child gambols like a lamb and keeps holiday with "every Beast"). Now, in that case, presumably, the *techne* of maturity, however calm and masterful, will still accommodate, or at least bear traces of, the conditions from which it emerged. But Aristotle resists this probability. He takes such care to separate the rude improvisations of art from its maturity that he ends by weeding out whatever seems at all unruly, or even dynamic.

Another passage in which Aristotle draws a line between human beings and beasts is the one at the beginning of the chapter on *lexis,* where he declares that the smallest unit of verbal imitation, and also the most fundamental, is the "letter." It may seem odd that he goes to such trouble to define a component that has no intrinsic value, but he does so with reason. In turning to language, a far more satisfactorily closed system than the tendencies of human nature can ever be, he seizes the occasion to distinguish men from beasts more categorically than hitherto: "A Letter is an indivisible sound, yet not every such sound, but only one which forms part of a group of sounds. For even brutes utter indivisible sounds, none of which I call a letter" (ch. 22). Feeling and emotion cannot enter into the definition of language because brutes too make noises expressing pleasure and pain, as Aristotle makes clear in a passage (*Politics* 1253a) that excludes not only brutes but also, presumably, children, from the polity: "Mere voice" belongs to all beasts, who use it perhaps nearly as well as the poets whose improvisations comprised the infancy of literary history, but "the power of speech is intended to set forth the expedient and the inexpedient, the just and the unjust . . . and the association of living beings who have this sense makes a family and a state."[9] Thus one can advance very quickly from the mere letter to the whole family of values that is represented in the kind of tragedy Aristotle admires.

The letter parallels the very largest units of tragic structure in being an "indivisible" unit, not in itself significant, which fits according to certain rules with other units to make a significant whole—just as a person who is properly *philos* fits into a family or a state. Thus, from the smallest to the largest unit of Aristotle's materials for poetic making, every precaution is taken to show that tragedy is the best form of human art because it is from that form, *as* a form, that everything we are inclined to call "tragic" in life— whatever disrupts our existence or wounds us—is necessarily excluded. As John Jones has remarked, "It is the fact of change which Aristotle finds essentially tragic, not the direction of change."[10] As we shall see at length, the function of action in Aristotle is not only to subdue the volatility of character but also to negate itself, in effect, by reducing movement to pattern.

The *Poetics* reads most coherently as a set of syntagmatic rules. Had Aristotle been a modern semiotician, he could have simplified his task considerably by starting from the letter and declaring that all six parts of tragedy are "lexical" and therefore encoded in both parallel and overlapping ways. He could have spoken of Plot, which, even as it flashes upon the mind of the poet, is nonexistent apart from the words he rehearses it with (as the last paragraphs of chapter 7 seem to concede); of Character and Thought, which are either expressed in the *lexis* or else manifest only as functions of plot, which in turn is manifest only either in the words which recount it or in the stylization of masked gestures; of the *lexis* itself, considered in this case not merely as Diction but as the system of signs within which the other five "parts" must appear; and finally of Music and Spectacle, which are systems of signs in their own right, like "plot" understood as a dumbshow—of all six parts, in short, which are thus homologous if not, in fact, very nearly interchangeable. Accordingly we speak of the "enactment of character" or "the embodiment of plot."

Aristotle could have effected all these reductions without serious violence to his idea of poetry, then, except in one respect: for him, mere "parts" at every level of organization must be subordinated to something not themselves, to a "whole" (itself a part at a higher level of organization) that precedes, presupposes, and shapes their relations. For Aristotle, in other words, the whole alone has the force *(dunamis)* to make the parts significant. It brings them alive; or so Aristotle claims, for example, in the paragraph of the *Politics* that precedes the one quoted earlier; "The state is by nature clearly prior to the family and to the individual, since the whole is necessarily prior to the part; for example, if the whole body be destroyed there will be no foot or hand, except in an equivocal sense, as we might speak of a stone hand."[11] But one must presuppose a very great deal to conclude unhesitatingly that only wholes can be alive. Perhaps, indeed, it is only wholes that are not alive. Molière's *Dom Juan,* that un-Aristotelian serious comedy, with its stone guest that falls upon the criminal like Aristotle's "statue of Mitys at Argos" (ch. 9; the passage may be inserted by a scribe), would appear to have played a subtle but effective joke on the assumption that what is significant is always vital. In that play the stony hand of destiny is pointed toward the living clay on which it will soon fall. When it falls it makes a rubble of its own dust mixed with the dust of Dom Juan's mortal remains. What then is significant here, life or death, part or whole? The only unity Molière respects is the unity of pulverization. The *sparagmos* of the Stone Guest, like that of Humpty-Dumpty, is part of tragedy that Aristotle's insistence on the living whole cannot account for: no amount of effort can put such creatures together again.

The question at issue, which is a crucial one, is whether Aristotle's concept of form in the *Poetics* fosters the vitality of art, as he claims, or actually leaves out everything but its own mechanics. Aristotle always argues that the vital center—*psuche*—of a structure is a thing standing wholly apart from any system of signification. It is a First Cause. Partly for this reason, perhaps, he says that "recognition by signs" (ch. 16; *anagnorisis . . . dia ton semeion*) is "the least artistic form" of recognition—an assertion that is surely arguable, and one that will prove worthwhile to return to.[12] What he wants to do, here and elsewhere, is to identify form with force and to relegate mere signs to those outermost reaches of legitimate representation that even force can reduce to order only with the greatest difficulty. And yet the logic of his general definition of art consistently undermines this aim. In the *Metaphysics* (1070a) the making of art is distinguished from the mere inward metabolism of nature as "a principle of movement in something other than the thing moved."[13] What is not clear is the degree to which, in this case, the approaching force of art must lose its charge, as it were, when it comes into contact with its already dynamic raw material. Matter is elsewhere said to "desire" form and thus in some sense to rise upward toward it. But it is just as true, and a good deal more comprehensible, that form is the fixing in place of the sort of natural change, or metabolic process, that is perceived by the shaper as a too random recurrence. The more likely function of form must then be to inhibit movement, to impose from without a law of nature *(phusis)* where before there had simply been life *(bios)*. This being granted (if form, that is, is a generalized substitute for aimlessly varied repetition), we can no longer understand change *(peripeteia,* for example) as an occurrence in time.

Aristotle's sense of structure, then, *is* a semiotic one, but he is unwilling to accept the consequence of this viewpoint, namely, that structure will then appear as a system of finite relations exhibiting neither synthetic unity nor indeterminacy. He protests against a world made up of stone hands and yet, without having recourse to the Prime Mover (a deux ex machina except in metaphysical arguments), he cannot offer a satisfactory distinction between what is vital and what is merely somatic within the framework of artistic form. To return once again to his analysis of the *lexis*: is not the cost of "unity" life itself if in the following passage a "sentence," a literary text, and the definition of man can be codefined by strict analogy? "A sentence or phrase may form a unity in two ways,—either as signifying one thing, or as consisting of several parts linked together. Thus the *Iliad* is one by the linking together of parts, the definition of man by the unity of the thing signified."[14] This seems an excellent distinction between art and nature, with the unity of nature proving even more radical than that of art, until it occurs to one that the forms of both actually appear on the same plane, that of the sentence. Furthermore, if Aristotle is willing elsewhere to define the *Iliad* in terms of the thing signified, to say that Homer made the *Iliad* "centre round an action that in our sense of the word is one" (ch. 8), then he could also have defined a man, conversely, as the sum of parts in a sentence. Thus it is not clear whether the "form" of a man is in our art of evoking him or in himself.

What is often called Aristotle's "hylomorphic dichotomy" cannot be sustained in balance because it lacks an intermediate area of fusion. Surely it is life pure and simple, "this living hand, now warm and capable" (Keats) that is forceful and affecting, however fragmentary, while the rules of life, its physics, are stone hands indeed; and it is hard to know what a midpoint between these states could be like. The hylomorphic dichotomy, like Aristotle's division of the parts of tragedy, supposes that reality is partly formal, partly substantial—partly lexical, partly embodiment. But the logic of his insistence that structure is the constitutive principle of its parts shows rather that reality, depending on one's angle of approach, is either all lexis or all body. A structure is neither an ineffable principle apart from its material nor a concrete manifestation of its material which would itself need to be represented by a structure. Aristotle's concession, at the start of the *Categories,* that "Substance . . . is that which is neither predicable of a subject nor present in a subject" is sweeping in its implication, and forces the conclusion that *mimesis* is a purely intellectual event and not an activity that touches and incorporates the world by representing it.[15]

The first point of this chapter, then, is that Aristotle's celebrated emphasis on form is far more radical than is commonly thought and wholly deprives the work of art of substance. (The second and only further point will be that substance gets its revenge.) If there were a sliding scale between the structural and the phenomenal in the *Poetics,* as admittedly there sometimes is elsewhere in Aristotle, no great objection could be made against his formalism and its influence on later critical thought. But there is no such scale, and therefore his influence has been unobjectionable only when it has been greatly distorted.

II

A. E. Taylor was probably right to assert that there is no special division of science into which the *Poetics* is meant to be placed; even so, on Taylor's own supposition that "the *Poetics* was meant to be a collection of rules," we ought to be able to call this work at least a subdivision of physics.[16] It is a secondary physics, a physics concerned with the rules of merely human making, and thus of course it observes the inferior "standard of correctness" (ch. 25) that belongs to human things. But it is still essentially prescriptive.[17] In places it reads like a handbook, so much so that one may suppose the earliest Aristotelians to have been on the right track in treating their Stagirite as a lawgiver.

Of special interest in this regard is the famous "unity of time." Else has shown persuasively, in my view, that the mysterious "single revolution of the sun" (ch. 5) refers not to the fictive time represented in the play but to the duration of the performance.[18] Thus the Daciers and Corneilles all misunderstood Aristotle in this case, but they were quite right—and Butcher and his German predecessors wrong to deride them for it—in supposing that the "unity of time" is indeed a prescription. It is an earnest injunction that the action of tragedy constrain time.

The passage in chapter 5 cannot simply be a casual remark, as Butcher suggests, "a rough generalization as to the practice of the Greek stage,"[19] because it so clearly touches upon what is elsewhere said to be the one decisive reason for the superiority of tragedy to epic: "The art [of tragedy] attains its end within narrower limits; for the concentrated effect is more pleasurable than one which is spread over a long time and so diluted" (ch. 26). Time is formless, or in any case a falling away from the uniform, and the whole purpose of composition is to fix it in place. The most frequently stressed advantage of a tragic *muthos* over the mere seriality of existence is that it can be grasped "all at once"; its temporality becomes a shape, or else, if that fails, it will resemble a "picture" (or "creature," as some would have it) which is so long that "the eye cannot take [it] in . . . all at once" (ch. 7). The structural turns of tragedy bend sequence back upon itself lest the course of events stand revealed as sequence merely, as in "simple" or episodic plots. Thus recognition freezes time in the intensity of the moment; in recognition one feels the horror of retrospect loaded upon the unbearable present and preventing any thought for the future. And thus reversal cancels time; in an instant it undoes the entire gestation of a plan of action.

While Aristotle has a great deal of interest to say about the contributions of recognition and reversal to his plot against time, he has very little directly to say about the third and allegedly equal part of the plot, the *pathos,* or Tragic Incident, "a destructive or painful action, such as death on the stage, bodily agony, wounds, and the like" (ch. 11). Even though we do not look for elegance of style in the *Poetics,* which may be a set of lecture notes, it still is hard to disregard the feeling of haste with which the phrase "and the like" *(kai ora toianta)* dismisses the horrors that precede it, horrors that even in their mere enumeration are more vivid than nearly anything else in the *Poetics.* In the *pathos* there is none of the neatness of recognition and reversal, none of the chessboard elegance that has led H. D. F. Kitto to speak of the Aristotelian plot as a "cleaning-up."[20] The *pathos* as it is here described is a very untidy event. Aristotle has little else to say about it. Possibly he included it in his account of tragedy only because the data left him no choice. Contrary to what is often said, there is a fair amount of stage violence and physical suffering in the Greek theater that is left to us, and very likely there is more of it in the plays that were performed in the sixty years after the deaths of Sophocles and Euripides.[21] In any case, it seems to me, Else is not at all justified in saying that the *pathos* is the cornerstone of

Aristotle's tragic theory.[22] The wording of the passage in chapter 11 and the drift of the treatise in general suggest that, on the contrary, he might happily have wished it away.

The tragic incident as Aristotle describes it seems scarcely to be part of the plot, in fact, but rather to belong to *opsis,* or Spectacle, that least integral part of poetic making to which "signs," or tokens of recognition, also belong. It may be objected that *opsis* does not include the movements of actors onstage but refers only to their costumes and the sets. This may be true but it is doubtful: Aristotle says only that *opseos kosmos,* decoration for the eyes, is "more" the business of the stage machinist *(skenopoios)* than that of the poet *(dramatopoios).* He does not say that it is exclusively decorative.[23] Be this as it may, one nonetheless feels that Aristotle's *pathos* must perforce slide out of its assigned category, the plot, but that this shift in function will not relegate it to the periphery of tragic experience. On the contrary, in declining from the essential to the accidental, the *pathos* ceases to be conceptual and becomes actual. To suppress it, in other words, as Aristotle seems to do, is to bring it to the surface. The trouble with the *pathos,* and the reason for Aristotle's failure to identify it in decidedly structural terms, lies in its unavoidable lifelikeness. Thus the *pathos* cannot contribute to the philosophical excellence of tragedy, which consists in its potential independence from the illusionism of performance. Not only can tragedy "reveal . . . its power by mere reading" (ch. 26),[24] but it is also enough merely to "hear the tale" (ch. 14) in order to "thrill with horror and melt with pity." These last are highly emotive phrases; if even mere audition is thus exciting, it seems likely that for Aristotle the immediacy of spectacle and the enactment of a *pathos* will be very nearly unbearable. He would not be alone in this feeling: for every Johnson who cannot bear even to read the concluding *pathos* of *Lear* there must be hundreds of coarser grain who cannot bear to witness the blinding of Gloucester.

III

Having suggested that form serves to ensure distance in the *Poetics,* I shall also maintain, accordingly, that mimesis is not quite the vital moment of representation it is often said to be. *Mimesis* is a slippery concept that is not easy to capture. Little clarity is gained from saying that it is neither simple copying nor creation from nothing but—something in between. Many accepted classics of critical theory have faltered in trying thus to define it dialectically. Even Johnson does not seem to notice that his equally forceful demands for the low-mimetic "just representation," on the one hand, and for the high-mimetic observance of poetic justice, on the other, cannot easily be reconciled. The ancients themselves are not as consistent on the subject of imitation as one could wish them to be, and their remarks, taken all in all, only add to one's feeling that the concept is too elusive to merit the pivotal place it has always had in the theory of criticism.[25]

Despite Plato's greater preoccupation, in general, with the purity of form, the concept of mimesis in Aristotle is more closely dependent on form than it is in Plato. That is of course because Plato locates form exclusively in the realm that cannot be represented at all by mimesis. It is not too much to say that for Plato there is no proper connection between mimesis and form. Mimesis, he feels, is too unstable to represent the Forms, and for this reason it encourages emotional instability in the spectator. This is just what Aristotle, with his doctrine of cathartic pacification, is unwilling to admit. We have seen, without referring as yet to the issue of catharsis, that Aristotle distances the vividness of representation. Plato, on the other hand, insofar as he countenances mimesis at all—as in hymns in praise of the gods and illustrious men—refuses to recognize any formal principle of mediation; Platonic mimesis is by nature, for better or worse, an intensely dynamic activity. These assertions can be illustrated by contrasting Plato and Aristotle on the subject of reading. Aristotle seems, again, almost to prefer reading to performance; form for him is most clearly to be perceived through the kind of extreme mediation that removes things in themselves from view. For Plato it is just the opposite; for him form is obscured increasingly by every additional remove of representation. Distortion is worsened, as the passage on reading in the *Phaedrus* (276a) makes clear, by the introduction of every new level of secondariness, like that of writing to voice. Only the forms approximated in direct and living speech, says Plato, can be "written on the soul of the learner."[26]

Aristotle, who purports to have rehabilitated art in having drawn form down into matter, is still inclined, with Plato, to reject the vividness of phenomenal appearances in art. At bottom, one suspects, he agreed with his teacher that the arts are too seductive. Supposing, then, that it was against his own better judgment that he attempted to redeem mimesis, it would not be surprising to find the resulting viewpoint less than perfectly clear or consistent. There are times, in fact, when for Aristotle, as for Plato, the arts are at best a branch of Rhetoric—or what Plato would call sophisty. "It is Homer who has chiefly taught other poets the art of telling lies" (ch. 24), Aristotle says, conceding in that one place all that Plato could wish. But then he falls back upon the revisionary mysteries of his own doctrine. There may be white lies, apparently, errors of rendering or keeping. Thus drawing the legs of a horse wrong may not "touch the essentials of the poetic art" (ch. 25). Horseness is all that matters. But it should not be taken on faith, as Nelson Goodman has argued, that we can know what these essentials are.[27] In Aristotle horseness is not something one learns from riding a horse or being kicked by one or watching the *pathos* of a horse dying. One learns it from seeing a justly drawn *schema* of a horse and—simply recognizing it. With all the talk one can muster about quiddity or the *posse in esse,* it comes to that.

Plato can tell us little that is of interest about the nature of art because within the phenomenal realm he has no tolerance either for closure, which would be an imposture, or for indeterminacy, which is sadly the case. For this reason, however, he anticipates Croce's conviction that intuition is superior to expression and thus avoids the pitfalls of objective formalism. He knows that categories blur and disappear in proportion to their material realization. He is indeed hostile to art as a way of knowing; and yet, as long as the context of his remarks is a little facetious, his evident enjoyment of art comes to the fore, an enjoyment in the holiday spirit of knowing, with Oscar Wilde, that it is "quite useless." Art is a madness freed from restraints both proper and improper. Sometimes it is a divine madness, and then it resembles the formless *arche* that thinks the Forms themselves. Plato says this kind of thing ironically, but others have said it seriously. As I shall argue in later chapters, this view, although it is kept in check in Plato and is far too vaguely ecstatic in most of his descendants, has much to recommend it as a theoretical starting point.

But Aristotle's idea of mimesis is definitely shrewder than Plato's in one respect. Aristotle accepts art among the forms of worthwhile discourse because, unlike Plato, he understands verbal or pictorial representation of *any* kind to be only approximate, at best, in arriving at truth. The Platonic drama, which Aristotle admiringly calls "Socratic Dialogue" and then ironically classifies as a mode of mimesis (ch. 1), is justified by Plato himself solely on the grounds that it is a nonimitative language. Language of that kind, for Plato, pure language, is dialectic, the elimination in dialogue of increasingly sophisticated errors by means of what Socrates calls the "interrupting question" with the purpose of arriving finally at the truth. In this regard Aristotle's formalism is indeed less vulnerable than that of Plato. All language for him, not just that of art ("Language in general," the chapter on *lexis* pointedly begins), is generically more or less the same, and it is more or less persuasive depending simply upon whether it uses the rules of logic, dialectic, or rhetoric.

Up to a point, then, unlike Plato, Aristotle does not *seem* to mind the relative murkiness of the artistic media. In fact, however, as we have seen, he is by no means prepared to admit the contamination of artistic form by unmediated and undifferentiated material elements. Again one may wonder whether Aristotle's revision of Plato is not a revision in appearance only. Plot is the form of tragedy, to which the other five parts are subordinated; yes, but it would be most elegant to suppose that the "other" five parts, which are increasingly impure with respect to the formal element when ranged on a scale from Character to Spectacle, are not so much subordinated to as absorbed by the plot and assimilated to its ontological status. And the plot, an intuited invention in the poet's head, not on paper or on the stage, can only be understood "Platonically," as a transcendent form. Hence the tragedy which is wholly free of imperfection is the tragedy which is wholly freed from any mode of concrete existence.

Consider Aristotle's treatment of "Thought" in tragedy. Because he inherits from Plato a powerful contempt for mere opinion (the *doxa*), he derogates speech that is not functional in a course of action, awarding Thought *(dianoia)* only the place of third importance among the six parts of tragedy. It is not to be expected, he assumes, that characters in a play will succeed in speaking philosophically, or that they will even aspire to do so. Their speech belongs to oratory (ch. 6; chapter 19 refers the reader to the *Rhetoric* for a discussion of *dianoia*); that is, it is an art of persuasion that is practiced irrespective of the truth of its premises or of any pressing need for action. It is "the faculty of saying what is possible and pertinent in given circumstances" (ch. 6). This is one of Aristotle's most helpful ideas. It should deter us from the fallacy of sententious thematization. For example, we should not adduce the "theme" of *King Lear* from the morally blind Gloucester's "As flies to wanton boys are we to the gods" because statements of that kind are inevitably, to some extent, "in character," opinions colored by factors that do not all belong to the plot. No more will the theme of *Hamlet* be found in the advice of Polonius or the musings of the Prince.[28]

For all its corrective value, though, Aristotle's treatment of Thought still betrays a significant bias concerning the relation between structure and its materials. Behind his compartmentalization of Thought there exists a wish to abstract the essence of tragic meaning from the verbal texture of the play and to refer it solely to the hypostasized instant of the poet's mythic making.[29] Thus a fallacy is avoided, to be sure, the fallacy of taking an utterance, or "sentence," to be synecdochic rather than vaguely metonymic with respect to its discursive setting; but a problem is also evaded, the problem of how to be transported from the discursive to the purely phantasmatic realm. We cannot find an exit from the verbal plane, so to speak. There is no passage opened in the *Poetics* from the temporal medium of representation to the ideal space of mythmaking which Aristotle calls the *psuche,* or soul, of tragedy. He distinguishes among the objects, the manner, and the medium of imitation but he does not explain how the only palpable dimension of art, the medium, can incorporate an object in any manner. The "sentence" (medium), again, is defined not in *relation* to a manner (e.g., the way the parts of the *Iliad* are arranged) or to an object (e.g., the unity of the human being) but rather in *equivalence* with them, which is to say that the three terms do not coexist with one another but rather substitute for one another. If the fallacy of sententious thematization is indeed a fallacy, it is still hard to know where to discover a thematic dimension of any other kind. Having insisted that the plot is the soul of tragedy, Aristotle leaves the reader to guess what kind of perceptual sphere a plot of that kind could possibly appear in.

It is no use looking for it in the real world. The presence of a fashioned plot is the one necessary criterion for grouping together all the works in the broad canon of imitative modes that Aristotle cannot name (ch. 1), the canon we call "literature." In distinguishing between the imitator Homer and the nonimitator Empedocles with respect to their objects, Aristotle implies that these objects cannot both be phenomena in the real world at once; if they were, no firm distinction between mimetic and nonmimetic writing would be possible.[30] Because there is clearly no tolerance for a subtle scale of differentiation (e.g., between selective and exhaustive representation) at this propaedeutic stage in the text, Aristotle must then be making silent use of the common Greek dichotomy between the image of real things and the phantasm of imaginary ones. In that case he is contrasting the presentation by Empedocles and others of images of existing phenomena, which is not mimetic, with the representation of the intellectual forms or fixed patterns of action (as in Homer) and of thinking (as in Plato's "dramas"), which is mimetic. Hence, with one of Aristotle's modern translators, we must define imitation as the making of fiction.[31] This will oblige us to disagree with the compromise formations of most commentators, who try to make out that *hule,* the material world, plays some part in the process. How could that be so if in fact it is just those who present the data of natural science and of history who are expressly denied the title of imitators? It must be an intellectual form that poetry imitates; yet the form, we are told again and again, is the imitation itself and can only be inferred, therefore, from existing poems. Is it not the case that in a sense— an important sense—mimesis, the soul of art and the theoretical foundation of Western realism, is finally nothing other than a Crocean intuition-expression?[32] Croce would agree, in any case, that "the power of Tragedy . . . is felt apart from representation" (ch. 6).

The first sentences of chapter 9 are perhaps the cornerstones of aesthetic thought. Poetry, Aristotle says there, is more "philosophical" than history. It reflects the universal, and above all it relates what may happen as opposed to what has happened. Here the defense of Aristotle's realism often entrenches itself. What may happen, it is said, *can have happened* and must therefore at least sometimes exist objectively: "If the poet chances to take an historical subject, he is none the less a poet" (ch. 9). Therefore, it might be argued, the assertion that Aristotelian mimesis is utterly lacking in substantive or material content must be invalid. But no: *as* poetry, even if it is copied with minute fidelity, the historical event ceases to be itself. It is lifted from its proper time and then placed, not even in a later time, but outside the flow of a later time. As we perceive the historical event in that condition, it is subject to countless ironies that are absent from our perception of events in time.[33] Aristotle himself would not only admit all this but insist upon its importance, reminding the defenders of his realism that no event in history as such has a beginning, a middle, and an end. If any event had these features, it would be imitative poetry, both secondary to its forsaken identity and timelessly insubstantial in its new identity.

The *Poetics* begins by isolating the "essential quality," the artness, of the several arts. Where there are no essences available for scrutiny, however—and I take it that most persons today would agree that there are none—there are no grounds for any categorization that is not openly heuristic. By the same token there are no forms inhering in any material object, such as a tragedy onstage, other than its actual material shape. Aristotle's hylomorphic balance must perforce give way to some monistic reduction. Perhaps he had no "common term" for poetic imitations because there is "essentially" no such category. There are fictions, if you will, or else representations, if you will, but with respect to art, the "principle of movement in something *other than* the thing moved" (italics mine), there cannot be both at once in the same sphere of perception.

IV

For Aristotle, then, art is a means of distancing reality, if not a kind of defense against it. Thus he anticipates the Kantian aesthetic distance, and not only in the remarks about catharsis. There is also his one reference to the actor's mask, which is "ugly and distorted, but does not imply pain" (ch. 5). Or again there is his oft-quoted assertion that "objects which in themselves we view with pain, we delight to contemplate when reproduced with minute fidelity" (ch. 4). In these instances art is evidently an anaesthetic. But here one must use care: It is not right to say that Aristotle thinks forms are defenses; it is more accurate to say that he wants to think forms are defenses but cannot quite do so. As we have just argued, masks and represented objects are *not,* in fact, forms. Not form in the abstract, form as *muthos,* but concrete representations would appear to be the actual defenses because they alone can plant themselves before one and thereby ensure the absence of what one does not wish to experience directly. But concrete representations are not "forms" at all; they are only material shapes. On Aristotle's own showing, then, contrary to the position that seems appropriate to him, art is either "philosophical" but not anaesthetic or else it is concretely realized and keeps actual suffering at a distance.

Aristotle's emphasis on intellectual form as a means of neutralizing pain must therefore be somewhat forced; but in truth the idea that the substance of art can have this effect would not have been very persuasive either. One wonders, indeed, both about the possibility of distancing of any kind in art and also about its value, supposing it to be possible. Surely there is in fact no delight for most persons in viewing reproductions of what is painful.[34] Son of a doctor and naturalist that he was, Aristotle was well accustomed to cadavers both real and pictured. Is he fairly evaluating his own experience when he generalizes from his tolerance of "the forms of the most ignoble animals and of dead bodies" in pictures (ch. 4)? With what delight would he view a picture of himself, or someone recognizably like him, killing his father? Here we approach the question of identification on the part of the spectator, which in my opinion Aristotle and his followers to this day handle somewhat unrealistically.

Although it is possible to venture an interpretation of *katharsis,* it remains unclear just what the term means in the *Poetics.* One hopes, in any case, that it does *not* mean the achievement of aesthetic distance through the purgation *or* the purification of dangerous emotions. Both these classical interpreta- tions, either of which may well be correct, are rather insensitive. In experience we "achieve" distance only from that to which we are or have grown indifferent. If Aristotle is used to cadavers he will certainly have no trouble looking at their pictures. Hence we are either indifferent in advance to the issue of a given tragedy or else, as Plato had hitherto claimed (rightly in my view), the very opposite of catharsis will occur through the process of identification: "From the evil of other men something of evil is commu- nicated to [ourselves]. And so the feeling of sorrow which has gathered strength at the sight of the misfortunes of others is with difficulty repressed in our own" (*Rep.* 10; 606b; trans. Jowett). When we identify with another we are hard put to resist imitating the other. If we are not indifferent to the tragic experience, our distance, aesthetic or otherwise, from the protagonist must narrow rather than increase through the duration of our exposure to the *pathos.* It does not matter whether we know the story in advance; it is one thing to know that "x dies" and another to watch him die, even in pretense. To "enjoy," aesthetically or otherwise, the expiation of a scapegoat must therefore have something of the pharisaical about it. Not sufficiently identifying with the scapegoat, we do not accept the premise that labels him, namely, that he is atoning for our own goatishness.

In *Oedipus the King,* neither Creon nor the chorus shows any sign of "identifying" with Oedipus in the long run. Creon is more cold-blooded in the last scenes than we expect or want him to be. Oedipus himself, at the outset, neither identifies nor identifies *with* his criminal self. Somebody else is the pollutant; that total stranger will be banished, and all will be clean again. The audience must keep itself suspended in this same ignorance, at this same immense distance from the truth, if it is to "enjoy" the spectacle. If we identify with Oedipus, on the other hand, if we feel that he has suffered for our sins, we may feel a certain tawdry relief at having been passed over, but apart from that we are apt to feel oppressed by a mixture of uneasiness and indignation.[35]

If distance tempers identification in Aristotle's view of spectatorship, it is hard to understand what he can mean in saying that tragic characters should be like ourselves. Else's proposal that catharsis is a structural concept, not an affect in the audience but an effect in the play (the purging of Oedipus that purifies a terrified Thebes, for example), has not met with the approval of those who wish to keep up the illusion that what Kenneth Burke wickedly calls "vicarage,"[36] the vicarious connection with the suffering of others, is a pleasant experience. However, Else's interpretation, whether it is right or wrong, does serve to protect Aristotle from the suspicion of insensitivity. For Else, *katharsis* is no different in kind or kind of effect from recognition, reversal, tragic incident, or *hamartia*.[37] All these features are interlocking differentia at the level of plot that have no necessary affective implication. Catharsis, the outcome of the plot, is typically some form of suffering for the pollution of blood guilt, and nothing more. Fear and pity themselves are structural features, being, as one commentator has said, "important controls in determining the kinds of actions depicted in tragic poetry."[38] Within the play, one aspect of catharsis is indeed emotional; it leaves a state of complacency or satisfaction distributed evenly among the characters such that there can be no more retributive turnings of the plot—which is thus at an "end." Whether the feeling of catharsis should happen to spread to the audience, and whether that eventuality would be a good thing, is, as Aristotle would say, outside the province of the poet, whose sole business is to fulfill his plot. It is safest, though, to keep the discussion structural. Even to suppose our "calm of mind, all passion spent" at the end is also to imply our having been more upset beforehand than was quite comfortable. Aristotle says nothing about catharsis as affect with good reason because his formalism serves to defer all questions of this sort, questions that force us to admit—or deny—that Oedipus is "like ourselves."

Before coming to reconsider Aristotle's "realism," the putative basis of his art in nature, and especially in our nature, it will be necessary to address a special but central issue within this topic, that of "character." The Aristotelian attitude that was inherited and transmitted by Theophrastus in his *Characters* (mostly from the *Rhetoric* insofar as this attitude carried with it an art of description) understands character as a fixed, mask-like entity that is allowed one change but only one—and that one not a random change but a simple inversion of identity. Apart from that one change, "a person of a given character should speak or act in a given way" (ch. 15). In later critical theory this dictum survived more or less unquestioned in the abstract, although the psychologists of Humours and the practicing playwrights often disagreed as to what it meant, until the study of Shakespeare began to give theory pause. There are hints of rebellion in Dryden, but it was not until Johnson's liberation of Character from the criterion of truth to status, or role, that Aristotle's view was finally gainsaid, never to recover prestige except in the recurrent form of a paradox calculated to unsettle received ideas about inwardness or "roundness" in characterization.

Johnson overthrows Aristotle on character by realigning Aristotelian terms: "*Shakespeare* always makes nature predominate over accident."[39] Whereas for Aristotle the mere accidents of a character reside in his idiosyncratic nature, for Johnson they are constituted by his role or office— by his assigned place, in short, in the plot. Thus Shakespeare willingly flouts the Aristotelian *muthos:* "His story requires Romans or kings, but he thinks only on men" ("Preface," p. 303). Except, again, for highly calculated recrudescences in such texts as Arnold's "Preface to *Poems*" and Sarraute's *L'Ère de soupçon,* the Aristotelian subordination of character to plot has never recovered from Johnson's sentence, which seems specifically to be retorting against Aristotle's "For Tragedy is an imitation, not of men, but of action and of life, and life consists in action, and its end is a mode of action, not a quality" (ch. 6). Nature is "general" for Johnson, "universal" for Aristotle. Whereas for Johnson Nature inheres to some extent in phenomenal appearances (although not in the tulip streaks of Dutch painting), Nature for Aristotle is inferred from but not manifest in appearances. His Nature (or "physics") is constituted by the unvarying forms that infuse but also survive the generations of things.

What is significant for the present argument in this contrast is its indication, again, that the hylomorphic compromise in Aristotle is an illusion. We can have no means of recognizing that a structurally conceived entity is "like ourselves." Suppose that some essential quality marks each of our characters, and that that quality is determined by our status. If I am essentially a King, then, will I recognize my royalty in a tragic character by any means other than by being shown a duplicate of my staff of office? But what is worse, suppose I am *not* essentially a King, can I then be persuaded in any way that Oedipus with respect to the formal enactment of his role is "like" myself? To be sure, Aristotle, who in discussing character is speaking, willy-nilly, of concrete representations, must recognize that characterization will have a phenomenal, accidental side (despite masks, repertories of formal gestures, and so on), and perhaps he recognizes further that it is on this side that a likeness to ourselves must almost certainly appear if it is to appear at all. The difficulty remains, from his standpoint, that it is on just this side that character springs free from its structural determination by plot. It is only the modality of character in *praxis,* an intellectual object existing regardless of the quality of the character's "motive," that is purely and directly a function of the plot. Thus even though Aristotle concedes that "Character" is "that in virtue of which we ascribe certain qualities to agents" (ch. 6), he means only that empirically our ascription of qualities is unavoidable, an impure deference to phenomena, like the practice of scene painting. Or rather it is nearly unavoidable: in a passage that is as startling as the passage about the adequacy of reading, Aristotle says that there *can* be a tragedy "without character" (ibid.).

Dramatic characters are "like ourselves," then, in proportion as they are irrelevant to the structure of tragedy. What counts for the plot, though, first and last, is not the fallibility of the agent but the functional efficiency of the agent's fallibility. For this reason the widespread view of *hamartia,* that it is an abiding or ingrained moral weakness, seems untenable. Moral weakness is a "quality," obviously, and thus it will almost inevitably be represented in a tragedy, yet it cannot be said to bear directly on the *psuche* of tragedy. The alternative opinion, that *hamartia* is essentially structural and signifies a blunder or miscue, has the best of it. Philip Harsh attempts to uphold the tragic-flaw thesis on the grounds that in a universe where qualities are irrelevant to action there can be no question of moral responsibility.[40] Of course this is true, and clearly Harsh maintains his hazardous ground only because he is unwilling to believe that Aristotle would assign this sort of universe to tragedy. It is the logic of Aristotle's position in the *Poetics,* one must suppose, and not a normative attitude toward the conduct of life or even toward the influence of literature upon the conduct of life, that forces him to such an extreme of formalism. Just as the fact that the structural outcome called catharsis may—but need not—affect the emotions of the audience is not intrinsic to the nature of tragedy, so the fact that the structurally necessary mistake of an agent may—but need not—arise from a responsibly held moral defect is not intrinsic to the nature of tragedy. Barring groundless conjecture, we cannot assume that the tragic mistake arises from a responsibly held moral defect unless somebody in the play says that it does ("Those who are quick of temper are not safe," says the chorus in the *Oedipus*); and if we accept hearsay of that kind, even if it is self-accusation, we lapse into the fallacy of sententious thematization. Repeatedly, and for the best reasons, an interpreters of Aristotle we adapt him to our needs by compromising the "aesthetic intellectualism" (John Jones) of his scheme.[41] If Aristotle were committed to placing the psychological causes of action within his "structure of incidents" (ch. 14), he would surely rate the *Medea,* in which "the deed" is perpetrated in full knowledge and with a full power of choice, more highly than he does. The fact is, on the contrary, that the exercise of free choice, either in acting or in refraining from action, marks the two worst of Aristotle's four types of plot (see ch. 17).

If too many qualities of character are represented, the result is not merely irrelevant; it actually harms the plot. This is only partly because if there were a "unity of the hero" (ch. 8), with the whole course of his behavior rehearsed from birth to death, there could be no structure of incidents but only a series of episodes. Even supposing the unity of action to have been more or less preserved, but containing within it a surplus of motive, the structural clarity of the action would still have been obscured in deference to considerations merely performative and phenomenal: "Such structures are composed . . . by good poets [only] because of the actors: in composing contest pieces for them, and stretching out the plot beyond its capacity, they are forced frequently to dislocate the sequence" (ch. 9; Else's translation, *Aristotle: Poetics,* p. 34). The real drawback in giving scope to the players is that the poet's art will be contaminated by the showiness (the opsis) of histrionics. To say that too much play-acting goes on and that too many motives are given is to say much the same thing, because from the poet-maker's standpoint actors and the characters they play share the same indispensable but still regrettably incidental and secondary claim to exis-tence.

The poet himself may be, and often was, an actual player, while in epic he is not only a character of necessity but was, in original redactions, the sole performing character.[42] Paradoxically, therefore, his own character can have none of the consistency he is supposed to maintain in his created characters because his identity qua "maker" and his identity qua player or narrator or rhapsode do not even belong to the same perceptual sphere. Clearly the greatest self-betrayal a poet can commit is to project himself into the realm that is extrinsic and inessential to the structure of his work. Modernist, and of course formalist, proclamations of the impersonality of the artist will seem relevant here. To enter one's poem would be to lyricize an objective structure, to return to those first "rude improvisations," dithyrambic, monodramatic, in which the *telos* of tragic form, although present, was scarcely perceptible. Thus in Aristotle's view it was the genius of Homer, so early in the evolution of the poetic arts toward impersonality, to bring in a character other than himself after only "a few prefatory words" (ch. 24). What Aristotle could not be expected to have noticed, or in any case to have admitted, is that the voice of the poet continues to speak through his characters, stand-ins whose personalities are highly volatile. We shall soon see how little Aristotle makes of the prince of these characters, Odysseus *polutropos,* the man of many turnings in word and deed.

Aristotle supposes that the characters who are better or worse than we are (ch. 2; *spoudiaoi* or *phauloi,* "worthwhile" or "low-life" types[43]) are at the same time, in some way, "true to life" (ch. 15) and "like ourselves" (ch. 13). In other words, as characters, though not as agents whose excellence is solely functional, they are not perfect. It is often thought, and with good reason, that "better" must refer mainly to the social status of a character because, whereas the tragic protagonist should be "one who is highly renowned and prosperous" (ch. 13), he should also be "a man who is not eminently good and just." It may appear at first that with this distinction Aristotle belies his Theophrastean followers and anticipates Johnson's contrast between character and role. This might be the case if Aristotle's understanding of structure did not depend precisely upon canceling this contrast by means of the tragic plot. Johnson's contrast between character and role exists for Aristotle as an improper state of affairs at the beginning of a tragedy. What removes it is *hamartia*. This term does essentially signify a "mistake"; only as a mistake can it appear at the level of action. At the same time, though, it is clear that perfect persons do not make mistakes and that therefore, after all, *hamartia* does entail moral weakness. But the bearing and importance of this qualification remain extremely limited; from the standpoint of the plot maker, the tragic flaw is simply the prerequisite for a "change in fortune," or social status. The most precise definition of *hamartia,* then, would be that it is the measure of initial discrepancy between the status and the merit of a protagonist. The resolution of a complex tragic action would thus be the achievement of parity, through reversal, between status and merit. Hence the complacency of those whose status is just what they merit and who willingly assist at a scapegoat ritual; their mediocrity, their adherence to the Mean, is vindicated by the abasement of pride they have witnessed.

V

In a complex plot, to which this argument has been largely confined because Aristotle thinks that it is the "natural form," if anything is (ch. 4), of tragedy, catharsis is the revenge of reversal on hamartia that is carried out by means of recognition. So apparently, then, catharsis is a kind of poetic justice and provides us with a structural explanation of how plots transform things as they are into things as they should be. But the very need for this transformation shows that the *Poetics* harbors a critical challenge to Aristotle's usual view of the efficacy of natural laws.

Elsewhere he maintains that *phusis* is the essence or immanent form of things. In that case the science of life is in no sense prescriptive or corrective but merely descriptive. But what then of tragic science, which begins with the premise that things are not as they should be and must be righted by tragedy, which can do its work only by imposing the external "principle of movement" called art on the otherwise self-motivating course of nature? Of course in other contexts nature too has a Prime Mover. But whereas in other discussions Aristotle can insist, as Thomas Gould puts it, that in nature " 'chance,' and 'necessity' . . . are pseudo-causes,"[44] in the *Poetics* he says that in nature things do occur by "mere chance" (*tuche;* ch. 9) unless tragedy is available to give them "an air of design." W. K. Wimsatt has confronted this problem by glossing it from the *Physics:* "Chance . . . and what results from chance are appropriate to agents that are capable of good fortune."[45] In the *Poetics,* however, there is no evidence that nature helps those who help themselves. It is not surprising that Aristotle's formalism tends to float free of its nominal basis in nature. If we had only the *Poetics,* we would have to conclude that for Aristotle nature in itself, like its reproduction in history-writing or Empedoclean science, is merely episodic, and very sloppily so: "The question why god allows iniquities is not answered, or even asked, by tragedy as Aristotle understands it."[46] Tragedy simply goes about setting iniquities right. One could imagine an idealist turn of argument whereby the corrective world of tragedy reveals the true shape of the natural world beneath appearances, but this saving turn will not be found in the *Poetics.*

And yet Nature viewed as a kind of arbitress keeps recurring in the text of the *Poetics,* as if to challenge Aristotle's confinement of form to the intellect of the artist. It is nature in all its evident imperfection, for instance, which keeps offering itself in the service of perfection: "Following, then, the order of nature, let us begin with the principles that come first" (ch. 1); "Nature herself discovered the appropriate measure" for the diction of tragedy (ch. 4); character must be "true to life," and so on. It is as though things as they are were the end of mimesis after all. Even in figures descriptive of form, Aristotle at times still echoes the main idea of his natural philosophy, which is that patterns in nature are dynamic, upward surges of becoming ripe with potential for being. Many commentators exaggerate the evolutionary idea in the *Poetics* in order to protect Aristotle from the charge of "mere" formalism. But this idea is really perfunctory, and when it does appear it tends only to suggest the pattern of development, not development itself. There is an analogy, for example, between the "history" of tragedy (ch. 4), with its theoretically reconstructed coming-to-be of a "natural form," and the shape of a tragic plot. First there is the emergence of the complex plot, which is like the "complication" within a plot, and then there is tragedy's recognition of and coming to rest with its natural form, which is like the unraveling of a plot. It has been argued that Aristotle's "history" is based on research; even so, it need no more resemble nature than a tragedy with a historical subject resembles nature.

The *Poetics* contains two—and only two—passages that directly concern "organic form," one of which I will put off considering. The meaning of the other is disputed. Butcher has "[Epic] will . . . resemble a single and coherent picture of a living being" (ch. 23). Else, whose Aristotle is usually a much dryer soul than Butcher's, still has "like a single complete creature,"[47] thus seeming to leave out the mediation of a *schema;* but his note on this passage reminds us that the term *zoion* is apt to denote a biological diagram showing either "the unified living creature" or the creature's "inorganic structure" (*Aristotle,* p. 109). So there need be no implication in this passage that epic should germinate from within itself or offer a full-blooded and variegated appearance to the audience.

Even if there were such an implication, however, it is still notable that Aristotle puts off using this simile, which some readers expand in importance until it fills the whole treatise, until he has finished discussing tragedy. On the one hand, epic is performed with more restraint, is less dependent on histrionics, than tragedy, and thus perhaps Aristotle can safely assert its vitality without undue concern that it will prove superabundant. On the other hand, however—and this is why epic is inferior to tragedy—the animation that epic dispenses with in stage business it doubly requires in the sprawling length of its plot; even in the case of Homer Aristotle can only halfheartedly praise the epic for the unity of its action. The result of these two tendencies is that in epic the distinction between mimesis and presentation is less sharp than in tragedy, the former quality being formally imperfect and the latter less hectic and colorful than its tragic counterpart. Because this distinction is blurred, then, and because therefore there is no purely intellectual mode of total realization for an epic, this inferior form, which is prior to drama in the evolution of forms, is actually more suited than tragedy for the "organic analogy" that readers from Coleridge to the present have taken to constitute Aristotle's highest praise of art. On reconsideration, Aristotle might well have devised still richer organistic similes for the "rude improvisations" with which, like protozoa, the poetic arts gropingly began.

VI

Tragedy bends nature toward the "probable," which may be impossible, as well as toward justice. "The probable" designates some event with a universal and not merely particular relevance. And if, indeed, the probable belongs to the sphere of universals, we must prepare to encounter the purely intellectual notion that there may be an impossible universal, like an extra dimension, say, in mathematics. Aristotle's preference for probable impossibility to possible improbability in his tragic plots leaves nature even further behind than formalization merely in itself, without bias, could ever do. It would be wrong to suppose that the organic aspect of nature is reflected in Aristotle's preference by appearing in that form of the probable impossible called the "monstrous." Monsters from the standard myths like centaurs, minotaurs, chimeras, and sphinxes are not organic at all. They are made up of parts mechanically fitted together, not for symbolic but for allegorical purposes—to borrow Coleridge's distinction for the moment. It is only in being thus allegorical that the universality of monsters, that is, their probability, can appear: They all "mean," in one way or another, that there is a beast in us all.

For Aristotle all monsters, gods, and supernatural coincidences such as the fall of the statue of Mitys can be adapted to the rational structure of tragedy as long as they are not used to resolve matters that should depend on the interlocking of human purposes. This "as long as" must be a rather sweeping proviso, however; it is hard to imagine an adequate plot by Aristotle's standards that would require any intervention by beings whose nature would preclude the effects of *hamartia,* recognition, and the other increments of plotmaking. It would be irrational for the monstrous to have a function, and in that case we must assume that it can come in only when it is not important. Aristotle is willing to admit the "Wonderful" (though never from the *mechane* except to clear up "externals") only because he has forestalled and, as it were, desensitized what is "irrational" (*alogos*) in the Wonderful by means of allegory. Thus, as he might argue, Athena may appear in the *Eumenides,* which is only an "ethical" play in any case (see ch. 18), because she so clearly stands for and affirms a gloriously abstract principle. Dionysus in *The Bacchae,* on the other hand, whose being and agency are too volatile to yield a determinate meaning, must appear "disguised as man" and marked, as Cadmus complains, by "human passions," in order that, in agreement with Pentheus, we can rationalize the god's presence as an allegory showing mankind foolishly aspiring to godhead. But *The Bacchae,* though Aristotle could scarcely have avoided thinking of it in calling Euripides the best poet at making unhappy endings (ch. 13), is not the sort of play that the *Poetics* would be likely to mention.

I have been trying to make good the assertion that Aristotle's formalism is tenuous and fragile yet rigid: brittle, in short. I have also suggested that it is "intellectual" and far closer to the formalism of the master he is trying to refute than is commonly recognized. His bias in favor of structure considered as the soul of a thing undermines the rational dichotomy between form and matter that he is normally said to maintain. Either the form is intuitive and everything material is extraneous to it, including performance and even the lexical basis of reading, or else the form is embodied within material, and the material in its turn is either wholly somatic or wholly semiotic, with no implicit principle of intentionality. I have suggested that the logic of Aristotle's argument in the *Poetics* tends to enforce a material understanding of form, but Aristotle himself pretty clearly inclines toward the distinction between "form" and "content" that has been presupposed in most subsequent critical theory. So far I have countenanced the notion of intuitive, or architectonic, from in order to show just how far tragedy, governed by such a notion, becomes a problem in structural poise with no necessary concrete or affective dimension. In turning now to Aristotle's remarks about existing literature, I shall have more to do with concrete embodiments, immanent forms of the kind that he either ignores or handles equivocally because everything about them jeopardizes rational detachment.

The Wonderful is permissible, again, because it inspires so little wonder. Gods are bound by metonymy to their machines and monsters are cast-off parts bolted together so obviously that they do not seem disturbing and strange. Monsters are more apt to seem ludicrous, rather, as when the topic of Chaeremon's "Centaur" is mirrored by its mode of composition, a combination of "all meters" (ch. 1). Clanking their joints as they go, these meters articulate so clumsily onstage that Aristotle recommends reserving them for narrative. But that is not the only reason why monsters are least frightening when they present themselves to the audience. Sophocles in the *Oedipus* has other reasons for keeping the Sphinx and Apollo offstage.

What is missing from Aristotle's Wonderful is the "irrational," the truly *alogos*, those aspects of the god in the machine which are not merely mechanical or gratuitously determinant but have to do at once with the "manic" inspiration (ch. 17) of poetry and the radical beastliness in man that cannot be disregarded as a casual homiletic topic.[48] Aristotle either subordinates the irrational to some system of reason within which it makes sense (as in chapter 25) or else he calls attention to its trivial, academic side: the departure from the surd or from the inferentially probable. Thus he says that the irrational factor in the *Oedipus* that is properly kept "outside the scope of the tragedy" (ch. 15) is the fact that Oedipus never heard how Laius was killed. Nothing about this observation seems quite right. The anomaly in question is *not* really outside the scope of the tragedy, and it is scarcely singular: it is neither more implausible nor more important than a dozen other unlikelihoods. Aristotle mentions this one anomaly twice (see also ch. 24). He is indeed so careful to associate the irrational solely with questions of verisimilitude in plotmaking that one is reminded the more forcibly of irrational issues in the *Oedipus* for which his poetics is not suited.

One of the two other literary happenstances to which he recurs more than once in the *Poetics* is the "Bath Scene" in the *Odyssey* (three times), and if anything his treatment of that is even less satisfactory. (It is tempting to think that Erich Auerbach began *Mimesis* with this scene in order to supply the defect.) No one has convincingly explained why Aristotle says that Homer does not "include" Odysseus's "wound on Parnassus" in the *Odyssey* (ch. 8). Most scholars have supposed Aristotle to mean that Homer does not include the youth of Odysseus in the present time of his narrative, thus preserving the Unity of Action. This seems to be a plausible explanation as far as it goes, especially as one cannot imagine that Aristotle has so far forgotten his Homer. Still, his phrasing in this passage is unusually awkward. His point could have been put more clearly with no difficulty; as it stands it is not only ambiguous but it is bracketed with the mention of an event, "the feigned madness at the mustering of the host," which is indeed not in the *Odyssey*. It is as though, by contagious magic, he were wishing the Parnassus episode out of the text; not surprisingly, because in all respects, both in theme and structure, this episode seems one of the most primitive and rudely improvised moments in the poem. The "wound on Parnassus" concerns the theme of initiation to manhood: that theme in turn is a displacement of the Adonis myth ritualized by the annual sacrifice which constituted, in the now widely discredited opinion of Gilbert Murray and his colleagues, the origin of tragedy itself. Aristotle, the Pickard-Cambridge of his day, preferred to think of solemn dithyrambs as the precursors of tragedy, and banished the "phallic songs" (or perhaps songs about *phauloi,* or low-life characters) to the time preceding the birth of comedy.

There are important similarities between the wound of Odysseus and the wound of Oedipus. Like the sun at night, both characters are at once out of their proper sphere and closer to the place of their true ancestry when they receive their wounds. The totem of Odysseus becomes the boar (compare Odysseus under the bushes and protected "from the sun's blaze" in book 5 to the boar in a thicket and protected "from the sun's blaze" in book 19), and thus he can be said to have wounded himself, like Oedipus. Neither hero is required to perform a full-scale dismemberment of himself because the offensiveness of both before the gods (Poseidon and Apollo, respectively) is completely atoned for in the long run by the punishment of extended exile and wandering. If we add, finally, that Aristotle mentions the discovery of Odysseus's scar in the Bath Scene as having been effected in different ways by the nurse (an older woman) and the herdsman (actually there are two of them, a swineherd and a cowherd, just as there are two herdsmen in the *Oedipus*), then we shall notice the parallel of these roles with those of Jocasta and the herdsmen-messengers, all of whom help to "discover" the identity of Oedipus in different ways.[49] Now, there is no more need to take sides concerning the real origins of tragedy (evidence indeed suggests in any case that Murray was wrong) than there is to insist that Aristotle has forgotten his Homer. It suffices to notice the gingerliness with which, on repeated occasions, he approaches the ritual content of the literature he admires. This material appears very prominently in tragedy, whether it qualifies as the origin of tragedy or not, and it still shows its power of upsetting in modern commentaries, where it is either inflated by Nietzschean rhapsodies or dismissed, still more tellingly, I think, in a patronizing parenthesis.

Aristotle cannot decide whether he likes or dislikes the Bath Scene. It is scarcely a "unified" scene by his ordinary standard of temporal economy. Narrative interruptions are common in Homer, but there are few this long or this startlingly digressive; Aristotle's apparently having forgotten this tearing open of the narrative by the recollection of a wound restores continuity to the sequence of events in present time. Even then, however, having stitched it up, Aristotle still wavers concerning the value of the scene. It contains a fairly good example of Recognition, he says (ch. 16); yet this recognition, based on Eurykleia's groundless assumption that the scar on the stranger's thigh is that of her old master, is just the kind of "false inference," after all, that Aristotle has in mind when he says, "It is Homer who has chiefly taught the poets the art of telling lies skilfully."

Eurykleia is about to cry out the name of Odysseus when he lives up to that name, "Quarrelman,"[50] by threatening to kill her if she makes a sound. Oedipus, another quite needlessly violent and ill-natured hero whose special penchant, like that of Odysseus, is to bring grief to those who love him most, assaults the second herdsman and threatens him with death if he does *not* speak. These are opposite ways of handling the intuition of shame— opposite in keeping with the specular relation between Odysseus, whose disclosures of identity are happy ones, and Oedipus, whose discoveries are the reverse. The atmosphere of the parallel recognitions in the *Odyssey* and the *Oedipus* is decidedly sexual. In each instance a younger man shows, or tries to show, an older woman both his manhood and its wound. In the *Odyssey* this happens all at once, while in the *Oedipus* Jocasta is no longer alive to witness her husband's removal of his *kukloi* or (eye)balls with the brooches that hitherto he had always seized in order to unfasten her robe. Even without connecting Homer's Bath Scene to the "tragic incident" of the *Oedipus,* we can see that the focal interest it is given in the *Odyssey* is occasioned by the surfacing of sexual themes. Like the interrupting flash-back to the wound, the whole scene is a monstrous breach of decorum.

No other incident in the annals of poetry is mentioned three times in the *Poetics*. The interruptedness of the Bath Scene may finally be what interests Aristotle about it, and what links his treatment of it with his equally wavering and uncertain remarks about the *Odyssey* as a "whole." It is difficult to credit or even to understand his assertions that the poem and its main character are "unified." In the first place, the character of Many-troped Odysseus must merit all the censure Plato reserves for it if steadfastness and consistency, both in the character himself and in the narrative treatment of him, are to be the cardinal if not the sole virtues of portraiture. Odysseus is memorable because of his many-sidedness; he is master of irony, trickery, and lying—among other "ways of contending." This is what Aristotle seems to miss, despite having said that Homer was a master liar, in assuming, for example, that Odysseus's weeping during the song of Demodocus is wholly sincere and has no tactical purpose (see ch. 16). Most readers would agree, I think, that Odysseus indeed cries readily, grief-stricken as he is by the memory of the war, but that his tears have deliberately been planned nevertheless, planned in accordance with his request for a particular story, in order to give the Phaeacians a clue as to his identity. Granted that this is so, then Odysseus clearly remembers nothing he did not already have in mind when he requested the song. This scene, which Aristotle singles out for comment as a recognition scene, is not a recognition scene at all.

"Recognition Scenes run through" the *Odyssey,* Aristotle says (ch. 24), apparently to justify the complexity of the poem without jeopardizing the repeated claim that its plot is unified. It is as hard for Aristotle to maintain this latter position as it is for him to account for the Bath Scene or the hero. Having specifically excluded the episodic from his concept of unity, he later recounts the plot of the *Odyssey* and concludes: "This is the essence of the plot; the rest is episode" (ch. 17). It is true that epic is elsewhere said to be a looser mode than tragedy, but in yet another place Aristotle refuses to say that Homeric plots are episodic: "He made the Odyssey, and likewise the Iliad, to centre round an action that in our sense of the word is one" (ch. 8). In other passages he seems to hedge between these positions. Thus in chapter 23, "the Iliad and the Odyssey each furnish the subject of one tragedy or, at most, two." Still elsewhere, when arguing that epic is inferior to tragedy, he seems to forget his defense of Homer's architectonic skill altogether and speaks of a "poem . . . constructed out of several actions, like the Iliad and the Odyssey" (ch. 26). No doubt these passages are not absolutely contradictory and all could be reconciled without much ingenuity. In such instances it is enough to notice what is not necessarily a lapse or blunder but simply an awkwardness of expression that seems to accompany these topics and not others.

VII

Not only in mentioning the *Odyssey* but throughout the *Poetics,* Aristotle stresses one sort of unity, I suspect, in order to keep another, less praiseworthy sort of unity out of the picture. I am not suggesting, that is, that Aristotle's formalism keeps chaos at bay, as there is never an easy dichotomy to be found, either in the *Poetics,* in the history of criticism, or in the present discussion, between form and chaos, unity and randomness. It is always instead a question of the difference between artistic unity and the kind of unity that is unconsciously imposed, between the architectonic and the archaic principles that seem alternately to account best for one's experience of art. To put it another way, there appear to be two forces that shape poetry, the imposition of order on process and the radical motive underlying process. Aristotle and his successors allow that there are unconscious factors in the making of poetry (Aristotle even acknowledges the inspiration of madness), but they do not in general accept the idea that those factors may still be present even when the poetry is "successful," and they do not admit that covert determinacies, to an extent that cannot be known, may modify or even undermine artistic determination. It must be especially vexing, from Aristotle's standpoint, that this latter idea itself is both the theme and the unifying principle of his favorite play, the *Oedipus.* What keeps him clear of such issues, with what degree of consciousness on his part one cannot say (I suspect more than a little), is the fact that his lack of attention to interpretive detail is as pronounced as his lack of attention to the syncretistic patterns of the common epic and tragic plots.

Following Plato in the *Phaedrus,* Aristotle in the *Poetics* affirms the unity of artistic form definitively—though to my mind unfortunately—for the history of criticism. He talks of the impossibility of substituting for, transposing, or doing without any of the parts in a unified work of art (ch. 8). This conception is weaker than it appears to be on first view, being at once too demanding and not precise enough. It is too demanding in that probably one could move around certain choral odes in Greek tragedies or quatrains in early English ballads or descriptive passages in Victorian novels without *seriously* damaging the respective structures of those works. And it is not precise enough because serious damage causing obvious disunity is the only kind of damage Aristotle has in mind. His concept of "organic form" apparently does not include the minutiae of a work, its diacritical, lexical, or even imagistic features.[51] There is no evidence in the *Poetics* of the subtlety of modern formalism or of the attention to detail traditionally lavished on sacred texts and eventually on Shakespeare by German and English Romantic readers. Such developments as these were not merely baroque embellishments of established techniques. Each of them changed the way people read—making a certain amount of willful historicism necessary, I think, for most of us not to feel the inadequacy of reading the way Aristotle reads.

Even from the standpoint of the heirs to his formalism, for instance, Aristotle must be faulted for showing no awareness of the affinity between microcosm and macrocosm in artistic structures. Although it becomes an important matter in reading the *Oedipus,* Aristotle does not remark upon the connection between great and small in his own word *kosmos,* which recurs several times in the *Poetics.* For Aristotle, as in English today, a *kosmos* was a universal order or design; but in Greek a kosmos was also an intricate miniature design, an ornament, or piece of fancywork.[52] In other words it was both micro- and macro-, and could easily have served as a descriptive term to bridge the smallest and largest units of artistic structure for any observer who felt the need of it. Aristotle apparently did not. For one thing, he criticized recognition by tokens or amulets *(semeion kai deraion)* as recognition of the poorest sort on the grounds that it is least intrinsic to the logic of the action in tragedy. This would suggest that no object can ever serve as a symbol and that it is impossible for isolated figures to repeat and embody the action in which they appear. Here again, Aristotle makes phenomena fall outside the intellectual sphere of mimesis.

One of the best examples of recognition by tokens, one that Aristotle might with difficulty have disapproved of had he mentioned it, involves the handkerchief whereby Electra recognizes Orestes in the *Choephori* of Aeschylus. One misses a good deal in passing it over. Most readers would agree that the *Oresteia* is about the emergence of civilized jurisprudence from the primitive atmosphere of the lex talionis. With the coming of enlightenment to an archaic world, juridical mediation distances and channels the violence of endless retribution. Aeschylus illustrates this societal movement from bad fortune to good, in Aristotle's terms, through various recurrent symbols that undergo a parallel change in significance. The most prominent of these is that of the net, which at first is wholly sinister: it appears as the toils of Helen's beauty and as the web of destiny first cast over Troy and then spread out at home, both purple tapestry and shower curtain, to trap an unwary king. In the primitive world, with its "mind of the past" (*Eumenides,* 838; trans. Lattimore), art is always a destructive artifice, tainted by its connection with the spinning of the Fates and with bloody chains of events. Then comes an avenger for Agamemnon whose *agon* will consist of incurring and then being exonerated from a blood guilt that had augured violence for all futurity. The conferral of innocence on Orestes marks the coming of an orderly civilization to Argos. Now art becomes politics, the use of skill to keep the peace, a branch of politics being theater itself, with its rehearsal of dialogue in the public square. Athena's last speech removes all taint from the figure of weaving and the related thought-figures of mastery and authority; she commands that the women of the city reverence the Eumenides "In the investiture of purple stained robes" (1028). Hence it is wholly fitting that exactly at the turning point of this masque-like plot, the recognition that enables the action to go forward should be effected by a "token," as follows. After Electra has asked, true to the old ways, "Is this some net of treachery, friend, you catch me in?" (*Choephori* 220) Orestes produces his sign: "Look at this piece of weaving, the work of your hand / with its blade strokes and figured design of beasts" (231–32). Orestes' token symbolizes the containment of savagery (martial and bestial violence) by the refinement of culture through just the process—the pleasurable imitation of the painful—that is discussed by Aristotle in chapter 4, and thus it prefigures the outcome of the trilogy.

All this is elementary but (I should think) useful interpretation. It helps students to come to terms with Aeschylus, especially in that it lends motive and direction to the dense imagery of his choruses. There is little doubt that Aeschylus "intended" everything that has just been said—which is certainly not anachronistic, in any case. It should be a matter of concern, then, that Aristotle's poetics not only ignores but in fact discourages interpretation of this kind on the grounds that it lingers over mere externals or "necklaces" *(perideraia)*. The "voice of the shuttle" alone (ch. 16), which he mentions as another instance of Recognition that is "wanting in art," should demonstrate the eloquence of objects and their way of wedging as much significance as possible into a course of events.[53] But for Aristotle that sort of figural delay, like naturalism in characterization, only obscures and upstages the perfection of form. These last are old complaints against Aristotle, who is defended against them from time to time, for example by Arnold in his 1853 "Preface" and implicitly by Yvor Winters and other opponents of "qualitative progression" in poems, but nothing that is said in those places persuades me that such complaints should not be taken seriously.[54] In matters of poetic taste Aristotle simply does not accept the *kosmos*. Macrocosmically, for him, the *kosmos* is mere *opseos kosmos,* the opsis or spectacle that is the least central part of tragedy. Microcosmically, the *kosmos* appears in chapter 21, fourth in a list of eight noun-types, as the "ornamental"; of these eight, the seven others are discussed later in the chapter, but, as Else says, "a lacuna in the manuscripts has swallowed up the discussion of *kosmos,* the ornamental word."

"Fear and pity," writes Aristotle contemptuously, "may be aroused by spectacular means" (ch. 14), in other words, by *opseos kosmos*. Later in the same paragraph he strengthens his attack on "those who employ spectacular means to create a sense not of the terrible but only of the monstrous," persons who "are strangers to the purpose of tragedy." The distinction that is implied here would be difficult to exemplify. Spectacles of suffering, "bodily agony, wounds, and the like," are legitimate *pathemata,* and it would be nearly impossible to present those spectacles in ways that are not at least somewhat gruesome. Given the nature of the spectacle that arouses fear and pity in behalf of Oedipus, it is no wonder that Aristotle again shows his leaning toward mediated experience and says that "hearing the story of Oedipus" should be enough to move us (ch. 14). Safe from the assault of *opsis,* "he who hears the tale will thrill with horror and melt with pity at what takes place." But on the other hand, the spectator who actually sees the blood-stained mask will see no reason to discriminate between the horrible and the monstrous. Oedipus the pollutant is monstrous, even less fit to be seen than to see, but Sophocles compels the spectator to endure his presence.

Oedipus the King is the play that Aristotle takes to be the most elegantly formed of tragedies, or so we may legitimately gather from the number of his references to it.[55] It is an extraordinary play, and an intricate one, but one would not have said that it is elegantly formed. Once the eyeballs of Oedipus have been gored with the brooches of Jocasta, everything is burst open. The *pathos* and the spectacular element prove to have been so all-absorbing that there can be no further action, and for the remaining several hundred lines the play simply elaborates on what has happened. Further-more, although the recognition of the hero is neatly accomplished, it does not quite find an objective correlative in what has happened. The visceral and the uncanny have played their parts too devastatingly. To be sure, there is a sense in which the *Oedipus* is at least as well constructed as Aristotle says it is.[56] There is, for instance, the outermost symmetry, the chosen tyrant's initial greeting to his "children," which balances the exiled king's last farewell to his children, and concentric ironies of this sort could be pursued inward. What Aristotle does not remark, though, is that in this play it is precisely those things that are formal—"good form," order, mastery, judicial procedure, logic—that are treated with the greatest irony of all. Just where Oedipus is strongest, as Tiresias says, he proves weakest. His preoccupation with due order helps make him the vessel of corruption.

Aristotle prizes tragic plots that achieve "narrowness" and "concentra-tion" (ch. 26). His standard is the *Oedipus,* in which the plot is complex, certainly, like the orderly mind of the hero, but in the long run it is a plot that tightens beyond bearing and bursts open, like the double doors of Jocasta's bedchamber. Its tightest screws, as Aristotle says, are Reversal and Recognition (ch. 6), both of which are ways of fastening loose sequences of events back upon themselves and thus creating a too close encounter. Just as plot brings agents into relation, so its chief operative features serve to bring out resemblances. The Recognition Scene, Aristotle insists, does not expose just any forgotten thing but brings some resemblance to light. Hence recognition functions smoothly in the realization of the proper subject of tragedy, which is a transgression between *philoi,* or "related" persons. Again we can observe Aristotle omitting to enforce the parallel between large and small that presents itself in his work. The threshold of the tragic moment, the moment of recognition, certainly requires "an eye for resem-blances" (ch. 22),[57] and is thus the making of a metaphor. The eye-opening fate of the protagonist, in that case, is also the "mark of genius" (ibid.) in the protagonist's creator and binds the two of them together with the "natural sympathy" that Aristotle speaks of elsewhere (ch. 17).

Aristotle's silence concerning the interaction of metaphor, recognition, and kinship is of a piece with his not calling attention to the connection between the architectonic unity imposed by mimesis and the underlying unity discovered through anagnorisis. If he had said that recognition disrupts formality, he would have staged his own recognition scene, with Oedipus, who realizes that "It was Apollo there, Apollo, friends, / who brought my sorrows, vile sorrows to their perfection" (1329–30). The Apollo who is "Paean," patron of healing and thus of the Aristotelian purgation, is also the *apollon,* or destroyer, who ruins Oedipus where he is strongest.[58] He is strongest at making metaphors, happily, but unhappily he tends to *be* the metaphors he makes, if we take metaphor, with Aristotle, to be "the application of an alien name by transference" (ch. 21). The identity of Oedipus can be encompassed only by a perfect labyrinth of transferred names: tyrant to king, husband to son, father to brother, magistrate to criminal, and so on. His name itself is an overly compressed metaphor that makes untoward connections between intellectual knowledge (*oida,* to know) and carnal knowledge (*oida-pous,* or "Swellfoot," as Shelley called him).

At first the metaphors that Oedipus makes are successfully Aristotelian. In the *Rhetoric* and again in the *Poetics* (ch. 22), Aristotle associates metaphors with riddles. An author's style, he says, is "a riddle, if it consists of metaphors." This is the style of the Sphinx, "the harsh singer" (36) who plagued Thebes until Oedipus came along and made her riddle an intelligible metaphor by completing the transference of names: her "creature," with its several attributes, is "man," the same who was later to be so carefully distinguished by Aristotle from brutes. Unfortunately Oedipus not only solves but also exemplifies this metaphor. Because he has been weakest when his limbs (that is, when the number of them) were largest, Oedipus absorbs into himself the subnormal or beastly (and also infantile) side of man even as he proves in himself, through his sacrifice, the supranormal or godlike side of man. Like the riddle as Aristotle defines it, Oedipus at once reflects "true facts" and embodies "impossible combinations" (ch. 22). Although the *Oedipus* seems, then, to present figures of both the "harsh" poet and the good poet by Aristotle's standards, these figures finally merge: plaguing Thebes and at last recognizing his own animality (when he sees the dead Jocasta he bellows like a bull), the transfigured Oedipus must identify himself with the Sphinx.

"Or, again, the deed of horror may be done, but done in ignorance, and the tie of kinship or friendship be discovered afterwards. The Oedipus of Sophocles is an example" (ch. 14). Here Aristotle seems almost to bring recognition, kinship, and the riddling quality of metaphor together. Strangely enough, however, this passage does *not* refer to the climactic moment of the *Oedipus.* For the second time, Aristotle adverts to the death of Laius, a deed of horror that falls "outside the drama proper." He seems continuously to turn away from the *pathos* at the heart of the play to a pathetic event that is old news, a narrative with the emotional impact, at most, of a play that is read and not seen in performance. The closest approach Aristotle makes to the central scene is in his first citation of the play, a peculiar one wherein he illustrates "reversal" with reference to the first messenger's tidings. Not to dwell on the question that has troubled many scholars, the question of just what kind of reversal this is and with respect to whom, one simply wonders how this incident comes to be singled out, as it is neither more nor less important for its element of surprise than several others.

His discovery about Jocasta is a much more devastating one for Oedipus than his discovery that he has killed Laius, even after he has learned that Laius was his father. Aristotle never mentions the former discovery and shows no awareness that in dramatizing the myths of families playwrights are likely to come across incest. Aristotle's list of the violated *philia* that make the best tragedies includes the killing of a father by his son, but there is no mention of incest. The omission is surprising because that crime appears, at least as a hint, in every one of the "few houses" (ch. 13) Aristotle mentions: Alcmaeon and Orestes killed their mothers, Meleager's mother killed him, Thyestes violated his brother's wife, and Telephus, having learned who his parents were from the Delphic oracle, forthwith journeyed to join his mother. Be these matters as they may, however, the fact remains that Aristotle never mentions the dramatic *present* of the Oedipus story. The reader who surveys his scattered remarks about the play, especially recalling those about its "irrational element," will find that they gather to a startling degree around the figure of Laius. Aristotle, patriarch that he is and never sure how he stands toward his predecessors, especially toward Plato, seems to have in mind a play of his own invention in which the *pathos* happens to a father, possibly a good play although a much simpler one, to be called, say, "Laius at the Crossroads."

VIII

To return at this point to the assertion that the bias of Aristotle's description of literature reveals what Hulme called "space-shyness": Possibly thinking most of the well-knit *Oedipus* when he says that "the whole will be disjointed" or torn apart (ch. 7; *diapheresthai*) if the parts are moved around, he does not consider that that play, and many others too, are finally about the breakup of relations that are too closely established. Here another connection between large and small presents itself, that of the articulation, at both levels, which is also disarticulation. Speeches, for example, are jointed together by "connecting words" that are called *arthra* in the chapter on *lexis*. The description of the *arthron*, which essentially means "joint," is a little surprising. The *arthron* is not, as one might think, a focus of concentration but a sort of catalyst. Although it makes connections possible between other words (without predetermining their order), it has, like the "letter," no significance itself. The "connecting word" does not necessarily help piece together a living body. In itself it is inarticulate, and if it is used incautiously it is disarticulating. Thus it is related to the blinding of Oedipus, the removal of whose *arthra* (1270), or eyeballs, undoes a falsely articulated structure of perception. When Oedipus reappears onstage, he complains before all other things of being dislocated: "Where am I carried? Pity me! Where / is my voice scattered abroad on wings? / Divinity, where has your lunge transported me?" The voice of the dismembered hero is in turn dismembered, like the "voice of the shuttle." This, it seems to me, is the voice one hears at last in tragedy. The chorus wants no part of it and replies to Oedipus that he has been transported "To something horrible, not to be heard or seen" (1308–12). This resembles the response of Aristotle. It is better to hear the play than to see it, he allows, but it is best of all simply to conceive it in its pure pattern.

When one comes to question the extent to which Aristotle's idea of the "whole" can be of use in interpretation, his account of the *lexis* will again provide a point of departure. In speaking of a poet's style, he notes that "the metaphorical, the ornamental, and the other kinds above mentioned, will raise it above the commonplace and mean, while the use of proper words will make it perspicacious" (ch. 22). There is an analogy between the style recommended here and the best tragic plots. "Metaphor" is equivalent to the recognition of kinship; "ornament" admits that degree of the *opseos kosmos* which is unavoidable; but the whole, finally, is still subject to the norm of perspicuity. What takes place, in other words, must be wholly intelligible, leaving no residue either of the uncanny or of inarticulate animality in the mind of the spectator. But from the standpoint of both playwright and interpreter the very severe limitation of this view is that, as I have tried to show, the inexhaustible meaning of the scapegoat necessarily appears in every facet of a tragedy *except* near the norm.

Despite the figure of "untying" that Aristotle associates with tragic endings, the fact is that in formal endings as he works them out everything must be tied up. This is done by making sure that there is nothing left unexplained, and also that nothing is out of scale. When Aristotle speaks of the perspicuity of the whole, he speaks chiefly of its size, its perspicuity in space: "A very small animal organism cannot be beautiful; for the view of it is confused, the object being seen in an almost imperceptible moment of time. Nor, again, can one of vast size be beautiful; for as the eye cannot take it all in at once, the unity and sense of the whole is lost for the spectator; as for instance if there were one a thousand miles long" (ch. 7; it is possible that pictures, not animals, are being described). Here as in all topics Aristotelian there is a Mean to be observed. In this analogy we see that the tiny organism is a *kosmos*, too bewilderingly ornamented in its microscopic world to be perspicuous, while the vast object seems horizonless—seems, one might suggest, to be sublime, though admittedly it is grotesque also. It is in the nature of the Mean not to extend to the horizons of insight. To support this declaration I have suggested that the *Oedipus*, Aristotle's "test case" for excellence in tragedy, is so tightly compressed in structure and yet so forcefully scattered abroad by that very compression that every detail (crossroads, double doors, brooches, eyes, all converging, Oedipus complains, on a "field of double sowing") becomes both sign and seed (*sema* is the word for both) in the replenished fields. Most of this is not registered, and seems furthermore to be denied, by Aristotle's formalism.[59]

Relatively little has been asserted in this argument about the nature of whatever it is that a poetics of order banishes from its purview, except that it cannot be described in formal terms. It includes the actual, material world, it includes the sublime, and it also includes points of contact and divergence between these horizons of representation. Such factors, which are difficult if not impossible to assimilate into any theory of manifest form, appear interchangeably and with the greatest vividness at the extremes of the minute and the boundless. The formalism we inherit from Aristotle is, as it were, Newtonian. The minute and the boundless cannot be inferred from the formal Mean any more than Relativity and its offshoots can be inferred from Newton's mechanics.

Furthermore, the Mean is not even "all right as far as it goes," because in the very idea of the Mean, as I have indicated in analyzing Aristotle's treatment of literature, there is a pressure, not just of exclusion but of distortion. The Mean can appear only as the measured distance between extremes that *it* must identify and delimit, extremes which, having thus been cut to size and classified as error or imbalance, are not the same as the extremes the imagination encounters in its experience of literature beyond formalism. It is for this reason that schools of criticism never quite manage to exist in harmony. Few readers rest wholly content with pluralism, with seeing "different parts" of the "same" work. The "literal" or "intended" meaning prized by hermeneutic conservatives and textual scholars coexists uneasily at best with "antithetical" meanings because these latter disturb, challenge, and purport to undermine the former. The material furnished by the unconscious, the Zeitgeist, or the social realities of a period cannot be subtracted from, factored out of, or even set alongside the "valid" semantic interpretation because such material exists in an ironic, iconoclastic relation to that interpretation. Antithetical senses, in other words, impose a dramatic irony, an internal source of dissent, on plain senses.

But the relationship between form and interpretation is still more complicated, more so than could be indicated even by criticizing Aristotle's point of view in the preceding argument. Both the plain and the hidden senses, perhaps, can be said to have forms, or what I earlier called unities, but if so they have very different forms that are never identical or parallel and are very unlikely to be mirror opposites. There is no form, furthermore, that can result from the effort to chart the course of their divergence. We do not know enough about the difference between outside and inside to know what is imposed and what dictates itself in any work. But even if one grants the "unity" of interpretations that undermine the Mean, they too are only partial and distort matters just as much as interpretations that are based on the concept of poetic making—although perhaps no more so. None of these uncertain issues gives us any reason to think what the revelation of form need be the final purpose of interpretation. The collision of the two forms may be, itself, the tragic *agon*, or else the contact between them may be relatively insignificant. It is this confusion that necessitates untold reserves and reservations on the part of the interpreter. Such irregularities as these in the meaning of literature can never be purged or purified by the catharsis of interpretation, especially because all these confusions cannot actually appear, as we shall now see in turning to Longinus, except when they are repeated, with a difference, in the mind of the interpreter.[60]

TWO

Longinus at Colonus: The Grounding of Sublimity

The capacity to be able to act theoretically is defined for us by the fact that in attending to something it is possible to forget one's own purposes. . . . Theoria is a true sharing, not something active, but something passive (pathos), namely being totally involved in and carried away by what one sees.

Hans-Georg Gadamer, *Truth and Method*

In undertaking to show the relevance of Longinus to the concerns of criticism at the present time, it may be useful to begin by considering opinions of his treatise that are recorded by two modern theorists of criticism. W. K. Wimsatt thinks that *On the Sublime* is incoherent in every way, that Longinus is incapable of distinguishing clearly among author, text, and audience and incapable likewise of distinguishing between such pairs of terms as nature and art or thought and language. The result of these confusions is, according to Wimsatt, that Longinus cannot sufficiently distinguish even between his own five "causes" of the sublime, the two that are inborn (the power of forming great thoughts and the ability to feel passion) and the three that can be learned (use of figures, use of diction, and word order). It is imprecision of this sort that augurs poorly, in Wimsatt and Brooks's *Short History*, for the future of author-oriented criticism.[1] As far as Longinus is concerned, according to Wimsatt, a verbal work is only an accidental spark of contact between two souls, like a piece of loose wiring.

Elder Olson agrees with this last view, in effect, but he feels that the spark is a happy occasion. As he puts it, the Longinian sublime is "the communication of nobility."[2] Apart from this point, Olson's view of Longinus is almost entirely in disagreement with Wimsatt's. He tries to make Longinus a kind of Aristotle, with the result that in his hands *On the Sublime* becomes so coherent that even the contents of the massive lacunae can be inferred.[3] Olson neatly determines that the "great thoughts" are the province of the author, the strong passions belong to the audience, and the three rhetorical categories refer the work to its own composition, to the author's choice of words, and to the affective quality of the words as sounds, respectively.

47

I think it inadvisable to attempt the rehabilitation of an obviously intuitive writer by stressing the well-ordered complexity of his ideas. Olson saw something he liked in Longinus but had to distort his author's way of proceeding enormously in order to bring it out. Wimsatt saw nothing he liked, but he saw the way Longinus's mind worked very clearly. He saw that Longinus is always talking about the same thing no matter how various the headings he devises may seem. I should like to make use of Olson's sympathy and Wimsatt's insight in order to show that the tendency of Longinus to slide from category to category and to leave large areas of overlap between his terms is in fact a highly desirable approach to theory, and one that is preferable to the formalism of Aristotle.

As theorists, both Olson and Wimsatt are primarily concerned, in their different ways, with structure: Olson to establish generic structures within which works can be identified, Wimsatt to define structure as an intrinsic quality of the works themselves.[4] This common concern brings both of them, but especially Olson, closer to Aristotle than to Longinus. Longinus takes a Chicagoan view of the accidental or intermediary function of language, but he takes a decidedly anti-Chicagoan, agnostic view of the conceptual structures, if there are any, that exist apart from words. As Wimsatt points out unsympathetically, text and soul seem to be analogous in Longinus;[5] neither has any definite shape or identity because each tends so easily to merge with other texts and other souls. Here too Longinus can be shown, however, to have taken a wise course. For him the question that has plagued Aristotle and his descendants never arises, the question as to whether structures are extrinsic or intrinsic to embodied works. The main question for Longinus is whether the knowledge that passes through discourse is finally to be understood in structural terms at all.

I do not wish to speculate, here or later, about the degree to which the argument of Longinus as I will interpret it is self-conscious, or cognizant of the implications that I will find in it. The *Peri Hupsous* is a series of fragments written by an unknown author; I will not deny that I take advantage of the vagueness that both characterizes and surrounds this work in order to build a poetics out of its hints and obliquities that can preside over the rest of this book. I will say, though, that I have paid more attention to the continuity of detail in the text than any commentator before me, and that I have not ignored or deliberately slanted any of it. To summarize what follows, then: I will concentrate on Wimsatt's observation that the difference between text and soul is very slight in Longinus. His *hupsos*, which means "height," or, in context, "elevated language," must be understood both as elevation *and* as language, difficult as it is to do so. His thinking can be viewed in two different but closely related ways. Either it is a theory of the interaction of consciousness with a phenomenal world that is perceived almost as another consciousness, or else it is a theory of the fluidity with which utterances can move from one consciousness to another. The quality that gets transmitted can be understood either as language or as spirit but it cannot be divided into language *and* spirit, language and thought, or language and reference. Once these distinctions are set aside, it will become apparent that it is much the same, though never wholly the same, whether one speaks of nature or art, author or audience; or whether one speaks—to return to the distinction that emerged at the end of the last chapter—of unconsciously or consciously imposed form.[6] Thus I will show Longinus to have accommodated, without by any means cathartically "resolving," the difficulty concerning the place and function of form that disturbs the argument of the *Poetics*.

I

In comparing Longinus and Aristotle it would be most appropriate, per-haps, to align the rhetoric handbook called *Peri Hupsous* with Aristotle's *Rhetoric*, especially because in the *Rhetoric* Aristotle allows more vividness and energy to the oratorical performer (1413b–14a) than he allows to the players in the *Poetics*. Speechmaking in the *Rhetoric* requires pathos and spectacle before all things, whereas dramatic imitation uses these aids as sparingly as possible. However, although in some ways the *Rhetoric* resem-bles the treatise of Longinus more closely than the *Poetics* does, the *Peri Hupsous* itself can be as readily considered a poetics as a rhetoric. Longinus maintains no distinction between modes of utterance, at least not in a systematic way. At the outset he speaks of his topic as a special quality that belongs to "the very greatest poets and prose writers."[7] On two occasions later he does discriminate between poetry and prose (15.8, 30.2), but at these moments of greater specificity he has evidently remembered suddenly that he is supposed to be a *rhetor*—which would imply, of course, that oratory must be a special discipline.[8] If it be granted, though, that the *Peri Hupsous* is both a rhetoric *and* a poetics, in this respect being yet another reflection of Longinus's failure, or unwillingness, to make distinctions, then the *Poetics* will not appear to be an inappropriate text for comparison after all.

Longinus intermittently discusses tragedy. He twice mentions *Oedipus the King*, once apparently to concur with Aristotle that it is supreme among tragedies (33.5) and once again to quote it, to quote as an instance of the sublime a central passage of the sort that Aristotle never considers:

> Weddings, weddings,
> You bred me and again released my seed,
> Made fathers, brothers, children, blood of kin,
> Brides, wives, mothers—all
> The deeds most horrid ever seen in men.
>
> [23.3; trans. Russell]

Longinus cites this passage as an example of troping singular objects with plural endings. That is what it is; it stresses the multiplicity of horrors that befall Oedipus as if to remind Aristotle that misfortunes rarely come singly: they are not "one." There is nothing in Longinus about tragic structure,[9] but still, on the strength of this passage alone, he inspires confidence in his ability to get at what is tragic in general, irrespective of what may be tragic in genre. In Aristotle, art, which is a movement external to the thing moved, traces a curve of order; in Longinus, as his plunge into the midst of the *Oedipus* would signify, "disorder goes with emotion, which is a disturbance and movement of the mind" (20.2; *ataxia de to pathos, epei phora psuches kai sunkinesis estin*). If the mind moves at all, if it transports or is transported, its movement is disordered and traces a disorder.

Longinus is not quite the rhapsodist that his cooler readers have made him out to be but he certainly lacks the Peripatetic neutrality of voice. His own consciousness of this difference is plain in his one citation of Aristotle, whom he makes to say, with Theophrastus, "that there are ways of softening bold metaphors—namely by saying 'as if', . . . Apology, they say, is a remedy for audacity." "I accept this doctrine," Longinus continues, "but . . ." (32.3).[10] No one can either be or give the impression of being inspired who thus says "as if." *Si vis me flere*: he who expresses emotion must not just move but be, if not always witlessly possessed, at least greatly moved in his turn. Thus in moments of emotion the writer has "no chance to delay," as the onrush of what he says will have "outstripped its creator" (27.2, 1). Although Longinus is capable of sarcasm concerning the affectation of madness (see 15.8), this is not because madness or a state like it is extravagant but rather because its affectation in the wrong place is *not* extravagant. It is one form, "the pseudo-bacchanalian" form, of the false sublime (3.5). To be transported we must first have our feet on the ground; we cannot be duly and unflaggingly inspired, after the perfunctory suggestion of Aristotle, "by a strain of madness" (ch. 17).

Although he willingly turns to the tragic literature of the Attic period for his examples of the sublime, Longinus appears to have little use for "the trappings of the stage" (7.1).[11] His distaste for the excitements of performance seems even more extreme than Aristotle's and may at first confirm one's fear that the "sublime" (as Boileau translated *hupsos*, following Latin translations) will prove to be nothing but a fancy word for sublimation. Here, ostensibly, is the closest agreement between Longinus and the *Poetics*, to the effect, namely, that characterization, or the mere portrayal of "manners" *(ethe)*, is inferior to, is indeed inessential to, the highest kind of expression. Narratives of manners, says Longinus, are the pastimes of old age: In the *Odyssey* the dotard Homer returns to the mere imitation of character which, as Aristotle had said, is also natural to childhood. (Whatever one may think of this judgment of the *Odyssey*, one should notice that at least it safeguards Longinus from emulating Aristotle's attempt to isolate a single course of action in that poem.)

For Longinus, as for Plato, greatness is steadfast, perhaps even inflexible; it eludes the many-talented Hyperides, for example, and appears instead in Demosthenes, who "has no sense of character" (34.3). Character in Longinus cannot be as freely varied as it is even in Aristotle. Slaves and women are permitted to speak by Aristotle as long as they speak in character, whereas in Longinus the drunkards of Herodotus (one who could arguably be released, as a historian, from the precept of poetic heightening) are censured for having spoken at all, even though, or rather because, they spoke in character (4.6–7). Longinus evidently feels, with Plato, that an ignoble taste for ventriloquism estranges the soul from the singleness of purpose it should cultivate. Even though Longinus easily violates this viewpoint in both taste and practice, it remains the most rigid, least thoughtfully integrated, and, I would say, least original feature of his thinking. That this view of character is what unfortunately leads to the facile indictment of his contemporaries in the last chapter is a disquieting aspect of Longinus's approach to art. It authorizes the Superman at certain moments; but in general, as I will try to show later, the sublime threatens more than it consoles autocracy of all kinds.

Not only is Longinus uninterested in the symmetries of dialogue and conflict that are made available by the imitation of character, but he also disdains, again in company with Plato, the group of emotions that carries drama forward. "Emotions, such as pity, grief, and fear" (8.2), he says, are "divorced from sublimity and [have] a low effect." These are just the emotions that determine the tragic structure in Aristotle. Again, though, this judgment is probably connected with Longinus's dislike of the ventriloquistic part of dramatic composition. His "fear" (*phobos,* as in Aristotle) refers only to cowardice, for example the cowardice, one may conjecture, of the suppliant Lykaon in the *Iliad,* which draws forth the famous response of Achilles: "Come friend, face your death, you too" (book 21; trans. Fitzgerald). But the fear involved in this exchange is not only dramatic; it is not only Lykaon's fear. There is fear for *any* listener in the reply of Achilles, and fear even for Achilles himself, perhaps, in having come to fathom the apathy of his own clearsightedness.[12] In a nondramatic setting, where emotions like fear can become ontologically charged rather than merely pragmatic, they could probably be restored, with the approval of Longinus, to the circle of emotions "without number" (22.1) that do readily supplement the sublime. But in rejecting pity and fear Longinus still does tellingly reverse the judgment of Aristotle. "In ordinary life," writes Longinus, "nothing is truly great which it is great to despise: wealth, honour, reputation, absolute power" (7.1). These are the "trappings" of status upon which the interest of the drama, considered as a representation of society, must solely depend. For a king who is not allowed to have developed a real personality, these possessions make up the whole of what is lost in the moment of tragic reversal.

As Longinus almost certainly did not know the *Poetics,* it is remarkable how precisely he inverted Aristotle's values.[13] But to what end? Would it not seem again that Longinus, even more than Aristotle, is bent on doing away with the last contingencies of human life in criticism? I would say decidedly not. It is most important to qualify and delimit his distaste for the material things that have enslaved his sottish contemporaries and that the dramatization of despotism relies upon. Longinus describes the domestic atmosphere of the *Odyssey,* to take up a case in point, as a "realistic" one (9.15); that is, it is made up of *biologoumena,* the stuff of daily life that every theory of criticism until 1800 or thereabouts may be said to have banished from the precincts of all but the lowest genres. Now, this stuff cannot be what is missing in Longinus's earlier complaint that in the *Odyssey* "the mythical element [*muthikon*] predominates over the realistic [*praktikon*]" (9.14). Admittedly, it is not the details of reality but the Aristotelian "probable" that is in question here, a factor that I took to be purely intellectual in the last chapter. But in the case of Longinus there is, in the *praktikos,* a bias toward actual experience.

It is difficult to agree with Longinus that myth outweighs reality in the *Odyssey.* Instead we would want to say that the poem quite amazingly holds the mythical and the realistic in balance. The all-too-human gullibility of Polyphemus and the fireside knitting of Calypso are "natural" (for that is perhaps a better word than "realistic") whereas the massacre of the female domestics, on the other hand, is savage on a scale that is plausible only in myth. Perhaps, though, for Longinus, this interdependence of the real and the fantastic is just the problem. Homer's realism, he may feel, is not in good faith because it is not made interesting for itself or its determination of the action but only for its meretricious connection with the mood of folktale. If this is what Longinus means, it will not redeem his judgment of the *Odyssey,* but it will provide us with some reassurance that, for him, reality is indeed the basis of the sublime. And this basis is crucial, as I shall argue everywhere in the present book; without it the sublime is merely the quaint remnant from the rhetoric of ahistorical aestheticism that its critics suppose it to be. Longinus does not care for moonshine; he dislikes the fabulous in Homer because one cannot discover it either in "real life" (3.2) or in any religion that truly inspires awe, like that of "the lawgiver of the Jews"—"no ordinary man" (9.9), says Longinus, but certainly, he must suppose, a real one.

II

The sublime is "grounded," then. There is a necessary connection between sublimity and the earth, or more necessary in any case than the connection between art and nature in Aristotle. The Longinian sublime is also more closely connected with the earth than the Kantian sublime, which is the opposite of the beautiful precisely in not being given but only implied as an absence by the natural world. What makes this connection possible in Longinus is the absence of radical dualism from his thinking. The effect of his penchant for sliding categories is to promote mergers.[14] There are mergers between genres, as we have seen, and there is also the merger of gods and men. This occurs in a passage that is mildly critical of Homer for having promoted the merger himself, but I think that too much has been made of Longinus's Platonic piety in this instance.[15] Homer exalts even while he demeans: In the *Iliad* he has made "the men of the Trojan war gods, and the gods men" (6.7). It is quite a different matter to have blended superstition and folkways in the *Odyssey;* in the *Iliad* the stakes of existence, and its conditions, are fought for at the height of human potential, which is figured forth in the attacks of Diomedes and Achilles on the gods and in the appearance of the unarmed Achilles, under the aegis of Athena, that fells twelve Trojans with heart failure. This height (*hupsos*) of human strength merges in turn with the voice of the poet, whose *Iliad* was composed "at the height of his powers" and at a "consistent level of elevation" (9.13).

It is this last sort of fusion, in which the person inspired takes on the qualities of what inspired him, that is most often noted both by sympathetic and by hostile readers of Longinus. The commentator in turn is inspired. The sublime, understood as the "echo of a noble mind" (9.2), is transmitted from the text to the voice of its author to the voice of the commentator, who can stand, as a result, in the place of the author: "Filled with joy and pride, we come to believe we have created what we have only heard" (7.2). As it is effected rhetorically by Longinus, this identification may remind one of the fallacy of imitative form, with the important proviso that it is *not formal.* Thanks to the looseness of his categories, Longinus can subordinate the structure even of his own insights to the continuousness of experience. He does not deliberately constitute himself, or so he would imply, as one who is inspired—as the great sublime he draws. We are conscious of his rhetoric not as the imposition of a pattern but as a movement;[16] first there is the interjection into his own text of some fragment, which is often broken up still further by misquotation; then Longinus reminds us of the force of heroism—or divinity—that is mirrored in authorship; and finally there comes an onrush of commentary, tumbling out, confused, in every way the record of experience, not of reflection (see 9.6–7, 10.3). The sublime in the theory and practice of Longinus is not infinite, though it may intimate boundlessness; it is always an experience in time, and thus restores to reading what formalization, which is necessarily spatial, has removed.

I have made no proper distinction, so far, between intention and accomplishment. I have spoken of "false" madness as though sincere madness were easy—and desirable—to single out, and then again I have spoken of sublimity and "rhetoric" in the style of Longinus as though there were no difference between them, or as though the difference did not matter. It does matter, but perhaps only when it is considered as success or failure in the representation of perceptiveness. All the least futile discussions of sincerity, from Johnson on *Lycidas* to Richards on *The Chinese Classics* to Lionel Trilling on Jane Austen, have touched only lightly on the question of hypocrisy and stressed, instead, a correlation that can be demonstrated, at least in part, between the occasion of an utterance and its manner. Thus in Longinus insincere madness is "untimely . . . emotion where none is in place" (3.5). If madness is appropriate to an occasion, however, one is then free to affect it in all sanity. If the real Erinyes should attack an orator where he stands as though he were Orestes, then even if he is calm at heart he may resort hypocritically to the figure called *phantasia,* or "visualization," which is said to betoken madness.

There is no necessary connection, therefore, between sincerity—considered as spontaneity—and the sublime. Even the noble Demosthenes could scarcely stand trial for sincerity in Longinus's reading of his rhetorical questions: "Emotion carries us away more easily when it seems to be generated by the occasion rather than deliberately assumed by the speaker. . . . The figure of question and answer arrests the hearer and cheats him into believing that all the points made were raised and are being put into words on the spur of the moment" (18.2). On the other hand, however—and this is a crucial distinction—at the affective end of the sublime experience sincerity is essential. For the reader or commentator it is not enough even to be persuaded, "for persuasion on the whole is something we can control" (1.4). If we are free to disregard the sublime, it is not the sublime. With respect not to one's reading but to one's reader, however, as the chain adds links, one is again freed, having taken the place of the author, to dissemble enthusiasm if need be.[17]

The very complexity of this issue, which is scarcely allowed to arise in the *Poetics,* must show that in Longinus there is no easy way to subsume art in nature or nature in art. There remains evidence in his own text, instead, of the conflict between the two which is just the conflict between design and compulsion that I discussed earlier. One reason why no clear relation can be established between art and nature is that for Longinus they are not easy to distinguish. He vacillates in his treatment of them but his vacillation is rigorous, I think, rather than weak-minded. For him the issue is at bottom a moral one, touching as it does on the question whether "we can develop our nature to some degree of greatness" (1.1)—the question, in other wrods, whether we can improve our nature by art. As a teacher justifying his own existence, he must part company with the widespread opinion, dating from Pindar, that greatness is solely "a natural product" (2.1), but he plainly feels that he must also stop short of the Sophists' notion that there are rules for all things given that all things are unknowable and must therefore be devised by artifice as need arises. The former view is typically that of the poets and the latter that of the rhetors, and Longinus, as usual, takes his stand between them.

Although his eventual assignment of two natural and three artificial causes to the sublime suggests that nature and art are fully separable, the discussion that leads up to this list is more complicated and—apparently—more confused. Of the "three points" (2.2) he makes to refute the contention that genius is artless, the second anticipates the later headings and the third is mostly cliché, but the first is significant: "Though nature is on the whole a law unto herself in matters of emotion and elevation, she is not a random force and does not work altogether without method." If this is so, nature is partly art and can receive from art, in that case, only a supplement of itself. The last sentence of the next paragraph (2.3) again undermines the standard contrast, this time not by merger but by dialectic: "The very fact that some things in literature depend on nature alone can itself be learned only from art." Whether by "art" here is meant criticism, or the reflective judgment, or the recognition of having failed to achieve nature by artificial means, is not wholly clear. What is clear, though, is that the sentence is reversible: "Art" and "nature" could change places, with "nature" now meaning "experience."[18] This possible reversal would point to an exactly complementary moment in the learning process, and would suggest, in its very exactness, that nature and art are not casual aids to each other but two facets of an indivisible dynamic. The exemplary Demosthenes later illustrates this dyad more than once, showing, for example, that "sobriety is needed even under the influence of inspiration" (16.4).

A more interesting later outgrowth of this interaction of categories occurs near the end of Longinus's by and large conventional contrast between genius and mediocrity: "We may say that accuracy is admired in art and grandeur in nature, and it is by *nature* that man is endowed with the power of speech" (36.3). Thus, language belongs to man's natural course of development and is not an art implanted in man by fiat. The notion that man differs from the animals in possessing inborn art, the chief sign of which is his conversion of random sounds into the articulate sounds of speech, was perhaps the most crucial presupposition of Aristotle's formalism in the *Poetics*. Longinus's view is neither that art complements nature nor that it is nature but simply that it comes to us along with the rest of our inheritance. If this is so, art cannot be an activity we perform but must be instead an activity that takes place in us—like nature. Longinus cannot quite say, then, with the formalist tradition from Aristotle to the present, that art, "in cooperation with the conscious will" (Coleridge), defends the fortress of the self against the siege of nature. He appears to suggest, rather, that both art and nature come as strangers to hold their combat in a remote corner of what at first we may not even recognize as the self: "Do you not admire the way in which [Sappho] brings everything together—mind and body, hearing and tongue, eyes and skin? She seems to have lost them all, and to be looking for them as though they were external to her" (10.3). This difficult response to the so-called "Ode to Anactoria" is drawn forth in particular from Sappho's "My tongue is broken, a subtle fire runs under my skin."[19]

III

The "broken tongue" of Sappho could be an emblem of the Longinian sublime. Her alienation from herself resembles the sudden switch to apostrophe whereby Demosthenes "divides a single thought between two persons in his passion" (27.3) and thus parodies the course of the sublime from transmitter to receiver: "this shameless monster, who—you vile wretch!" Longinus says that Demosthenes is touched by genius because, unlike Hyperides, he "lacks fluency" (34.3). But it is not only this loose application of Sappho's trope that merits attention. There is also the more precise metaphor in which the broken tongue represents the lapse into incoherence, the disarticulation of syntax or "semiotic discontinuity," as Thomas Weiskel has called it, that is caused by certain figures of speech.[20] *Polyptoton,* the term that designates all repetitions of a word in different inflections, is also the general term that includes Demosthenes' change of person, and it is one of the figures that Longinus stresses most.

The sublime figures and tropes, which I shall now survey, are not quite sublime in themselves any more than art is quite nature, although, as we have seen, neither of these paired sets of terms constitutes a clear dichotomy. Just as Sappho's broken tongue is not itself her speech—neither her allegedly inarticulate stammerings nor the well-formed "sapphics" that record them—so in turn speech itself is not the sublime.[21] If the sublime were indeed a property of words themselves, it could be quantified with respect to their combinations. It might prove, for example, to be some "principle of equivalence" like that of Jakobson and would in any case certainly appear as a function of structure. In other words it would be part of the matrix of continuous, orderly composition by which, according to Longinus, the orator effects "persuasion." But "persuasion" in Longinus is just the opposite of "transport," which is caused by the sublime (1.4).

Persuasion is an affect that we are free to resist. It arises from the "ability to order and arrange material" and takes its effect, such as it is, "when we see the whole context" (1.4). The sublime, on the other hand, is what we cannot resist. It is not surprising that we can stand aloof from persuasion. It is more surprising that we can be persuaded at all, except by the most translucent of styles, because carefully organized discourse forms a lattice-work that seems to resist *us;* it proclaims its autonomy far more than its authority. In recognition of these characteristics, the New Criticism affirms the autonomy of the work of art. The sublime, on the other hand, as Longinus's descriptive terms for it will show, is that which forces its way through an opening it has widened in the latticework of persuasion. It has no other way of appearing; as Kant also showed, its occasion is natural, but it cannot appear in or through nature without a prior appeal to a formula-tion of the mind—an inner discourse—that arises in response to nature. Thus it is not a quality of words, but it does depend on their close proximity.

Just so in criticism, I would venture to add, the sublime will not appear in formal discussion as such, but it cannot appear without the context of a formal discussion. The sublime is "what is left to the imagination"; it is not the words in the text or a paraphrase of them but it is still prompted by them. Where the text has left words out or transposed or delayed them, the imagination must supply them. I shall try to demonstrate that this familiar exercise of multiple choice has all the attributes that Longinus and his successors call sublime. Far from cloaking itself in a nimbus of ineffability, the sublime is closely related to interpretation itself. "It is only through inevitable omissions," writes Wolfgang Iser, "that a story gains its dyna-mism."[22] These omissions are the reader's share. The sublime (to continue to call it that for the time being) is potential in any interpretation that does not suppose that it can either leave a text as it found it or else exhaust it by assigning it a form. The sublime that is closest to interpretation responds to a text by augmenting it. What Longinus calls *auxesis,* or "amplification," is not the sublime, he says, because, like persuasion, it is determined finally by quantity; but it is still close to the sublime, close enough to call for a fine discrimination. "Sublimity depends on elevation, whereas amplification involves extension; sublimity exists often in a single thought, amplification cannot exist without a certain . . . superfluity" (12.1).

Amplification, about which there will be more to say in another place, is not a "broken" figure. One of the few exceptions to the criterion of fragmentation in Longinus's survey of figures, it remains close to the sublime because it overloads "persuasive" composition as much as the sublime disrupts it. A more typical figure that generates the sublime is asyndeton, which presents words or phrases "without connection" (19.1). There is nothing deliberative or slow, nothing spondaic, as it were, in the wide spacing of this figure; rather it rushes by in order to get beyond an impasse which is passed along, in the process, to the reader's effort of reconstruction: "Disconnected and yet hurried phrases convey the impression of an agitation which obstructs the reader and drives him on. Such is the effect of Homer's asyndeta" (ibid.). The passage Longinus has quoted just before this observation marks a crisis of speech in the *Odyssey* which is also a crisis for the status of speech as a means of persuasion. The breathless Eurylochus returns to tell Odysseus that Circe has turned their comrades into "squealing," inarticulate swine, "though [their] minds were still unchanged" (book 10; trans. Fitzgerald). Panic-stricken as he is, Eurylochus is unable to imitate in his asyndetic speech the well-knit construction of what he saw: "We went as you told us, noble Odysseus, up the woods, / We saw a beautiful palace built in the glades" (ibid.; trans. Russell, 19.2). As befits its ambiguity for men, Circe's palace is both persuasive *and* sublime, a contexture in a "glade" or gap; but in its outward structure it is like the figure that constrasts with asyndeton in Longinus, polysyndeton, which creates "smoothness by conjunctions" between phrases (21.2) and thus undermines the "harsh character of the emotion" (21.1) one would find in the same phrases written without conjunctions.

Another figure conducive to the sublime is hyperbaton, which is an arrangement of words that differs from the "normal sequence" (22.1). This figure creates gaps not in syntax but in expectation, whether by delay or by prematurity. From the standpoint of the author, however, hyperbaton is fully unified, not in the arrangement of its parts but with respect to the ground of thought or feeling from which it arises. More than any other figure, hyperbaton implies spontaneity and brings the problematic terms *art* and *nature* into their closest possible conjunction: "Hyperbaton is the means by which . . . imitation approaches the effect of nature" (22.1). Again, *ars est celare artem*. Yet, working under this concealment, the art of hyperbaton actually disrupts the nature it pretends to resemble: Thucydides and Demosthenes "show ingenuity in separating by transpositions even things which are by nature completely unified and indivisible" (22.3). Thus it is not the figure of speech itself that the sublime thunderbolt gaps (as one gaps a sparkplug) but rather the natural ground of the figure. Hyperbaton opens abysses, vacancies. If we recall the full play of the word *arthra* in Aristotle, which according to usage means both the presence and the absence of jointure, we may also grasp the significance for Longinus not only of Sappho's broken tongue but also of the antifeminist trope, quoted from Plato's *Timaeus,* that labels "the seat of the desires 'the woman's quarters' " (32.5). The sublime thus can be further understood as a condition of desire, an intimation of presence transmitted not only through a figural rift but also through a "cleft in the ground" (13.2; the phrase appears in an important passage that will occupy us below).

The topics of Longinus's quotations nearly always reflect, in some way, the rhetorical devices they are chosen to illustrate.[23] This is to some extent a consequence of the "representative" form that Pope was inspired—partly by Longinus—to illustrate in his *Essay on Criticism*. But in the case of Longinus the pattern of representative form is so continuous that it seems, irrespective of purpose, to be a necessity of expression. Evidently Longinus is drawn as much to a certain view of nature as to a certain group of tropes and figures. As hyperbaton reveals, nature itself is noble, impassioned, and broken. We noticed before that Longinus, unlike Aristotle, stresses the plurality of Oedipus's misfortunes; he assumes that the heart of tragic experience is the moment of dismemberment, not resolution, and he expects that that moment will be represented in language that risks inarticulateness. The language that prepares for tragedy's bloody sowing will likewise be scattered abroad; hyperbaton, asyndeton, and polyptoton are all present in the passage about careening flight that Longinus quotes from Euripides' lost *Phaethon:*

> "Steer towards the seven Pleiads."
> The boy listened so far, then seized the reins,
> Whipped up the winged team, and let them go.
> To heaven's expanse they flew.
> His father rode behind on Sirius,
> Giving the boy advice: "That's your way, there:
> Turn here, turn there."

Equally characteristic are the passages that describe in nature the wound they illustrate in syntax. Under the heading of "ordinary words" and how to use them, Longinus indulges in an outburst of rapid-fire quotation: " 'Cleomenes in his madness cut his own flesh into little pieces with a knife till he sliced himself to death.' 'Pythes continued fighting on the ship until he was cut into joints [i.e., steaks]' " (31.2). The effect of slicing is just the same in hyperbaton as Demosthenes uses it: "Now, for our affairs are on the razor's edge, men of Ionia . . ." (22.1).

Nothing could have a more overtly rhetorical effect than the violence in these "ordinary words." At present among critics there is a tendency to discredit the discipline of "rhetoric" as it has been traditionally practiced because it is so difficult to imagine a "pure" employment of language that would not be rhetorical.[24] If to some degree nature is revealed as art by the ubiquity of rhetoric, it is equally true, however, that in the absence of a zero-degree or full transparency in language, art disappears back into nature simply for the reason that the province of art has no discernible boundaries. One wonders whether Longinus, whose technical categories so readily dissolve, might not agree with this recent view. Is there an Ordinary

Language (*idiotismos;* 31.1) whose idioms are not cut to pieces by use? What is the "normal sequence" that the artifice of hyperbaton disrupts?

IV

Although for the most part Longinus's observations about the need of art to conceal art are commonplace, there is one moment at which he seems to become fully attentive to Horace's maxim. In preparing to assert, *inter alia,* that hyperbaton approaches nature most nearly of all the figures, Longinus declares that "figures are natural allies of sublimity" (17.1). "Allies," here, is a precise metaphor. Longinus is about to describe with surprising, almost digressive, amplitude the adversary relation between the orator and the prince or judge who listens to him. What the orator must avoid, says Longinus, is the danger of making the figural gaps, or "fallacies," of his oration look like subterfuges; he must not "raise the suspicion of a trap, a deep design." For Longinus, again, the irregularity of figures reflects the violence in nature, and now he seems to perceive that with a provenance thus shocking figuration itself will appear to be an evil that must be concealed. And certainly, for all his complaisance, the orator is indeed an aggressor.[25] Except in epideictic oratory, which Longinus does not discuss, the orator is always trying to prevail over opposition while frequently pretending not to be hostile. If his eloquence fails, the violence of nature, of his nature, and of the nature of his speech, will have a colorful outlet indeed: "Such a person [as "tyrants, kings, governors . . ."] immediately becomes angry if he is led astray like a foolish child by some orator's figures. He takes the fallacy as indicating contempt for himself. He becomes *like a wild animal*" (italics mine).

Here a complication arises. Although there is violence in all figures, evidently it is not the studied figures but the ones that are most wildly irregular that will seem the most natural and hence irritate the hearer as little as possible. The inkhorn techniques, on the other hand, the ones that are conducive to the unity of composition and are therefore not sublime, bring on a violent reaction—the reaction, say, of Wordsworth to "poetic diction" or of Whitman to "the *beauty disease*" ("Poetry To-day in America"). The force of figures that are themselves broken by violence goes unnoticed but does so only because it has overwhelmed and disarmed opposition without the knowledge of the opponent. "Amazement and wonder exert invincible power and force and get the better of every hearer" (1.4). The sublime stuns the hearer, spends its aggression in so doing and becomes, once it has entered the hearer, the appreciative condition known as "transport" *(ecstasis).* This process is parallel to, and I think more generally useful in criticism than, the process of catharsis in Aristotle.

The Longinian catharsis is a conversion of power into light, and in this

Longinus differs from later theorists of the sublime. The difference between hupsos and the sublime of Edmund Burke is not so great as it is sometimes said to be,[26] but there is, in tendency at least, one important distinction to be stressed. Burke's sublime wears many guises but in general it inclines toward mist and obscurity, whereas the sublime of Longinus begins in darkness but then bursts forth into clarity and illumination: " 'God said'— now what?—'Let there be light,' and there was light" (9.9). The illustration that comes next makes the pattern clear while showing what the triumph of light in the sublime is like. The "sheer brilliance" (17.2) of the sublime speaker may be a cruel light but it is also honest; without sublimation it shows even death for what it is: "Darkness falls suddenly. Thickest night blinds the Greek army. Ajax is bewildered. 'O Father Zeus,' he cries,"

> 'Deliver the sons of the Achaeans out of the mist,
> Make the sky clear, and let us see;
> In the light—kill us.'

It is as if, through the premature expiation of having asked to be killed by his "Father," Ajax is hoping that in coming to light prior to its manifestation as force, the oedipal situation need never develop.[27] The wished-for moment will be violent, certainly, but at least the suppliant will have deferred to authority, just as the orator must defer to the ruler who will become "a wild animal" if he suspects that he is being mocked by the evasions of figure. In each of these three instances the coming-to-light is a purification of aggression: of divine omnipotence heretofore without an outlet, of blind rage in battle, and of rhetorical guile, respectively. It is a blazing forth that is apt to be followed by a general diffusion of force once pressure has been released by the cleft in the ground. Power becomes light in an allegory of acculturation.

Longinus's famous list of natural analogies for the sublime includes the brilliant light that issues from "the craters of Etna, whose eruptions bring up rocks and whole hills out of the depths, and sometimes pour forth rivers of earth-born, spontaneous fire" (35.4). It also includes the force of the ocean, which elsewhere has the might of a god, as when Poseidon causes Hades to quake in the underworld "for fear the earth-shaker . . . might break through the ground" (9.6). In every analogy Longinus can think of, some force breaks through a natural barrier, just as the sublime breaks through the contexture of figures. But what Poseidon threatens in this last instance is in fact such a powerful rupture that even Longinus wishes to channel it. The threat of "the whole universe overthrown and broken up" makes Homer's battle of the gods "blasphemous and indecent unless it is interpreted allegorically" (9.7). "Much better," says Longinus in the next paragraph, are the passages in which the gods, like the orator or like his judge bemused in a state of transport, are no longer hostile. Even then, in an episode Longinus prefers to the battle of the gods, the image of the gap appears once more, this time constructively, with the coming of Poseidon: "The sea parted in joy, and the horses flew onward" (9.8). The effect of these two passages about Poseidon when they are read in sequence exactly parallels the progress of the sublime from the broken ground of chaos toward the benign channeling of its force. Longinus's next two examples, to confirm the pattern, are the one given from Moses, in which "now what?" makes a gap in the quotation, and the one from Homer's speech of Ajax, who longs for the incisiveness—"kill us"—of the light that pierces darkness.

In keeping with this same pattern, the effect of Demosthenes' oratory is at first violent and then less so. Longinus quotes the passage beginning "The aggressor would do many things" (20.1), and then shows how Demosthenes responds in kind: "The orator is doing here exactly what the bully does—hitting the jury in the mind with blow after blow" (20.2). By the end of the paragraph, which concerns the mixture of a regular, recurrent figure, anaphora, with an irregular one, asyndeton, Demosthenes has somewhat diffused his force: "His order becomes disorderly, and his disorder in turn acquires a certain order" (20.3). Demosthenes, who has "divine gifts, it is almost blasphemous to call them human" (34.4), always subjects the hearer to an "abrupt sublimity" (12.4) which has the effect of being "catapulted out" (21.2) from the gap or opening we have been keeping in view. The effect he has on his audience is twice compared with thunder and lightning (12.4, 34.4). This simile as Longinus uses it is not at all novel in ancient literature, even with reference to Demosthenes, but in Longinus it becomes a motif and recalls the crucial preliminary definition of the sublime: "Sublimity . . . tears everything up [panta diaphorese] like a whirlwind [1.4; Prickard: "lightning flash"; Roberts: "scatters everything before it like a thunderbolt"]." When Aristotle expresses his fear that if one part of a tragedy is moved from its place "the whole will be disjointed," he uses the word diapheresthai. Once again, then, Longinus can be seen to have planted his unstable compound in the very midst of the Aristotelian order.

V

It is not clear whether Longinus's "good friend" the philospher in the final chapter is an opponent putting a wrongheaded argument or simply Longinus himself varying his delivery, good orator that he is, by putting one of two equally valid arguments in another voice. I incline to the second possibility, in part because to suppose that the two speakers are one will bring into consideration a special effect of the Longinian sublime, namely, the identification of the listener with the speaker, which I shall now discuss from various standpoints. Whatever the diagnostic merits of the friend's case (which will be found in Tacitus and many others), the rhetoric of his closing comment provides the essential background for the sublime: "I understand that the cages in which dwarfs or Pygmies are kept not only prevent the growth of the prisoners but cripple them. . . . One might describe all slavery, even the most justified, as a cage for the soul, a universal prison" (44.5).

Although this speaker does retain a conception of "justified" slavery (meaning only justified imprisonment, perhaps), we can still infer from his remarks a state of culture in which, despite the overthrow of democracy by despotism, the institution of slavery could be subject to criticism as it never really was in the thought of Plato or Aristotle. For them, each person, even if he is not officially a slave, must understand his station in the social and moral order to be fixed within justifiable restraints. Especially in Plato, this narrowness (adherence to one vocation, for example) is good for the soul and best suits its natural, uncorrupted wish for conformance with the Good. Hence Plato cannot share the rather complex opinion without which the idea of the sublime cannot be entertained, the opinion of Longinus that the soul by nature craves freedom whether its constraint is justified or not. Supposing that there is merit in this opinion, either man is an entity divided against itself or else his soul is a visitant from without, longing for escape from an oppressive host. Either of these views makes a sublime object of man himself: no longer a whole or a unity, man is divided by a fault through which what is sensed as alien and senses him as alien comes and goes.

There is unquestionably an element of the uncanny in the sublime, a quality which has been convincingly evoked by Freud as the sudden appearance of oneself as another.[28] It is by his sense of the uncanny, arguably, that Longinus's ascription of sublimity to speeches favoring the oppression of aliens is dictated. In light of these remarks, here is a long passage in which it is hard to decide, as one reads, who is the slave, who the governor, and who the liberator, or to decide which of these is the host, at the present moment, of the sublime in transit:

> It is when it [visualization] is closely involved with factual arguments that it enslaves the hearer as well as persuading him. "Suppose you heard a shout this very moment outside the court, and someone said that the prison had been broken open and the prisoners had escaped— no one, young or old, would be so casual as not to give what help he could. And if someone then came forward and said 'This is the man who let them out,' our friend would never get a hearing; it would be the end of him." There is a similar instance in Hyperides' defense of himself when he was on trial for the proposal to liberate the slaves which he put forward after the defeat. "It was not the proposer," he

said, "who drew up this decree: it was the battle of Chaeronea." (15.9–10)

The first emphasis falls upon fact—ironically, perhaps, because the facts will be very difficult to pin down. It is "visualization" *(phantasia)* that "enslaves" the hearer, that much is clear, but we do not know whether this device works for or against the facts. Neither do we know, as yet, why the sublime is said to be an enslavement of the hearer that cooperates with rational persuasion, when hitherto in the *Peri Hupsous* transport and persuasion have been treated as alternatives that are practically synonymous with rebellion and conformity, respectively.

All these questions are answered, but in a very surprising way, in a later passage: "We are diverted from the demonstration [of fact] to the astonishment caused by the visualization which by its very brilliance conceals the factual aspect. This is a natural reaction: when two things are joined together, the stronger attracts to itself the force of the weaker." In short, might makes right, but *only* when might is subversive. Whatever the opinion of Demosthenes concerning slavery and whatever sympathy his idolator Longinus may have for it, the force of the sublime as Longinus records it covertly transfers power from the oppressor to the oppressed. The "enslaved" hearer, in the first place, is the citizen who has custody of the prisoners; or, if he is a first-century reader of Demosthenes, he is a slave by virtue of the despotism he lives under. (Longinus's interlocutor Terentianus was possibly a Roman senator in prospect,[29] but he would nonetheless merely have been one of the emperor's "flatterers in the grand manner" [44.3].) Furthermore, in the first quotation, a voice from "outside the court" penetrates it with tidings of escaping prisoners, and the prison in turn is said to have been "broken open." Liberator, prisoners, messenger: these in turn burst through some barrier and thereby prove themselves, and not the possessors of temporal power, to have carried out the movement of the sublime exactly.

The situation of Hyperides, who is not elsewhere considered to be sublime (see 34.1–4), is equally complex. He was once a liberator and is now on trial for his temerity, an outcome which in the previous citation Demosthenes declares to be impossible (so great is his respect for lawless force). Thus enslaved, Hyperides would appear to have transmitted his power to the slaves he released, and yet he is now speaking with sublime effect on his own behalf because the power of yet another has been transmitted to *him*: It was not me, he says, but the disruption caused by the battle which did this thing.

All the confusion in this long passage arises, then, from the unexpected discovery on the part of each speaker in turn, including Longinus, of the self in the other. If perhaps in some cases it is the other way around, if it is the self that seems to have been invaded, that is because the sense of demoniacal possession Freud speaks of in this context is sure to appear where there are political passions. It is the rule of "transport" in the sublime, as this passage also shows repeatedly, that to have power one must be enslaved, possessed by another. As an instance of this intimation of Hegel's master–slave dialectic in operation, one may cite the subversion of Edmund Burke's politics by his aesthetics. In his *Reflections on the Revolution in France*, the established throne and all the other "fixed forms" of government, especially the pitiable queen, exactly conform with Burke's condescending notion of the Beautiful in the *Enquiry*, whereas the mob in full cry on 6 October is much closer to his notion of the awesome Sublime. Cattle are nothing much, he says in the *Enquiry*, but the wild ass in *Job* who knows no master is sublime.[30] What then, in the *Reflections*, of the "thousands of great cattle reposed beneath the shadow of the British oak," who commendably "chew the cud and are silent"?[31]

By "visualization," Longinus means that in phantasy, as hearers, we subvert our own identities. We conjure up presences that usurp our places. The hearer neither sees Demosthenes nor remains conscious of his own freedom but sees instead the hitherto unknown liberator of the slaves and becomes himself a slave to what he sees. He discovers himself to be Oedipus as surely as the Aristotelian audience does not. But in this discovery there is strength. If the sublime is a possession that is distinguished by a coming-to–light, and thus casts out the uncanny almost in the instant of evoking it, its effect may be "amazement" (12.5) and clarity all at once, an epiphanic moment of presence that quickly becomes self-presence. When what is absent stands before one, even takes possession of one's consciousness, first there is a recoil, as from an invader, and then there is a surge of empathy, as in the "momentary checking of the vital powers and . . . consequent stronger outflow of them" that accompanies the sublime in Kant's *Critique of Judgment*.[32]

Common and nowadays somewhat ineffective rhetorical devices for this making present in Longinus are the sudden switch from past to present tense in narrative (25) and the sudden apostrophe to the hearer (26.1–2). We can still be affected, though, by the skillful use of a third device, conjuration. Demosthenes' oath, "By those who risked their lives at Marathon" (16.2), is remarkably glossed by Longinus: "He was suddenly inspired to give voice to the oath by the heroes of Greece." Demosthenes does not call up the past, then; past voices call through him, thus enacting the course of the sublime from speaker to speaker. The finest event of this kind in Longinus is "the appearance of Achilles to the departing fleet over his tomb" (15.7). The heroic past, which is in a sense the whole text of the *Iliad* and the other cyclic poems, stands above a gap in the ground whence it has come, still alive with, or revived by, the charge for posterity it carries. The past in the person of Achilles haunts the puny survivors whose victory has been won and who are now launched, a "departing fleet," upon the historic decline Longinus laments in his final chapter. "Greatness of mind wanes," he says there (44.8)—unless it should return to possess the living.

VI

The sublime is chthonic, "earth-born" like the volcano, yet it is also divine—or else it is the human euhemeristically exalted. It appears at the horizons of perceptual experience that are left out of the *Poetics*. Hence Longinus's touchstones frequently bring extreme conceptions of matter and spirit together. He quotes, for example, the Homeric account of the rebellious giants, who themselves are heavy and dull and make heavy work of their climb into the sky: "Ossa on Olympus they sought to heap; and on Ossa / Pelion with its shaking forest"—shaking like the beard of a giant— "to make a path to heaven—" (8.2). In their lumpishness these giants must use the arithmetical *auxesis* rather than the true *hupsos* or *megethos* (greatness) to serve their purpose. At the same time, however, their instinct cannot be taken lightly if it enables them to forge a "path" toward their goal: "And they would have finished their work. . . ." This coincidence of the animal and the divine is repeated, not so much in the next Homeric passage itself— "So long is the stride of the gods' thundering horses,"—as in Longinus's response to it: "If the horses of the gods took two more strides like that, they would find there was not enough room in the world" (9.5).

The oxymoron of measureless substance is exemplified for Longinus by the ocean. He himself takes its measure, thinking perhaps of a strait or bay that becomes a lake at low tide, in the course of assigning an inferior place to the *Odyssey*: "We see greatness on the ebb," he says, glancing forward again to the waning of greatness in his last chapter: "It is as though the Ocean were withdrawing into itself and flowing quietly in its own bed" (9.13). When a vast, possibly boundless expanse becomes a self-contained structure, it stops flowing out of itself. It no longer *influences* in the way the ghost of Achilles, representing Homer, can influence, not to say inundate, a departing fleet. There is no "outpouring" (ibid.) from the *Odyssey* that can affect us. In a passage that wholly anticipates Kant, Longinus identifies the sublime as something illimitable in the mind, something that must overflow and appear in contrast with the finite objects in nature: "The universe therefore is not wide enough for the range of human speculation and intellect. Our thoughts often travel beyond the boundaries of our surroundings. If anyone wants to know what we were born for, let him look . . . above all [at] the Ocean" (35.3–4). Just as boundlessness and measure are closely interdependent, so also, it will be recalled, art and nature, words and thought, are nonidentical word pairs that are nonetheless inseparable.

Freedom, to repeat the essential homily concerning the sublime, needs its obverse in confinement. We could not identify the "abundant, uncontrolled flood" of Archilochus if it were not a "bursting forth of the divine spirit" from "under the rule of law" (33.5).

The sublime, again, is neither a great mind, precisely, nor the words of a great mind but rather "the echo of a noble mind" (9.2).[33] If we are to take this turn of phrase seriously, the sublime must then be the reverberation, or resonance, of words. That characterization may bring it a shade too close to language, however, too close to uttered language, that is, and for this reason Longinus's ensuing sentences seem to counteract the sense of the word *echo*: "This is why a mere idea, without verbal expression, is sometimes admired for its nobility—just as Ajax's silence in the Vision of the Dead is grand and indeed more sublime than any words could have been."[34]

The distinction between silence and the echo in this passage is as crucial as it is subtle. Again Longinus has turned to a crisis of communication in the *Odyssey*. An attempt to open a path between heroic ghosts and present needs, the crisis begins when Odysseus invites the sublime by making a wound in the earth. "With my drawn blade / I spaded up the votive pit," he recalls, all for the purpose of speaking with Tiresias, "the prince of those with gift of speech" (book 11). All the women and men who are allowed to approach after Tiresias has spoken his fill are echoes of the seer, reverse echoes, as it were, which confirm the authenticity of his prophecies with the accuracy of their recollections. The eloquent silence of Ajax, which is balanced as a motif by the vagueness of Tiresias's forecast beyond the moment of planting the oar, is made possible by the eloquence of Tiresias on all prior topics, without the exhaustion of which Ajax could not have approached the pit.[35] Furthermore, the silence of Ajax is itself pregnant with speech, as even the snubbed Odysseus realizes: "Who knows if in that darkness he might still / have spoken, and I answered?" The silence of Ajax, in short, is wholly dependent on words—on Odysseus's present narrative, on the speech Odysseus made to Ajax rehearsing the old grievance, and on our own feeling that even in that moment of growing darkness, which recalls Ajax's darkling petition for death quoted earlier by Longinus, the suicide could have said much.[36]

The sublime echo thus wavers between the aftersound of words and their negation. It is as difficult to locate precisely as the ghost of Ajax disappearing into Erebus. The "voice of the dead" in such moments is not really a voice; rather it is the speaker's memory short-circuited so that it seems as though the dead were now saying what the speaker has always known them to have said when alive. Even if the "dead" should in fact be living persons, the effect of astonishment brought about in the speaker by means of visualization, brokenness of figure, and his accession to "divine gifts" makes the speaker seem merely a mouthpiece for what is remote from his ordinary sphere. " 'The dead writers are remote from us,' " wrote Eliot, " 'because we *know* so much more than they did.' Precisely, and they are that which we know."[37] In the experience of the sublime they are not remote, however, but so vividly present that they take possession of consciousness.

The controversy that surrounds the theory of influence today has in part to do with the question of whether influence occurs in the form of words or thought, echo or silence. The early Humanists thought that it is the words of the past that either intimidate or educate us. Edward Young thought that the *spirit* of the past can liberate our own genius if we disregard the words. Harold Bloom imagines a powerful presence from the past, at once word and spirit, which will dominate the new speaker unless he contrives to sap its strength. Longinus can be helpful in ascertaining how far the idea of influence can be carried beyond the discussion of buried allusion, but more importantly he can show how far beyond this point it *needs* to be carried. If nonverbal thought is necessarily at least "colored" by reading, that coloring is not washable. It must be seen as a dye: "The choice of correct and magnificant words . . . makes . . . a kind of lustre bloom upon our words as upon beautiful statues . . . it is indeed true that beautiful words are the light that illuminates thought" (30.1–2). Allusion, then, which can be defined as words taken from their place in history, colors the whole mind. This is a far subtler view than the notion of words as the "dress" of thought, but it is also more troublesome when it comes to assessing originality. When it is difficult to discriminate between words and thought, it becomes more difficult to know how great a portion of what is spoken belongs properly to the speaker.

In that case more than ever, the speaker must fight for his share of credit as an originator or "author."[38] This is the point at which he ceases to be the "hearer" and assumes, in his turn, the role of orator. Whatever it is that reaches the hearer, and perhaps *echo* will have proved as good a word as any for it, he is at first stunned but then he reacts, and in so doing he passes into the speaker's role.[39] The aggression of the original speaker is met with counteraggression on the part of the listener. One such listener is Longinus, who cannot praise his literary ancestor Plato without some word of qualification. There is a measure of tension in his reverence for Plato from which his reverence for Demosthenes, for example, is wholly free. On several occasions Longinus taxes Plato with abuses of style. The "otherwise divine Plato" (4.6) too often exhibits the vice of frigidity, and he is also given to such needless and dull embellishments as periphrasis (29.1) and surplus metaphors (32.2). In these belittling gestures, which have the effect of pointing to something petty in Plato's nature, the reader will recognize one reflex of the anxiety of influence in the theory of Harold Bloom. It is hard not to conclude that Demosthenes is praised more unreservedly than Plato is because he is less important. Demosthenes commanded only one register of the sublime, and his style does not exert any direct influence on the sinuous and chameleonic style of Longinus himself. By far the more powerful influence upon Longinus is Plato, whose style and whose think-ing—his concept of nobility, his dislike of the theater—figure with great prominence in the *Peri Hupsous*.

There is an additional charge to be whispered against Plato. With Xenophon, says Longinus, Plato was "trained in Socrates' school" (4.4); or again, late in the passage toward which the present analysis is tending, Plato "diverted to himself countless rills from the Homeric spring" (13.3). In short, Plato can be charged with unoriginality as well as pettiness. Longinus is aware that his readiness to find fault is a fault—"I myself cited not a few mistakes in Homer and other great writers" (33.4)—but he goes on to argue, notoriously from the standpoint of his detractors, that the faults he finds in others are sure proofs of their genius; and in that case his own fault would prove that he himself is at least not insipid. Even in this gesture of restitution toward genius, however, there is a trace of malice. Take Caeci-lius, he continues, author of the treatise on the sublime against which he has pitched his present essay: consider what Caecilius says against Plato. Apparently Longinus is about to defend Plato. But then, with a devious stratagem common both in oratory and in neoclassical wit, Longinus faithfully repeats the indictment made by Caecilius: "Loving Lysias more deeply than he loves himself"—possibly the talk of *philia* here is meant to recall the *Phaedrus*—"[Caecilius] yet hates Plato with an even greater intensity. . . . In preferring Lysias to Plato he thinks he is preferring a faultless and pure writer to one who makes many mistakes" (32.8). Plato is ever so faintly damned, then, both by contrast with Lysias—for Longinus will not glorify mistakes until the next chapter—and also by comparison with him. In repeating the invidious comparison of Caecilius, Longinus himself causes Plato to appear merely as a competitor, and an unsuccessful one at that, for superiority in phrasemaking.

Longinus's attitude toward Plato is not in itself terribly significant. I have lingered over it to show further that captiousness of some kind belongs properly to the dynamics of the sublime (a point to which I shall return), and to suggest that this inevitably critical moment does raise an epistemo-logical question: Is the sublime firmly enough situated in the nature of things to survive criticism? It is the first premise of Longinus that the sublime is objectively verifiable. What he says to establish this point has a Johnsonian ring: "Reckon those things which please everybody all the time as genuinely and finely sublime" (7.4). Here Longinus differs from Kant, whom he anticipates in so many other respects, and rejoins the eighteenth-century "empiricist" writers, from Addison to Burke and Kames, who found the sublime indisputably to be present in certain works of art and natural objects.

At least, this is partly so. Coleridge, a Kantian whose *Biographia* attacks the premises of empiricism, still struggles whenever possible, more clearly so in other writings, to establish an objective ground of judgment,[40] and Longinus, no matter what he says, must undertake the same struggle. Although, again, nature plays a vital role in the production of the sublime for Longinus, it is not clear that nature, which "is not a random force and does not work altogether without method," can be very safely distinguished from art. It is not easy to decide whether the sublime passes from object to subject as a volcanic echo or from subject to subject as an oratorical echo. Coleridge, in the well-known anecdote of the lady he heard calling a waterfall "pretty," himself knew, absolutely, that it was "sublime." But the anecdote at least partly bears witness against itself because Coleridge's knowledge, absolute or otherwise, would not have been possible without information given by reading and by the oral tradition of the educated.[41]

The Longinian sublime cannot be located in words or things with confidence for similar reasons. His conviction that the sublime pleases all at all times must be undermined, furthermore, by the prevalence of the instinct he notices in himself and his predecessors, like Caecilius, for faultfinding. If the sublime is the most exalting experience one can have that is not purely religious, and if it must therefore be spontaneously desired by the soul (we can reasonably expect that Longinus would want to take a Platonic view of the question), then why do we act so aggressively toward it? Why do we decry its pretenders and even express doubts about the illustrations of it that we bring forward ourselves? It may be replied that vigilance is needed to protect the fane of the sublime from false priests who go about "poking the thyrsus in at the wrong place" (3.5; my adaptation of the term *parenthyrsus*). Yet it is troubling that such vigilance leaves so little intact. The *Odyssey,* the battle of the gods in the *Iliad,* Plato—all but the safely peripheral Demosthenes, peripheral both in style and in politics, are quite badly mauled. As Longinus himself would say, they are "dissected": "We have to ask ourselves whether any particular example does not give a show of grandeur which, for all its accidental trappings, will, when dissected, prove vain and hollow" (7.1).

It appears from this metaphor that the aggression of the hearer is an imitative aggression, corresponding as it does to the tearing apart that marks the appearance of the sublime itself. Although it takes place in a different mood, perhaps, the rending of the sublime still anticipates interpretation, the dissection that Wordsworth called murder. The listener's response to the sublime resists its assault. At first the listener is possessed, and then he bestirs himself to expel the alien voice, which ceases to possess him in the process and becomes his property instead: "It is our nature to be elevated and exalted by true sublimity. Filled with joy and pride, we come to believe we have created what we only heard" (7.2).[42]

After these last observations have been made, the dramatization of mimesis that follows will almost interpret itself:

> Many are possessed by a spirit not their own. It is like what we are told of the Pythia at Delphi: she is in contact with the tripod near the cleft in the ground which (they say) exhales a divine vapour, and she is thereupon made pregnant by the supernatural power and prophesies as one inspired. Similarly, the genius of the ancients acts as a kind of oracular cavern, and effluences flow from it into the minds of their imitators. . . . Plato could not have put such a brilliant finish on his philosophical doctrines or so often risen to poetical subjects and poetical language, if he had not tried, and tried wholeheartedly, to compete for the prize against Homer. . . . As Hesiod says, "this strife is good for men[.]" Truly it is a noble contest and prize of honour, and one well worth winning, in which to be defeated by one's elders is itself no disgrace.
>
> We can apply this to ourselves.   (13.2–14.1)

Possession, which is divine, comes from a cleft in the ground that represents the natural origin of the sublime. The priestess is then the "author" of the sublime, and we who receive her prophecies are hearers-turned-authors or hearers-turned-interpreters. After the Delphic comparison Longinus changes the subject a little, revealing from that point forward the aggression in the relationship between speaker and listener.

VII

Nearly all commentators suppose that there is a drastic narrowing of the Aristotelian *mimesis* in Longinus and other late Greek and Latin writers. Verbal imitation has replaced ideal representation, symptomizing the over-throw of true philosophy by the "Alexandrian" logomachy. But in the case of Longinus this judgment is unduly harsh.[43] In his treatise the spirit is not suppressed, leaving only the gaunt body of philosophy in view; rather spirit and letter are nearly interchangeable, and each very adequately embraces the *mimesis* of Aristotle. The common distinction we make between *mimesis,* alluding to Plato and Aristotle, and *imitatio,* alluding chiefly to Quintilian, Longinus, and the rise of Humanism, is a good deal more radical than it should be. Pope's lines on Virgil are perhaps closest to the equipoise of Longinus: "When t'examine every part he came, / Nature and Homer were, he found, the same" (Essay on Criticism, I, 134–35). The "nature" that Pope has in mind is the *phusis,* or "rules," of Aristotle, but the "nature" of Longinus, had he written this couplet, would have been more dynamic.

One way in which Longinus does maintain a slight functional separation between nature and art is in speaking, as he routinely does, of "mere" words. These are what the false sublime is made of: it looks sublime, but in the long run, for "the man of sense and literary experience . . . , it fails to dispose his mind to greatness or to leave him with more to reflect upon than was contained in the mere words" (7.3). Only the implications of the word *more* can save Longinus from saying, here, that the sublime itself is merely a matter of words. It is not solely because this conclusion would trivialize the sublime that Longinus is fortunate to have evaded it; he also escapes having to admit that as a "text-book" (1.1) his treatise must be a failure. And indeed it is a failure in that genre. Because by his own demonstration there is no trope or figure that is not subject to abuse, then truly, though Longinus has argued to the contrary (2.1), the sublime cannot be taught as a rhetoric. This he does later admit in an unguarded moment: "Evils often come from the same source as blessings; and so, since beauty of style, sublimity, and charm all conduce to successful writing, they are also causes and principles not only of success but of failure" (5).

If the sublime is not a rhetoric, and I think Longinus knows it is not, it cannot be identified with any structure. This article of belief must be kept in mind in turning to a number of passages that seem to undermine it by identifying the sublime with order and resolution. The first of these describes the *Iliad* during Longinus's contrast of that poem with the *Odyssey*. The *Iliad,* he says, has a "consistent level of elevation which never admit[s] of any falling off" (9.13). What is perplexing about this statement is that elsewhere Longinus has insisted that the sublime appears in disruptive fragments of less brilliant surrounding compositions. If "persuasion" is achieved by observing the Horatian decorum (see 1.4), the "transport" of the sublime must be a breach of decorum. There are several ways of resolving this anomaly. First, it could be said that a whole text, seamless in itself, would become sublime if it disrupted other texts. The reader of the *Iliad,* especially if he or she is a poet, might find that as a whole it overwhelms his or her own inspiration. It could also be said that for the *Iliad* to have unified the story of Troy is a feat that surpasses ordinary powers of composition. Thus the composition of the *Iliad* is an extreme instance of making the plural singular, which will always result, as Longinus says elsewhere, in "surprise" (24.2).

A third rationale for Longinus's suddenly holistic phrasing, briefly stated, might be this: When he speaks of sustained elevation he is not actually touching upon questions of structure or even of unity. He is speaking, rather, of a device that more closely resembles the blows of Demosthenes' bully, the device, namely, of repetition. This is the most satisfactory explanation for Longinus's praise of the *Iliad* because it can also be applied to his other totalizing figures. This I shall do in a moment, having first resisted the temptation to gloss over the anomalous passages prematurely. For they *are* anomalous. Recalling Aristotle, for example, Longinus claims that periodic structure in a sentence can be sublime: "The beauty of the body depends on the way the limbs are joined together, each one when severed from the others having nothing remarkable about it, but the whole forming a perfect unity" (40.1). He pursues this train of thought pertinaciously: "Similarly, great thoughts which lack connexion are themselves wasted and waste the total sublime effect" (*sundiaphorei kai to hupsos*). Because it is not evident how more than one great thought can appear in, or even be discussed with respect to, the structure of a single sentence, Longinus's notion of the "total sublime effect" continues, in this context, to be unintelligible. Perhaps he is affirming what is crucial, again, in any theory of the sublime that has subtlety: the principle that sublime moments need a formal context of some sort and cannot take their course in a vacuum.

If this is so, it remains only to characterize the interstices of the "great thoughts." It is not clear from this passage alone whether sublimities should come at us in a steady stream, creating, e.g., the *Iliad*'s "consistent level of elevation," or whether they should be indirectly but no less surely connected by decent intervals of decorum. Longinus himself begins to resolve this question, and to show how the sublime can indeed appear in formal composition, a few sentences later in this same discussion of periodicity. Having quoted a passage from a lost play of Euripides about Dirce being haled up and down by a bull, a passage that is as agitated as its subject ("it writhed and twisted round"), Longinus remarks that "the word-harmony is not hurried and does not run smoothly" (40.4). He means that clusters like *perix helixas* and *petran drun* slow one down in pronouncing them. For this reason "the words are propped up by one another and rest on the intervals between them; set wide apart like that, they give the impression of solid strength." Like Antony bestriding the world, they are colossal. It is in this manner, then, that Longinus can praise unifying effects in style without contradicting himself. Apparently neither sustained elevation nor periodicity is to be considered smooth or even fluent. The sublime elements of composition are like the stone slabs of an entryway before the invention of the keystone; up to a point, the strength of the arch is proportionate to the width of its base. Thus even in passages in which a sustained effect is aimed for, the composition should be, as Longinus puts it in the next section, "rough at the joins" (41.3; *skleroteta episundedemena*).

Longinus more than once resorts to architectural metaphors—rather surprisingly, it has been pointed out, considering that the Greeks did not rank architecture among the fine arts.[44] Having in general insisted on the need for a "cleft" through which the sublime can pass, Longinus at one point seems to change his mind. In a discussion of gathering details for a sublime effect, he says that good writers "have taken only the very best pieces [i.e., stones], polished them up and fitted them together. They have inserted nothing inflated, undignified or pedantic. Such things ruin the whole effect, because they produce, as it were, gaps and crevices" (10.7). But again there is really no contradiction. An architecture in which wedges of foreign matter (wood, perhaps, or roughcast) leave actual "chinks and crannies" in a wall would be much cruder than the rough architecture of the sublime needs to be or can be.[45] It would be ludicrous architecture, like the wall with its chink that separates Pyramus and Thisby in *A Midsummer Night's Dream*. The opening of the sublime must be well-knit to a certain degree in order to resist what will tear through it.[46]

After this review it can be asserted with some confidence that Longinus's fifth "source" of sublimity, which is "dignified and elevated word-arrangement" (8.1; *sunthesis*), is not out of keeping with the other four, at least three of which stress division and passion rather than composition and composure. But the exact nature of the linguistic "joins" under this fifth heading remains difficult to determine. Much depends, in any theory of form, on whether connecting links are thought to be interstices, like the cushion of air that keeps colliding bodies from touching in the physical world, or joints, like helical or chain structures. Whichever of these models may seem more accurate, there can be no question of a third, of the blending or ooze that is implied in the Goethean concept of "organic form." There is nothing liquid or even porous about those linguistic signs which are not themselves the sublime but remain necessarily its vehicle. A sign cannot merge with its neighbors without losing the syntagmatic features—the differences—that make it intelligible. This observation may be an instance of what the German hermeneuticians condemn as *Modernisierung,* but it still provides a convenient way of loosening the strong grip that the word *sunthesis* appears to exert upon the disruptive potential of the sublime. Even the evidence of the *Peri Hupsous* itself makes it clear, in any case, that *sunthesis* is not synthesis. Longinus's *sunthesis* is actually a somewhat limited technical term meaning the order in which words are written down; it is quite closely equivalent, that is, to the modern word *syntagmatics.*

Although the semantic possibilities of imitative form are not to be overlooked in studying word arrangement (one thinks of the poetic line in Virgil), the primary concern of Longinus in this regard is with rhythm.[47] This being so, the word *composition* that is used in most translations of the section on *sunthesis* is especially misleading. Rhythm may be syncopated but it cannot form an arc or return on itself. It is essentially repetitious, "the ticking of a watch made softer," as Yeats put it,[48] and thus has very little to do with the *techne* of the classical formalists. Longinus himself tips the balance between variation and repetition clearly toward the latter by devoting a section (20) to the sublime effects of asyndeton combined with anaphora. He stresses the need for variety "to save the sentence from monotony and a stationary effect" (20.2), but much more significantly he recommends that anaphora be used with asyndeton, which is percussive in effect, rather than, e.g., with hyperbaton, which would involve an unexpected deviance from norms of recurrence. At this point, furthermore, he expatiates on the bullying of Demosthenes, "hitting the jury in the mind with blow after blow" (20.3). It may be observed in addition concerning this point that Longinus later contrasts the "wonderful spell of harmony" cast by the "varied sounds of the lyre"—the mild spell of "persuasion," that is, or of the beautiful—with the Phrygian pulsation of the flute, which inspires one mood, though by no means the only one, of the sublime (39.2–3).

In short, repetition is more important than variety if one's purpose is to stun the auditor. Again we come to an aspect of the sublime that we may prefer to wish away. Mesmerism, demagoguery, Madison Avenue, ecstatic dancing, and the "meditation" on a name or a sacred mantra—all undertake to "enslave" the hearer, to bring about the identification of an audience with some transcendently authoritative voice by means of repetition.[49] But Longinus is able to show that repetition has more acceptable uses. A mature taste in the discrimination of sublimities, for example, comes from experiences that take place "many times over" (7.3). From this standpoint taste can be defined, very plausibly, as a superior force of habit, an informed, at least partly voluntary self-hypnosis. Repetition also provides a way, finally, of revealing what the sublime is and what it is not. Partly owing to the element of sameness in repetition, the sublime is *one*—and largely indivisible—but no version of the sublime is ever *unified,* anywhere in the *Peri Hupsous,* as an increment of structure or of harmony.

VIII

Some difference remains, however, between the repetitious sublime and the sublimity that takes effect with a single blow. Verbal composition is mainly a process of accretion, "building up" (39.3), a process that is equivalent to what Longinus describes, on the figural level of composition, as *auxesis,* or amplification. There are enough passages assigning repetition rather than singleness to the sublime to warrant the suggestion that Longinus anticipates Kant's distinction between the "dynamic" and the "mathematical" sublime,[50] which latter heading denotes the effect of being staggered by the sheer volume of something: too much information, too many anxieties, mountains too high, and so on. The addition of this category completes my discussion of the rhetoric, the conditions, and the modes of the Longinian sublime. Using the mathematical sublime as a point of departure, I shall now discuss some of the implications of the sublime, with an eye toward showing why I think it is preferable to the identification of form as an end in view for contemporary criticism.

The mathematical sublime has been analyzed by Thomas Weiskel, and more recently by Neil Hertz, as a frustrating buildup or sedimentation that finally causes the sensation of "blockage," the "checking of vital powers" noted by Kant. Hertz admires Weiskel's thesis but argues that Weiskel identifies the blocking agent in Kant—the Reason *(Vernunft)*, which implicitly rebukes the Imagination *(Einbildungskraft)* for failing to reduce the overload to proportion—too hastily and arbitrarily with the Father in the "family romance" of Freud.[51] Weiskel cuts his way through the blockage of his own knotty problem, in other words, simply in order to have got through it. Passed on from commentator to commentator, each time with a new qualification, the mathematical sublime renews itself according to the pattern described earlier: possession, resistance, response. Hertz's solution—not to cut through the blockage but to learn to live with it until its familiar presence ceases to frustrate—is designed to put an end to the game, but that may not be possible. It is too likely that one's orientation in the chain of audition along which the sublime is passed is, as Weiskel says, irreducibly oedipal. Any forfeit of that orientation would then simply become a promise that one will not mind being overwhelmed.

There is another topic in Freud, however, that brings one closer to the way it feels to cope with the mathematical sublime from day to day. This topic is the "mastery of repetition" that Freud supposes to be a constructive displacement of the death instinct.[52] At least one phase of the sublime, the initial phase that all the eighteenth-century theorists agreed in calling awestruck or frightened, is loaded with intimations of mortality. Freud described the favorite topics of the obsessional neurotic as those "upon which all mankind are uncertain,"[53] including the afterlife and the reliability of memory. The neurotic's repeated efforts to break through to conclusions about these topics, efforts which transfer to waking life the unpleasant doing and undoing that everyone performs during a feverish doze, are futile attempts at *auxesis*. Replete with its "great thoughts," on the other hand, the sublime can become a working through that makes the neurotic compulsion purposeful. The sublime reveals its power of sublimation even in what it does to the signals of repetition itself: a dripping faucet becomes the sound of waves, a metronome softens into meter, and the dullest monotony becomes "The murmurous haunt of flies on summer eves."

The issue of repetition dominates even Longinus's passing remarks about metaphor. A structurally oriented poetics is likely to make metaphor, whether Aristotle's "transference of an alien name" or Jakobson's "poetic function," the microcosm of its largest concerns. Both in the *Poetics* and in the *Rhetoric* Aristotle showed how metaphor is the most important trope in the repertory of the artist because the "eye for resemblances" that it requires is what is also needed to connect the beginning with the end of a composition. On the other hand, Longinus, whose poetics is disruptive, evinces no interest in the structural properties of metaphor.[54] What does interest him is the traditional question among the rhetors concerning the relation between metaphor and repetition:[55] How often should the trope be repeated in elaborating a single topos? The answer Longinus gives is that there should be no limit as long as the result of any repetition is the pathos, or mesmerism, that erases one's memory of repetition and "never allow[s] the hearer to count the metaphors because he too shares the speaker's enthusiasm" (32.4). It is not metaphors themselves, then, but their repetition that achieves the sense of identity—empathetic rather than semantic identity— that can be managed only by the "transference of alien names" from the standpoint of structural analysis. Because the temporality of tropes and figures is unrelieved in Longinus, the vertical structure even of metaphor collapses into sequence.[56] He says nothing about the synonymy and identity that are enforced by radical metaphor in formalist thinking.

Repetition in the mathematical sublime can function as a homeopathic cure and thus resembles one widely sanctioned interpretation of catharsis in Aristotle. Like the frenzied music mentioned as a *katharsis* in the *Politics* (1341b–42a) and as a form of repetition by Longinus in his section on rhythm, repetition in excess precipitates the hearer toward a state of calm. Such is the outcome, Longinus thinks, of the onslaught of metaphors describing the "bodily tabernacle" in the *Timaeus:* "Finally," writes Longinus, at once quoting the passage and describing the effect of it on the reader, "when the end is at hand, the soul's 'ship's cables' are 'loosed,' and she herself 'set free.' " This extended metaphor seems to invite death, and in that respect it can be compared with both homeopathic medicine (more poison) and homeopathic catharsis (more suffering). But the therapy of repetition does not depend on the suspension of life that is required by the unified structure of catharsis. Rather it comes about in keeping with the ordinary footfall of time, which is metric, rhythmic, and anaphoric. The dynamic sublime, a single thunderbolt, has somewhat different purposes, but in the mathematical sublime there is reassurance in knowing that "Hectors and Sarpedons came forth" and kept on doing so (23.3), and there is likewise a sense of being "renewed" by the Ciceronian discourse that is "repeatedly fed with fresh fuel" (12.5).

IX

I have tried to show in my analysis of the *Poetics* that the crisis—the "recognition scene"—of a unified structure exposes the function of the double, or projected self, at the crossroads of choice; sexual or otherwise, this choice is always equivalent to the "ambiguity" of the New Critics. The crisis that comes with the sublime, on the other hand, exposes the function of the double in the prefiguration of death; confronting the uncanny, the listener tries to wrest authority from what seems to be a former self. Just as Addison and Burke associate the Beautiful, which is soft, smooth, round, and well-formed with sex, generation, and the plenitude of earthly existence, so they and most other theorists incline to associate the sublime with darkness, solitude, the unknown, and the "checking of vital powers." The sublime seems always to have been viewed as a trial confrontation with death. Whereas the theme of the Beautiful is the destiny of others as it appears manifest in their forms (their shapeliness in life, their roles in drama), the theme of the sublime is the destiny of ourselves, which we confront in the act of trying to win an authentic self from the forms that stand in our way. When the contrast between these old rivals for aesthetic attention is put thus provocatively, awarding all sanity, vital health, and humanity to the Beautiful—which is the flesh of formalism—then anyone who is not merely morbid and still prefers the sublime as an objective for interpretation has a lot of explaining to do. The worst that can be said about the sublime is now said: In bringing the death instinct rather than the pleasure principle close to the surface of aesthetic experience, it is necessary for the sublime to risk the irresponsible and exhibitionistic courtship of danger. To this effect Longinus praises a Homeric passage about mariners in a storm: "He has in effect stamped the special character of the danger on the diction: 'they are being carried away from under death' " (10.7). However, the immediate danger attendant upon the sublime is not death, but ridicule. With the slightest overemphasis the sublime becomes the ridiculous: ham-handed, humorless, and provincial. This risk may be unavoidable unless the sublime is transformed into another, quieter quality, one that I think Longinus himself has anticipated.

The false sublime gets puffed up and loses control. The danger of visionary speech (the dynamic sublime) is Icarean, the risk of a great fall, as when "the writer's soul . . . shares the danger" with Phaethon (15.4) or when the listener must share "the speaker's peril" during the suspension of meaning in hyperbaton (22.4). The danger of interpretive speech (the mathematical sublime) is Daedalian, the temptation "to go too far" in the proliferation of tropes (32.7), to lose the sublime in confusion rather than achieving it by sustained attention. The mathematical sublime must turn out to have been pregnant and not dropsical (3.3). All its amplifications may be nothing but "puffy and false tumours" (3.4). These dangers, which once more show the close proximity of words and nature, have to do in general with bodily malfunction and monstrosity.[57] Expressions may be "incomplete and abortive" (14.3), constipated, as when the "bowels" of the too-literary mariners of Aristeas "heave in pain" (10.4), or dwarfed, hardened beneath the surface like chancres, by the pettiness of conception that dwarfs reality: vultures that are tombs for men (3.2), a book that compresses the conquest of Asia (4.2), and the forced synecdoche crossed with homonymity (in the word *kore*) that traps a maiden in an eyeball (4.4). The failure of the mathematical sublime, then, which is the failure of interpretation, results in monsters, grotesqueries, and misbirths of the study.[58]

Dangers of visionary speech, however, are not so easily dispelled, nor are they quite so clearly deserving as targets for satire. A transitional instance between the two kinds of sublimity, an instance of euphemism, runs a more complex risk: "The goddess struck the Scythians who plundered the temple with a feminine disease" (28.4), by which is meant, presumably, impotence.[59] We could classify this misfortune as a bodily disorder that is related merely to the collapse of the mathematical sublime, for there are certainly as many Scythians as Hectors and Sarpedons. There is a key difference, however: for a prior offense, a rape, the Scythians are now cast as victims of authority instead of hapless authors. The danger now becomes ethical, in other words, and returns us to the issue of enslavement. Originary power endangers audiences just insofar as it realizes itself. If Icarus falls, no one notices; that, I take it, is what Brueghel meant and Auden emphasized:

> the ploughman may
> Have heard the splash, the forsaken cry,
> But for him it was not an important failure.

But if Phaethon, having risen against the order of things and having succeeded in driving the sun, should survive, or transmit his blinding success as a legacy, we would then find ourselves at the mercy of a petulant and spoiled youth. "Persuasion" is a democratic, tolerant discourse that leaves the hearer free to choose whether to be persuaded. It may be a novel, a book of self-help, a primer in economics, a discourse on Method; in the marketplace the ploughman listens attentively and casts his vote. "Transport," on the other hand, as we have seen, whether it drives the hearer across the sky or drives him mad, casts him into slavery, robbing him even of his proper self.

It is "natural," as Longinus says, that "when two things are joined together, the stronger attracts to itself the force of the weaker" (15.11). The sublime seems too readily to belong in Plato's utopia; the integrity of the unenslaved individual counts for very little in either case. We cannot pretend that the concluding remarks of the *Peri Hupsous* as we have it are not in the main the sort of diatribe against the herd instinct that betrays a longing for tyranny. Longinus offers himself the chance to blame the disappearance of the sublime on the defeat of democracy but he refuses the offer—and is right, by his own lights, to do so. Always excepting Demosthenes, the oratory of "persuasion" that best suits the forum of democracy is not in any sense sublime. It is not certain, in fact, whether even persuasion is dependent on one political climate more than another: "In our age there are minds which are strikingly persuasive and practical, shrewd, versatile, and well endowed with the ability to write agreeably" (44.1). The more insidious enemy of the sublime, materialism, likewise flourishes regardless of most political changes; "most," that is, however, because the possibility of founding an austere tyranny, a reign of philosopher-kings or perhaps a theocracy, is the greatest temptation of those who are capable of "great thoughts."[60] Hence, again, there appears to be a bond of sympathy between tyranny and the sublime.

I think, however, that this sympathy exists in appearance only. In the course of its attack on materialism the argument of Longinus is almost undermined by a reversal of the values attached to certain metaphors. This reversal is inevitable and ultimately robs the austere tyrant of his authority, leading to the democratization of the sublime that I wish to propose. In Longinus's last chapter the tropes associated with materialism gradually begin to imply that materialism is an epidemic so far-flung that it must itself be accounted sublime. The grosser passions fight an "unlimited war," wealth and the lust for it are "measureless and uncontrolled," and we are "slaves" to the love of pleasure (44.6–7). The rout of the sublime being sublime, then, Longinus is almost prepared to acquiesce in things as they are, to let the inundation come in whatever form: "Perhaps people like us are better as subjects than given our freedom. Greed would flood the world in woe, if it were really released and let out of its cage, to prey on its neighbors" (44.10). The Longinian sublime is certainly a tyrant but it is not always, as we might have supposed, a celestial dictator, a sky-god or Platonic Houyhnhnm; it is not surprising, when one considers the intimacy between mind and nature that is revealed elsewhere in the text, that the tyrant is sometimes our own instinctual life. A Yahoo tyrant, at least nominally the oppressed rather than the oppressor, it is demagogic, revolting, universally in charge, so much so that it must be softened and coaxed into epicurean channels, sublimated like our "private parts," which nature "concealed as well as she could": "and as Xenophon says, [she] made the channels of those organs as remote as possible, so as not to spoil the beauty of the creature as a whole" (43.5). The term *beauty*—*kallos*—is no doubt a vague one here but it may serve to remind us that if the "creature" in question were sublime, or conducive to the sublime, all its gaps might be visible. It should be clear, in any case, that the sublime extends the lower as well as the upper reaches of the *Poetics*.

X

The bridge between the sublime, thus revealed in its role as a negative force, and the beautiful, a tenderhearted experience that could not in itself entail the possibility of being *critical*, is the mathematical sublime, or sublime of interpretation. The most elementary temptation of any antiformalist interpreter is to identify with all the darkest visionaries and to find dark values exclusively, with Melville in *The Encantadas*, on the only side of the tortoise he or she can see. But the interpretive sublime is on neither side. It exists as an alternative to alternation and reveals the lack of opposition in false dichotomies. The discovery of hidden meanings is no more adequate as an exclusive end of criticism than the summary of overt ones.[61] Derivative myth-criticism, "Freudian interpretation," and most of the merely rancorous modes of demystification oversimplify in this way. At the end of the last chapter I suggested that any criticism necessarily goes astray in some measure because it can never estimate the distance between the architectonic purpose and the instinctual purposiveness of its object—or of its own subjectivity. The "effect" of literature, the sublime or uncanny effect which sets it apart (but not categorically apart) from the relatively featureless discourse of practical exchange, does not appear squarely within either form or the negation of form but in the signs of estrangement, the gaps, between formal design and the form of its attempted negation. Neither of these forms completely occludes or represses the other; each harbors an unsubdued strength that deforms the other in ways that cannot be scientifically reduced any more than psychology can fully discriminate or arbitrate between will and instinct in the mind.

So the sublime is *not* identical with the unconscious, and its appearance is not properly to be described as sublimation, although that plays its role. Undoubtedly we have grown too familiar with our fictions about the fictions of the unconscious, with all their pathos and economy—so familiar, indeed, that the whole psychoanalytic romance may turn out to have sublimated whatever it is that is *still* wholly unconscious. The sufficiency of the oedipal explanation is undergoing attack from every direction—humanist, feminist, Marxist, deconstructionist—because too obviously it cuts the Gordian knot of interpretation. As Hertz argues, the oedipal explanation breaks through the mathematical sublime arbitrarily. I am not quite sure; in my view the oedipal explanation seems arbitrary because it overdetermines the language of desire, desire which is not for one thing, arguably, but for the sheer sensation of presence. But the oedipal explanation is still, if I may so put it, a valid allegory. Roughly the same objection can be made, followed by a roughly comparable defense, concerning the closely related explanations called "bourgeois ideology," *langue*, and the "precursor"—concerning any explanation, in short, that seems unequivocally to insist that poets are written, not writers.

Antithetical factors are not interpretive ends in themselves any more than the factors conducive to formal unity were before them. Systematically approached, antithetical factors will soon constitute an antithetical formalism. There is undoubted value in a science of this sort, which will certainly find ways of making whole dimensions of art visible for the first time, but I do not see how this or any other quickly exhausted way of processing literature—for that is what it is—can be heralded as the future task of criticism and recommended specifically as an antidote to interpretation.[62] It is under the banner of science, and not as a hindrance to science, that the interpretation industry has come to monopolize criticism in the last forty years. Interpretation has supplanted both judgment and taxonomy in scholarship; this triumph has been a recent one, not because interpretation had never been done before but because for the most part until this century it had seemed a simple job that could be done silently. It may be noted that the interpretation industry has always dominated theology, and always will dominate it, because where it really matters interpretation has never seemed easy. Interpretation is inevitable; it is thought itself, and it will seem exhaustible, not when it is supplanted by science, but only when it is itself mistaken for science.

The New Critics used to ask the philological historians how they could confidently classify ideas, terms, and texts without reading them attentively, without a due concern for nuance and irony. It seemed a good and fair question, and the answer came as too much interpretation—to the point of "blockage"—with that sort of concern. But ridicule and self-exhaustion alike have now done their work, and very few more new books with titles like "Ordered Flux" are likely to appear. The new blockage is more likely to consist of general rhetorics, revisionary histories, and narratologies, entitling us to ask, in behalf of interpretation, the same old question: How can the new anatomies proceed with confidence if they do not read attentively, openly, and to some extent unsystematically? The science of the greatest modern anatomist, Northrop Frye, has passed inevitably into eclipse, but rival sciences alone are churlish enough to scorn the grace of his interpretations.

The function of the sublime is to keep interpretation from closure. It persists between forms, as close to one as to another; it should be remarked in this regard that the most sophisticated operative terms of formalism, from Aristotle's "recognition"—duly interpreted—to Skhlovsky's "defamiliarization" and Sigurd Burckhardt's "disturbing element,"[63] point clearly toward what I mean by the sublime. A valuable instance of the necessary interaction between forms and the sublime appears in Longinus's reading of Sappho's "ode" to Anactoria. Self-convicted of fragmentation, her tongue "broken" by passion, Sappho "brings everything together," as Longinus says (10.3) with commanding metrical skill. If this were all, the topic of interpretation would still be "ordered flux," but Longinus has merely set interpretation in motion by suggesting an equipoise of motive. One would have to continue—to point out, for example, the consecrating excitement of love-anguish in contrast with an encroaching ennui that is intimated in the very composure and elegance of these sapphics, thus questioning the presupposition we have as readers that form is comfort. One would have to show, always inconclusively, how passion and control infect and finally disfigure each other in the course of their endless give-and-take of values.

The effect of a well-conducted interpretation along these lines, drawn out more and more finely in a dialectic that never quite repeats itself, is the effect of the mathematical sublime. But we still have not faced the imputation of tyranny in our victimage by the victim Sappho. Rumors of tyranny have followed the concept of the sublime ever since they were first prompted by the typical metaphors of Longinus himself. Perhaps it can be shown at least that they have been greatly exaggerated. Tyranny exists without legitimate authority but it still requires that some authority, however specious, be invoked for it. The sublime by contrast is unauthorized, as we have seen, a phantom of possession that is always in retreat from one site to another. Although the sublime never falsifies its nature *(quod semper, quod ubique, quod ab omnibus)* and thus evades the charge of fickleness leveled by Plato against both poets and democracies, yet at the same time it never regiments response; it always surprises and elevates, as Longinus says. Its tonic effect is not subject to conventionalization and it also lacks the monotonous insistence of obsession. Not at all necessarily suggestive of spectacular gloom but of the happy absence, rather, of inhibition, it is best seen, on reflection, as a grace beyond the reach of art.

In an article called " 'A Grace Beyond the Reach of Art,' " which is meant to supplement his book on the sublime, Samuel Holt Monk demonstrates that Pope's phrase is less directly indebted to Longinus than to a flourishing and longstanding concept of "grace" per se.[64] *Charis, venustas, gratia, je ne sais quoi, sprezzatura:*—roughly synonymous with all these terms, *grace* was very nearly equivalent in seventeenth-century poetics to *sublimity* in the century succeeding Boileau's translation of Longinus (1674).[65] (Hazlitt's *gusto* may offer itself as a nineteenth-century equivalent, while *indeterminacy* and *free-play* are somewhat unsatisfactory candidates for our own.) The very real difference between the two terms was that *grace* in the aesthetic milieu of the Restoration suggested nothing gothic, ponderous, or frightening. It encompassed the baroque fillip, the shining of a countenance, the unexpected twist of a period, or the simplicity of an epigram. Its effect, says Monk, was "sudden and surprising," like that of the sublime, and in its time it was, like the sublime, "a repository for the irregular and irrational elements in art,"[66] but apart from these parallels it was a very different quality, a carelessness in elegance (like Pyrrha's hair in Horace) rather than a breach of decorum.

Monk says ("Grace Beyond the Reach of Art," p. 134) that Lysias was the stock example of grace in literature, an example taken by seventeenth-century writers from Longinus's probable contemporary Demetrius (see *On Style*, 3, 128). When one considers what Longinus says about Lysias, one comes to suspect that he may be extending the terms *hupsos* and *megethos* to incorporate the *charis* discussed at length by Demetrius (127–42) and also in passing by Dionysius of Halicarnassus. It is important not only that Longinus compares Plato with Lysias while pretending not to, showing thereby that grace, whatever Plato may lack, is certainly what Demosthenes lacks. What is more telling is the fact that the concept of grace would rationalize the presence in Longinus's canon of Sappho's ode, a poem that many scholars, most notably Saintsbury, have refused to call sublime.[67] When Demetrius affirms that "one cannot sufficiently admire [the charm: *epicharitos*] in the divine Sappho,"[68] Longinus would certainly applaud the precision of his sentiment. All things considered, he would not demur unduly, I think, if one were to introduce grace into the domain of the sublime.

A modern essay that is splendidly Longinian, provided that one is willing to extend the meaning of *hupsos* in this manner, is "Language as Gesture" by R. P. Blackmur, whose examples, especially those taken from the plastic arts, have a quality resembling "grace." Blackmur reminds one of Longinus both in his virtuoso, paronomasiac style and also in his way of choosing and then sympathetically fusing his commentary with his examples. He concludes "Language as Gesture" with a tribute to Shakespearean gesture that could be a translation of Longinus: the power of implication in Shakespeare "must overwhelm us even though we realize as we consent to it, that we have made it ourselves."[69]

XI

I suggested at the beginning of my last chapter that the tradition deriving from Aristotle has tended to constitute itself as the only tradition. In recommending a different perspective I have tried (a victim, perhaps, of some obscure law of recoil) to recover nearly the whole field for Longinus, including much to which he never explicitly laid claim: a theory of representation, a rigorous understanding of the interplay among nature, feeling, and language, and a grasp of aesthetic qualities beyond the so-called sublime—the Burkean trombone—extending even to amplification, charm, and delicacy. For the moment I have not pressed these conclusions into a theory of interpretation, but in rough terms the orientation of such a theory will be obvious. Even though the theory itself should remain as evasive as the sublime, in practice it amounts to this: whenever possible, the interpreter should delay the semantic closure that is urged upon him by his or her own will to form and that of the text. The enterprise of interpretation is best honored by those who do *not* agree to go no further, to get no closer, to honor tenuous symmetries. Having arrived at a liminal understanding of form (both as the determination of consciousness and as unconscious determination[70]) by feeling along its edges like someone who is blind, the interpreter begins, at that point of exhaustion, to interpret.

The Sophoclean Oedipus disregarded by Aristotle but nonetheless present in the *Poetics* realizes that, as Longinus says, his misfortunes are plural. Because of his resolution to become a scapegoat he sacrifices the "external trappings" of his governorship—as helmsman and *tyrannos*—to the interior form of his family romance, scattering the symbols of his far-seeing guardianship on the ground in order to make the character beneath his role visible for the first time. In Longinus all of this seems a preliminary matter; it is a model for the structure of disruption that tells us very little in itself, "catharsis" notwithstanding, about the way the experience reaches the spectator. A fuller and subtler moment in the Oedipus story is commemorated by Longinus, just before he cites the apparition of Achilles over his tomb, as "Sophocles' account of Oedipus dying and giving himself burial to the accompaniment of a sign from heaven" (15.7).

In the messenger's speech recording this event, there are "clefts" in the sky, in the earth, and in knowledge, all of which regions at this moment, especially as Oedipus views them, are nearly indistinguishable. Although each region is sundered, there is still no point of division between them:

> Then very quickly we saw him do reverence
> To earth and to the powers of air,
> With one address to both.
> But in what manner
> Oedipus perished, no one of mortal men
> Could tell but Theseus. It was not lightning,
> Bearing its fire from God, that took him off;
> No hurricane was blowing.
> But some attendant from the train of Heaven
> Came for him; or else the underworld
> Opened in love the unlit door of earth.[71]

Longinus recognizes his affinity with a seer who can bring mind and nature so close together that one sudden obeisance will do for both. A sweep as unconfined as this cannot be imagined without some loss of categorical nicety. Theseus, like Horatio and so many others to come, survives to interpret the experience, reconstructing in his own person the monarchical form of Oedipus while passing on the family form to Hippolytus. Like Longinus, Theseus will aspire to the mathematical sublime; he will be concerned with the quality of life in society after the dynamic sublime has been buried. Leaving the sacred ground, he carries the vision of Oedipus into a community that is preserved, in all its necessary forms, by taking that vision to heart in order not to relive it. The power of Oedipus is now explanatory, descriptive, and perhaps lacking in magnificence, but in being recalled by the voice of Theseus it is made to return from its antisocial isolation. To follow and confirm that return is the whole art, or nature, of interpretation.

THREE

The Other Harmony of Dryden's "Preface to *Fables*"

In the first part of this book I have argued that the *Peri Hupsous* of Longinus is preferable to the *Poetics* of Aristotle as a point of departure for the development of a theory of interpretation. I have even suggested that the valuable insights of formalist thinking itself are if anything more readily to be inferred from Longinus than discovered in Aristotle. Henceforth I shall try to identify a Longinian mode of criticism which would not merely encourage the narration of new adventures of the soul among masterpieces (though it would not be as embarrassed to do so as much recent criticism has been) but would actually entail a serious, sympathetic, and adequately modulated response, fully circumspect in its assumptions, to the critical issues that have come to the fore in the past two decades.

In the last chapter I shall take up these issues as they are anticipated in a modern Longinian, Walter Benjamin, but for the next two chapters I want to show what was done with them in two classics of criticism that seem to divide the genius of Longinus between them. One of them, Shelley's *Defence of Poetry*, rivals any theoretical text of which I am aware in its metaphysical precision and range, but also succumbs in a good many places to the undue solemnity and curdling of expression that lessens the impact of much current writing—and on occasion lessens that of Longinus himself. The other, Dryden's "Preface to *Fables, Ancient and Modern*," to which I now turn, is theoretically precocious almost by accident, perhaps, although its intricacy of thought remains extraordinary however one accounts for it, but is written in the enviably casual manner that has been tacitly forbidden in modern criticism, especially in American universities, ever since *impressionism* became a code word for irresponsibility and laziness.[1]

The prose style of the late Dryden cannot be praised too highly; the fine things that others have said about it would suffice, however, did it not remain to say that his style is in fact motivated by his views of literature and criticism. It is the nature of that motivation that will form the main concern of the present chapter. I shall take Dryden's *beau désordre* as a starting point for an excursion through every other dimension of the "Preface"—its psychology, its natural philosophy, its view of other authors, its view of the self—in order to show that all these factors have a way of confirming and even changing places with one another: to show, finally, that in important ways the "Preface" itself is another Fable, is as much a translation as the ensuing translations are, and is very deliberately offered as a harvest, rivaling Chaucer's, of "God's plenty."[2]

I

It is doubtful that the novelty of Dryden's later criticism is owing entirely to the appearance of Boileau's Longinus in 1674; but Longinus, who is quoted at a key point in the "Preface" (II, 276), certainly does encourage tendencies that appear in Dryden from the beginning.[3] Consistently in the arguments of Neander, for example, but only in those arguments among many others in the *Essay of Dramatic Poesy*, we find Longinus unwittingly recalled and the author of the "Preface" anticipated—in the norm of the "large and comprehensive soul," for instance, that is applied to Shakespeare (I, 67). But Dryden's two critical masterpieces are fundamentally different. The early *Essay*, a carefully constructed drama, is formalistic. It is wonderfully open-minded, certainly, but in all its viewpoints it never strays far from the question of Rules. Its formality is most exquisite in the exordium, upon which I shall want to concentrate shortly, approaching the informal "Preface" by that route after a digression on the significance of beginnings in critical essays generally.

Formally preliminary and informally hazarded beginnings lead to two different kinds of coherence in the writing and the principles of critical theory. All beginnings, I have argued elsewhere, are insidiously proleptic.[4] They not only outline what is to come but also anticipate it almost to the point of preemption through some figure, emblem, or anecdote that insinuates its relevance into every corner of the text. The point I want to pursue here is that formal beginnings are less prescient in their handling of anticipation than informal beginnings. The first monsters in the irregular-seeming but still immensely calculated beginning of Horace's *Ad Pisones* prefigure the many negative examples that further his theme of decorum as consistency, and lead in the end to his portrait of a monstrously shaggy poet. This much is plain, but there is also a less well-monitored side of Horace's prolepsis that becomes evident in one of those monsters, the woman who becomes a "dark, grotesque fish below" *(turpiter atrum / desinat in piscem)*. She is one of "the dreams of a sick man" *(aegri somnia)* who cannot be distinguished clearly in this case from Horace himself. On the whole, though, one can only admire the casual shrewdness of Horace's beginning—the fact, for example, that his seemingly random first remarks have neatly exempted his poem from his own charge, a few lines later, that "Works with solemn beginnings" *(Inceptis gravibus)* usually fizzle out, while at the same time the very abruptness of these remarks, preceding even the address to the Pisos, suggests an unannounced rivalry with epics that begin *in media res*.

Despite Dryden's widely shared belief that Horace had "no method" ("Preface to the *Aeneis*," II, 232), there is certainly a great deal of method in the beginning of the *Art of Poetry*. But the evidence of method appears to be indistinguishable from the evidence that Horace is keeping some things out of sight, in one instance perhaps even out of his own sight. This secondary, repressive function of form, which we first encountered in the *Poetics*, recurs in the exordium of Sidney's *Defence of Poetry*. The horse that Horace engrafted to a man's head at the beginning of the *Ad Pisones* was to have a long career; it can be linked even to Swift's man-like Houyhnhnms if we recall that Sidney, whose first name means "horse-lover," nearly falls victim, like Gulliver, to a strange encomium that he recalls at the beginning of his *Defence*: "If I had not been a piece of a logician before I came to [the Emperor's stable-master Pugliano], I think he would have persuaded me to have wished myself a horse."[5] Here is the slip in Sidney's prolepsis, whether he be logician or no. It is true that he has not completely confused the horseman with the horse: having praised horsemanship, his spokesman Pugliano then turns to a distinctly new topic, the praise of horses, but that justification will not explain why Sidney delays his sudden outburst of identification—however ironic—until the topic has changed.

The explanation is, I think, that he is having a phil-hippine crisis. Afraid that his "self-love" ("Apology for Poetry," p. 83) may not be legitimate, he undertakes the vocational defense to follow. What Sidney will wish to say is that poetry, "the companion of the camps" (ibid., p. 99), is as active, heroic, and "right virtuous" a calling as equestrian knighthood itself, that both callings are equally good at producing a Cyrus or an Aeneas, an Edward Wotton or a Philip Sidney. The slip about horses, however, which shows man aspiring merely to equal the noblest of animals, reveals that Sidney will be unable to refute *The School of Abuse* on its own terms. Despite his Platonic veneer, Stephen Gosson himself had had no notion of attacking poetry per se but only poets, as his title shows, and Sidney in his turn has little enough to say merely in defense of poets. Man's "erected wit," noble horseman that it is, may aspire toward what Shelley was to call "beautiful idealisms" ("Preface to *Prometheus Unbound*"), but the "infected will," itself as unbridled as a horse in clover, Pegasus with neither curb nor bit, raises up a cavalry of evils that "can do more hurt than any other army of words" (ibid., p. 86).

In the "Preface to *Fables*" Dryden dispels this secret fear, which is brought into the open in part by the formality of Sidney's extended comparison, by seeming frankly to concede whatever Jeremy Collier can allege against the theater and against himself. This relaxation is anticipated, as we shall see, by the opening sentences of the "Preface." Even in the *Essay*, however, which has a formal exordium and proceeds to canvass—if not precisely to defend—the advantages of various rules and forms, Dryden has already learned to disarm the more destructive tendencies of formal prolepsis, providing a model of cognitive flexibility that looks forward in some ways, again, to his final poetics. For one thing, unlike Sidney, Dryden is a "new man" (Ne-ander) who is not obliged to keep up Sidney's tense vigilance over his country and his class. Thus in the dedicatory epistle to Buckhurst (the well-born "Eugenius" of the *Essay*), he good-naturedly confesses the irrelevance of Sidney's gallant equestrianism to his own social standing: "Sometimes I stand desperately to my arms, like the foot when deserted by their horse" (I, 15).

Just as this dedicatory epistle features alternating figures of military combat and love, so the exordium to the *Essay* launches a combat between friends that echoes, or seconds, a dispute between equal navies: as in a dance, the "most mighty and best appointed fleets" approach each other "in parallel lines." The elegance of dramatic resolution that is thus anticipated on these two fronts, both forensic and military, encourages the reader to hope for a happy outcome on yet a third front: for the success, after a "dreadful suspense," of the struggle waged by the English theater to "restore" itself under the new monarchy and to reassert its claims against rival theaters. In all three of these struggles—the battle, the debate, and the restoration—England will triumph owing to the ascendancy of "new men." At certain moments the *Essay* seems to propose itself as a model for the new theater, as when the disputants wish to avoid suddenly reappearing on "the stage, . . . which is against the laws of comedy" (I, 44). Even Neander's defense of rhyme, which temporarily seemed important enough to start a family quarrel over but which Dryden painlessly recanted only a few years later, is pursued at least partly for the sake of a figure that exactly mirrors the relation set forth in the exordium between conflict and conciliatory balance. Speaking of the function of rhyme in stichomythic exchanges, Neander addresses Crites: "You tell us, this supplying of the last half of a verse, or adjoining a whole second to the former, looks more like the design of two than the answer of one. Suppose we acknowledge it: how comes this confederacy to be more displeasing to you than in a dance that is well contrived?" (I, 89). In short, conflict is everywhere staged in "parallel lines" and purified by artifice until the agony of actual violence is no longer evoked by it. (In just these cathartic terms, Wordsworth defended verse writing as opposed to prose in his 1800 "Preface.") Staged conflict is like "those little undulations of sound, though almost vanishing before they reached [the hearers], yet still seeming to retain somewhat of their first horror, which they had betwixt the fleets."

The formality of these figures is delicate and unobtrusive, but it still reveals the calculated restraint, or perhaps repression, that informs Dryden's early work and distinguishes that work from what I could almost wish to call the "release" of his last "Preface." To begin with rhyme itself: In proclaiming its virtues, Dryden must suppress the fact, as he does even more egregiously in the bad-mannered and badly conceived "Defence of an *Essay*" (1668; see especially I, 115), that the great Elizabethans rarely used it. Here in small is the dilemma of the *Essay*. Dryden can easily engineer an English victory over the Dutch in real life and over the French, the Spanish, and even the ancients in literature, but how, in literature, can he bring the English to conquer their own ancestors in "the last age"? At times Dryden cheerfully confesses that writers in the present age have fallen off but he always hopes that a new "confederacy" of rival playwrights can win this last, most elusive victory. Still, the problem causes anxiety. The three formal debates—ancients vs. moderns, French vs. English, blank vs. rhyme—are set in place to keep a debate between the English before and the English after the Commonwealth from materializing. Neander makes the possibility of such a debate still remoter by making his set contrast of Shakespeare, "Fletcher," and Jonson a matter of national pride and not modern envy.[6]

Nothing he does can make the past seem less dominant, however. There is an occasional note of elegy in the *Essay*, especially in the exordium, which seems specifically to mourn the passing of the Elizabethans. The beauty of the prose in the first paragraphs comes from an apparently unmotivated surplus of pathos. In particular, this quality can be sensed in the prevailing silence. Getting away from the noise of the city (which Hobbes called the "scommatique" world of satire and comedy) and dropping below the natural noise of a waterfall (Hobbes's "pastorall" world of pastoral and pastoral comedy) in order to hear the "heroique" noise of epic and tragedy,[7] all Londoners alike are said, in a remarkable phrase, to be "seeking out the noise in the depth of silence." In part this is just a matter of not talking ("every one favouring his own curiosity with a strict silence"), but the moment also involves a silence in the atmosphere that seems not to help people hear but to function, rather, as a kind of acoustic muffler. It is a silence that must be listened *through*: the descent down the river, "dropping below" the falls from city life toward the greater "depth" of heroic life, passes through silence as if through a time warp. That is just what it is; it is the silence of the interregnum when the theaters were closed. What is veiled by Dryden's opening scene, then, is the intense effort of modern wits to catch the accents of "the last age" but one, the age prior to the artistic silence that was compounded by an unregulated and unresolved noise resembling a "great fall of waters": the noise of civil strife.

By straining, the characters of the *Essay* can hear the noise of "the giant race before the Flood," hoping even as they listen that the time will soon arrive that is finally announced by Dryden in his "Prologue to Congreve's *Double-Dealer*" (1694):

> Well, then, the promis'd hour is come at last;
> The present age of wit obscures the past.
> Strong were our sires; and as they fought they writ,
> Conqu'ring with force of arms, and dint of wit;
> Theirs was the giant race before the Flood;
> And thus, when Charles return'd, our Empire stood.
>
> (II, 169)[8]

If the unsung strife in the *Essay* occurs between Dryden's contemporaries and the age of Shakespeare, that may be why the navies at present are said to have "disputed the command of the greater half of the *globe*" (italics mine); and it may further account for the pathos of the prose. Like T. S. Eliot after him, Dryden nostalgically evokes the Thames of Spenser's *Prothalamion*. First he writes that the four companions "ordered the watermen to let fall their oars more gently" (I, 19), and then later, lest we miss his cue, he tells us that they have "given order to the watermen to turn their barge, and row softly" (I, 25).[9]

This series of instances, including that of the misleadingly casual Horace, is meant to show that the formal beginnings of critical essays set in place the resistance to undigestible material that shapes them overall. The chef-d'oeuvre in this kind, the "frame-story" of Dryden's *Essay*, shares this tendency to conceal things with its predecessors and thus serves to mark the distance Dryden will have come by the time he speaks his last words in the "Preface," which are contrastingly uninhibited—and informal.[10] Although he had always known Montaigne, one suspects that as he grew older and his essays more and more often included mock-apologies for haste, forgetfulness, and the garrulity of age, the taste for Montaigne, who began to affect senility not long after he turned forty, must have grown on him also.[11] Montaigne complained, perhaps disingenuously, that he could never compose formally, not even a business letter or note of introduction, but it is clear, throughout his work, that he held this failing to be a virtue. Master of nonchalance himself, he advised other writers to follow him in doing without "exordiums and perorations."[12] Eventually Dryden brought himself to take this advice. "The logical and Aristotelian arrangements are not to the point," Montaigne wrote elsewhere: "I want a man to begin with the conclusion" (*Complete Essays*, II, 10). What Dryden learned from Montaigne, who was the first to have gone some way toward achieving Rousseau's wish to tell the whole truth about himself, and who talks on as cheerfully about incest and cannibalism as about anything else—what

Dryden learned from him was an uninhibited manner which enables him in many respects to begin where others leave off.

To turn then to the informal beginning of his "Preface": in the past, Dryden had often had recourse to architectural expressions when he wished to affirm Judgment—the "master-workman"—or the regularity of art. Thus at the end of the *Essay* Neander argues that rhyme is "a rule and line by which [the poet] keeps his building compact and even" (I, 91). In the first paragraph of the "Preface," however, architecture begins, like the haunted houses of fiction, to ruin the composure of the builder:

> 'Tis with a Poet, as with a man who designs to build, and is very exact, as he supposes, in casting up the cost beforehand; but, generally speaking, he is mistaken in his account, and reckons short of the expense he first intended. He alters his mind as the work proceeds, and will have this or that convenience more, of which he had not thought when he began. So it has happened to me; I have built a house, where I intended but a lodge; yet with better success than a certain nobleman, who, beginning with a dog kennel, never lived to finish the palace he had contrived. (II, 269–70)[13]

There is a certain contempt for this nobleman's bungling which is not surprising in a "new man" who has had to court the great more often than he could have wished. It would be just like a slovenly specimen of the class Arnold later called "barbarian" to want to live with his dogs, say, and to find himself living instead in the only completed wing of a palace that no one else could afford. The bourgeois, on the other hand, has extended himself to finish a sensible house. But if there is contempt in Dryden's simile, there is also an understandable measure of identification: A lodge might have sufficed Dryden himself, but he feels that a dog kennel has been his lot ever since 1688. He dares affirm, however, giving notice of the immense pride that increasingly shores up his serenity, that he has not only designed a palace but finished it.

Or rather, he has finished a facsimile of it. Underlying his pride, without necessarily undermining it, is the awareness that his edifice has got out of hand and built itself beyond the poet's—or essayist's—power to control it. The palace in any case is not the one he had wanted. Just as formerly he had meant to write an epic and instead translated the *Aeneid*, so now, failing to the same degree in a lesser ambition, he has meant to translate the whole of the *Iliad* and instead become distracted among other works (II, 270). Like the *bricoleur* of Lévi-Strauss, an engineer in a time of dearth, he has learned to use what comes handiest, whatever is "lying next in my way" (ibid.), and trusts more and more to chance that the building will come out right. And that it will be finished in time: the nobleman "never lived to finish" his undertaking, and Dryden has just barely survived to finish his, he feels, having struggled through "several intervals of sickness" (II, 273). We cannot know his state of mind, of course, and indeed he speaks once of saving a quarrel until another occasion, but it is difficult not to feel that everything he says in the "Preface" has the ring of last words.

Although they are haphazard and although most of them are merely translations, the *Fables* are meant for neither a house nor a palace, after all, but for a monument. The entire volume, which is vast in extent, is a personal dwelling; everything in it is arranged to be "congenial" to the soul of the builder, to reflect him and his taste. He does not give the impression, however, that he has chosen his furnishings himself. They have chosen him. At large in his library, he is importuned by ancient voices and speaks them one after another. The builder "alters his mind," he says at first, but then on reflection he recasts the builder's role as a passive one: "So has it happened to me." The crowding in of last passages is so hurried that all distinctions based on judgment must be waived or run almost together: "Thoughts, such as they are, come crowding in so fast upon me that my only difficulty is to choose or to reject; to run them into verse, or to give them the other harmony of prose" (II, 273). Here, indeed, is God's plenty, with "such a variety of game springing up" that the author cannot "know . . . which to follow" (II, 284).[14]

II

With this sketch of Dryden's prolepsis I "conclude," as Dryden says, "the first part of this discourse," having laid down "the dead-colouring"[15] that can now be gone over again and placed in relief. To begin where we left off, with the subject of variety: For the aging poet, ripeness is all, and his "Preface" is a benediction upon final fruits and late "game." The imagery of hunting is not new to Dryden. In his first published prose, the "Preface to *The Rival Ladies*," the imagination is compared with "an high-ranging spaniel" (I, 8), and in his "Life of Plutarch" (1683), Dryden praises Plutarch as a master of the indirect approach in the handling of a topic: "the best quarry lies not in the open field" (II, 9). The aims and objects of literature offer a well-stocked preserve, then, but they cannot be expected to jump into one's net like the fish at Jonson's Penshurst or to wait submissively like the "painted partrich" that "lyes in every field." Dryden's is lively game "springing up" in profusion, not necessarily elusive but still difficult to flush out and snare in any consecutive order. It consists in a wealth of allusion, quotation, and translation, an excess flowing in from the literary medium itself, not unlike *auxesis* in Longinus or the "mathematical sublime" in Kant. Too many poets, too many ideas, too many characters in Chaucer; it is all charmingly too much.

Dryden's attraction to plenitude is spontaneous (and, quite precisely in the jargon of his day, against his better "judgment"). It is wholly natural that he would have little use for undernourished French plots, for Jonson's frugality of wit, or, we might add, for the lean prose of a Thomas Sprat or a Rymer. Much as he relies upon Scaliger for his etymology of "satire" in his "Discourse Concerning the Original and Progress of Satire," he still presents the alternative derivation from the *satura lanx* or "stuffed platter" of the Romans with evident relish (see II, 98). The dish is "full and abundant." It was "yearly filled with all sorts of fruits, which were offered to the gods at their festivals, as the *prémices* or first gatherings" (II, 105). Or again, the gods' plenty that satire holds out may be "a kind of *olla*, or hotchpotch, made of several sorts of meats" (ibid.). This pleasant attitude weakens the connection between satire and moral purpose that Dryden intends, on the whole, to promote. If satire turns out to be more like a good dinner than a bitter medicine for the vicious and foolish, Dryden can scarcely upbraid Horace, as he realizes, for not being as single-minded in his aim as Persius or Juvenal: "I know that it may be urged in defence of Horace that this unity is not necessary; because the very word *satura* signifies a dish plentifully stored with all variety of fruits and grains" (II, 145).

Unity is a virtue that Dryden always wants to praise, knowing that he should do so, but he has a difficult time fixing his attention, as a practical critic, on the notion of an organizing, purposive idea. His first "Preface," like his last, begins in disarray, with a "confused mass of thoughts" working their way "towards the light" of organization (*"Rival Ladies,"* I, 2). It is the *mass* of this movement that is fascinating and must be resisted, not so much because it might prove overwhelming or because the evil that comes of excess is easy to identify and define, but simply because duty lies elsewhere in an age of French-import criticism. Thus despite the fact that stuffing is clearly the soul of satire, Dryden dutifully brings the foreign criterion of unity to bear on it. That his genius is for excess is clearest whenever he encounters meagerness, as when he allows himself a private joke as a holiday from the labor of praising the Earl of Dorset's trifling satires: "There is continual abundance" in Dorset's writing, he says, "'Tis that which the Romans call *coena dubia*, where there is such plenty, yet withal so much diversity, and so much good order, that the choice is difficult between one excellency and another" (II, 94). Which is to say, Dorset's satires are dubious indeed.

It is the same with "Fars" (*ME* "Fars," stuffing; note that the French for *satura lanx* might be *écuelle farcie*), a word that Dryden appears to have learned from his kinsman Sir Robert Howard during their controversy over rhyme and then quotes against him in the "Defence of an *Essay*." The context is certainly "derisive," as George Watson notes (I, 145n.), yet there appears to be more fascination than condescension in Dryden's laughter.

Howard had complained that people who make rules and distinctions "will grow as strict as *Sancho Pancos* Doctor was to our very Appetites; for in the difference of *Tragedy* and *Comedy*, and of *Fars* itself, there can be no determination but by the Taste."[16] Appalled by this passage, Dryden sarcastically quotes it again and again (I, 145–46), but his fancy is caught by it nevertheless: "unless he would have us understand the comedies of my Lord L., where the first act should be pottages, the second fricasses, &c., and the fifth a *chère entière* of women" (I, 120). From the evidence of this well-stuffed dish, to which is added a dash of Restoration wit, it is clear how little Dryden himself cares for portioning out "rules and distinctions," and how much he is, after all, a creature of excess.

By 1700 Dryden knows that he loves plenty, excess, and every other sort of "hotchpotch,"[17] and loves them the more, perhaps, because they are bad for him. He scarcely bothers to conceal his irregular taste in the "Preface to *Fables*," even though it is just here that one finds his first unmistakably sincere apology for irregularity. Perhaps the reason for this anomaly is that he can turn this figure of thought, the apology for excess, to uses that in themselves offer a pleasant surfeit. For one thing, there are almost too many apologies. First he apologizes for such symptoms of senility as may appear in his writing—running afoul, once again, of Sidney's horsemanship: "I have the excuse of an old gentleman, who mounting on horseback before some ladies, when I was present, got up somewhat heavily, but desired of the fair spectators that they would count fourscore and eight before they judged him. By the mercy of God, I am already come within twenty years of his number, a cripple in my limbs, but what decays are in my mind, the reader must determine" (II, 272). Aside from the surplusage of weight and quantity, not the least excess in this passage is the protraction of gallantry into a time when it is no longer in character except as avuncular repartee, but even in that form it is just the sort of liveliness that draws comedies into censurable indiscretions. This apology precedes an apology for the author's failing memory—"which is not impaired to any great degree" (ibid.). That misfortune, such as it is, brings with it the compensation of yet another pleasing excess. The loss of memory is what makes room for the "thoughts" that "come crowding in." One sort of variety, that is, gives way to another, a garrulity that is no less copious than that of exact scholarship.

Possibly, though, it is not Dryden's memory for *fact* that is impaired: "Old men especially are dangerous," warns Montaigne, "whose memory of things past remains, but who have lost the memory of their repetitions" (I, 9). Later I shall take up the theoretical rationale for repetitiousness in Dryden's "Preface," noting only for the moment that a weak memory is a highly convenient pretext for the redoubling of abuse. The second time Dryden finds fault with Cowley (II, 286), pretending to have forgotten that he did so before, he rejoices in the redundancy of the occasion by cross-examining his own love of plenty: "One of our last great poets is sunk in his reputation, because he could never forgive any conceit which came in his way. . . . There was plenty enough, but the dishes were ill-sorted." For the lover of clear contrasts, it must be disquieting that Dryden's stock figures can be applied so indifferently to the purposes of praise or blame, but we can also admire a mind so crowded that its possessor is obliged to reduce all rules to their exceptions and to convert all the preestablished tropes of evaluation into more adaptable formulas of description: *"Inopem me copia fecit"* (II, 279) is for him a highly ironic expression of modesty. Another excess anticipated by Dryden's apology for his impaired memory is the rather startling margin of error he allows himself. There is practically nothing he gets right about Chaucer, partly because he trusts in and repeats the errors of Thomas Speght's 1602 edition,[18] but also because he simply forgets what he knows, as he disarmingly admits in the end: "When I had closed Chaucer, I returned to Ovid, and translated some more of his fables: and by this time had so far forgotten *The Wife of Bath's Tale* that . . ." (II, 290). Not only Chaucer but also Homer (the "machine" of Agamemnon's dream comes *before* the Catalog of Ships[19]), the Roman lyrists (he cites "Catullus" meaning Martial) and a good many others get mixed up in Dryden's immethodical progress. But unlike Aristotle's errors, for example those that concern the *Odyssey*, Dryden's forgetting appears not to serve as reinforcement for any systematic pattern of exclusion. It may not be forgetting at all—almost certainly it is not wherever there is a grievance to be repeated—but rather a skillful rhetoric of inadvertency, a show of confusion bearing witness to the author's easy familiarity with plenitude. In that case, it would bring one close to understanding the *consciously* revolutionary psychology of this, Dryden's last essay.

It is by pleading inadvertency (quite absurdly) that Dryden apologizes for the first of many times, each time seeming to have forgotten that he has done so before, for whatever there is that "savours of immortality or profaneness" in his writing: "If there happen to be found an irreverent expression, or a thought too wanton, they are crept into my verses thro' inadvertency" (II, 273). It is a little more to the point to argue, as he then does, that the authors of the indecencies he translates are the persons who should be held responsible for them (ibid.), but that is scarcely an adequate excuse either. Dryden himself refuses to accept Chaucer's apology for "ful broad" speaking in the "General Prologue" (II, 285–86), which consists essentially in saying that it is not he, Chaucer, who speaks, but his characters. In Chaucer as well as in Dryden, this excuse is grossly sophistical in most respects. From one point of view, however, the modern one expressed in Rimbaud's *Je est un autre*, it is perfectly legitimate. It seems to me—and I shall try to show this more fully later on—that both attitudes coexist in Dryden's thinking, the one according to which he is a responsible speaker and the one according to which, in some sense inadvertently, he is spoken through.

Dryden's apology for past literary indiscretions is probably heartfelt, but still he is loath to part with his errors. To bid them farewell, as he must, is to write finis not only to his own high spirits but also, from the retrospect of "this concluding century" (II, 270), to the heyday of the Restoration itself.[20] His clinging to gallantry in extreme age shows regret for a whole epoch, for the Cavalier horsemanship that has passed by. The culture of high-hearted profligacy had been literary as well as social and political. It had reached back to Montaigne—"I am one of those who hold that poetry is never so blithe as in a wanton and irregular subject" (I, 29)—and perhaps, through him, to Rabelais. To echo Bakhtin's treatment of Rabelais, "Preface to *Fables*" is a "carnival," a farewell to the flesh that becomes a last fling.[21]

III

How is that we sense Dryden's recantation to be sincere, even though it obviously resembles the sophistical apology of Chaucer's "General Prologue"? Dryden is convincing, I believe, because he seems so moderate in discriminating between his respectable critics and his traducers. "I shall say the less of Mr. Collier, because in many things he has taxed me justly" (II, 293). Collier seems to be cast as the "Good Parson" in Chaucer, while the execrable Luke Milbourn represents the bad divines. Nevertheless, Collier comes in soon enough for harsh treatment. The sentence I have just quoted is actually the only one that Collier would not have found offensive in one way or another. Dryden has said earlier: "Chaucer's Monk, his Canon, and his Friar, took not from the character of his Good Parson" (II, 282). But is this so? Does not the very quantity of rogues Dryden invokes here suggest that the few Colliers who exist are bound to be infected by the epidemic of Milbourns? "We are only to take care," he continues, "that we involve not the innocent with the guilty in the same condemnation" (ibid.). Collier is certainly the "religious lawyer" of the first digression on the clergy (this and the later ones really do put one in mind of the digression in *Lycidas*), and Collier as well as Milbourn must feel the sudden violence of a passage which should give one pause: "When a clergyman is whipped, his gown is first taken off, by which the dignity of his order is secured" (II, 282–83).[22]

Like *Lycidas*, the "Preface to *Fables*" is a triumphant defense of an author's vocation, proceeding positively by identifying the self with departed genius and negatively by means of a satiric "underplot." Both interjected satires, Milton's and Dryden's, are aimed against the clergy—against the hypocritical formalism of the clergy—but Dryden's, understandably more than Milton's, expands through a subtle matrix of allusion to encompass every class of person by which Dryden had ever been tormented. Having already touched upon the elegiac qualities of the "Preface," I shall now try to bring out the element of satire as further evidence that the "Preface" is itself a fable, an exemplar of the kind of criticism that is deliberately cast in a nonanalytic mode. I shall make use of Frank L. Huntley's contention, in an ingenious essay, that the unifying purpose of the seemingly haphazard "Preface to *All for Love*" is to abuse Lord Rochester, in part by repeated quotation from Juvenal's satire against the well-born.[23] Several of the details Huntley has configured reappear tellingly in the "Preface to *Fables*."

There are two points of special interest about the passage in which Dryden suddenly strips the clergyman and whips him: its sudden brutality and the accompanying detail of divestiture. Rochester is said to have instigated the cudgeling Dryden received in the Rose Alley in 1679, and though the culprit may not have been he, we have little reason to believe that Dryden did not think it was.[24] As for the removal of the gown, Rochester was known to be an exhibitionist, as Dryden slyly intimates in the "Preface to *All for Love*" when he laments that noblemen "must call their wits in question, and needlessly expose their nakedness to public view" (I, 226).[25] Now, although Dryden's violent outburst is nominally directed against the clergy, false priests and well-born prodigals are much more closely allied in his thinking than may appear. Shortly after this passage, Dryden turns to an analogous distinction between office and person: "Is then the peerage of England anything dishonoured when a peer suffers for his treason?" (II, 283). And when Dryden quotes Rochester— "*Not being of God, he could not stand*" (II, 280)[26]—his acknowledgment of a witty enemy who had been dead for twenty years is qualified by "though somewhat profanely." Thus in turning against the nobility, Dryden himself plays the part of a respectable clergyman shocked by the Restoration court and perhaps not much mollified by Rochester's eleventh-hour religious conversion. The "new man" surfaces again. Although the "dog kennel" in the first paragraph is commonly assumed to be the duke of Buckingham's, it is hard not to think of Rochester as well in glancing back at it. No one had more notoriously made a kennel of his palace than the sodden Rochester in the last months of his life, the time of Dryden's beating. Those of lesser birth, whom Juvenal was at pains to praise, continue to live better, more exemplary lives, but also more straitened ones.

Dryden reinforces the link between clergy and nobility by securing it from the other direction. Milbourn was only one of the two criticasters who had most irritated him in recent years. The other was the parvenu wholesaler of epics Sir Richard Blackmore, the "City Bard, or Knight Physician" whom Dryden delights to exhibit as "this noble Knight" (II, 292, 293). Clearly, "one N_____, or one B_____" (II, 291) are interchangeable vermin. Three of Dryden's four chief objects of aversion are now tied together by allusion: clergymen who try to legislate literature, noblemen who pull rank and patronize rivals, and literary hacks who attempt to ennoble themselves at Dryden's expense. To this collection of "parsons, critics, beaus" (Pope, *Essay on Criticism,* l. 459), a fourth class of enemy, indifferent monarchs, is soon added. Advance notice comes with the allusion to William's debts (II, 277–78), and from there the satire builds. Dryden soon casually remarks that Chaucer was "favoured by Edward the Third, Richard the Second, and Henry the Fourth, and was poet, as I suppose, to all three of them" (II, 281). He then extends the parallel between William and Henry, whose "title was not sound" and who was therefore happy to have Chaucer's voice in his service. But William joins the rogues' gallery in earnest when Dryden echoes his earlier violence against the defrocked clergy, this time in behalf of the murdered prelate Becket, and records "the whipping of his Majesty from post to pillar for his penance."

With these villains now set in place, Dryden contrives that all his enemies will be met, at the end of the "Preface," in the figure of Rochester. Huntley has shown that the quotation of Horace in the "Preface to *All for Love*" alludes unmistakably to Rochester.[27] There Dryden says that Horace has no use for "Demetrius the mimic, and Tigellus the buffoon:

> Demetri, teque, Tigelli,
> discipulorum [*sic:* discipularum] inter jubeo
> plorare cathedras"
> (I, 228; Horace, *Sat.* I, x, 90–91)

("You, Demetrius, and you, Tigellus, I bid you go and whimper by the lounge chairs of your girl students.") Admittedly, if Dryden's misquotation here is not a misprint (making the female students male), then my case is weakened because, as Dryden must have known, Demetrius the acting teacher trained women exclusively, just as Rochester had "trained" Mrs. Barry. Already in this passage, then, the bond is established between Grub Street curs and scurrilous noblemen. What Huntley does not mention is that this same passage, quoted anew, and this time accurately, constitutes the last words of the "Preface to *Fables.*" Blackmore, miraculously both Grub Street *and* "noble," was formerly a schoolmaster; the connection with Rochester is preestablished; King William was known to be uxorious. It remains only to add the clergy: "As for the rest of those who have written against me, they are such scoundrels that they deserve not the least notice to be taken of them. B_____ and M_____ are only distinguished from the crowd by being remembered to their infamy:

> Demetri, teque, Tigelli,
> discipularum inter jubeo plorare cathedras."
> (II, 294)

Here too is God's plenty.

IV

As befits a volume of last poems that are mostly translated, the last words of Dryden's "Preface" are quoted words. Increasingly he has found it sufficient, perhaps even necessary, to speak the words of others: *"Facile est inventis addere* is no great commendation, and I am not so vain as to think that I have deserved a greater" (II, 289). And if translation is a modest enterprise, so too is the writing of critical prefaces. In the "Preface to the *Aeneis"* (1967), Dryden contrasts the essay he is writing with the essay of Jean Segrais from which he has taken much of his material. The preface of Segrais is "full and clear, and digested into an exact method; mine is loose, and, as I intended it, epistolary."[28] But then, he says in the *Fables* preface, that is the way a preface should be: "The nature of a preface is rambling, never wholly out of the way, nor in it" (II, 278). The belief that nonchalance is the best style for a preface stems from the self-consciousness of Dryden's calling as a translator—from the conviction, that is, that there is no hope of rivaling or substituting for a text that is honored either by translation or by a preface: "My preface begins to swell upon me, and looks as if I were afraid of my reader, by so tedious a bespeaking of him" ("Preface to *Sylvae,"* II, 30).

Informality is thus a rhetoric of modesty, a mark of the sort of writing that is a satellite of the fully formed text to which it defers. Such writing is never far away from the text—because of dependence on it—but obviously is never "in it" either. Except for the *Essay,* which is composed as formally as a play (and has its own preface, the "epistle" to Buckhurst), all of Dryden's *essais* are prefaces or postscripts. They are on a threshold and preserve the deference that suits their marginal importance, while at the same time they realize the freedom of a frontier, patrolling the border between form (the ensuing text) and formlessness (the arbitrariness of having been "prefix'd"). There is a hint of boasting in Dryden's modesty. Because they are "rambling," prefaces are uninhibited, he says: "This I have learned from *honest* Montaigne" (II, 278; italics mine). It is owing to their honesty, their uninhibited frame of mind, that prefaces can begin to turn the tables on the texts to which they defer—and to restore the self-respect of translations as well. What makes the "Preface to *Fables"* unique is that in this, his last, essay, Dryden seems to have begun to notice that *all* writing is both preface and translation, in part because all writing of whatever "kind" is much more radically conditioned by the medium it shares with all other writing than commitment to generic norms had permitted his contemporaries to believe.

As we have mentioned, Montaigne discovers the privilege of age and of prefaces alike in their freedom from sanctions against repetition. He speaks of "handling . . . and going over" thoughts in order to "tame them" (I,

20)—to confine them to sense, presumably, as though they were Dryden's "confused mass of thoughts"—just as Dryden says, having finished his "dead-colouring": "In the second part, as at a second sitting, though I alter not the draught, I must touch the same features over again" (II, 273). It is easy to let an author's running commentaries on his own performance slip past when they are thus casual and not formally sustained like one of Fielding's interchapters, but it would be unfortunate to do so in Dryden's case, because in fact these particular touches in the building up of his self-image reveal an entire poetics based on premises that are rarely noticed in Dryden or any of his contemporaries—a poetics based on Associationism rather than formal composition. Although many scholars have concluded that Dryden was a Modern and a believer in progress (and certainly at times he was both) it is still undeniable that in passages like the one quoted above, which miniaturize a much broader idea, Dryden falls into a cyclic way of thinking. The "parts" of a text as he puts them together become superfices, mask upon mask, filter over ground, and no longer in the least resemble the consecutive but interlocking "parts" of Aristotle. The movement of composition is an overlay rather than an extension.

The late Dryden takes a similar view of movement in time,[29] although he admits that the cyclic outlook can take a superstitious turn. Having heard that Mlle Scudéry is also translating Chaucer, he writes that "it makes me think there is something in it like fatality; that, after certain periods of time, the fame and memory of great wits should be renewed" (II, 289). His view of the individual life in turn reflects his view of history. In the best-known of the epistolary poems printed in the 1700 *Fables* he modulates a classical commonplace in a way that overturns any and all humor-psychologies based on the "Ages of Man." For an instant, at least, there is no question of second childhood or the coincidence of birth and death; more subtly, Dryden says that age repeats youth, although in a different key: "For age but tastes of pleasures, youth devours"—and then some game springs up, representing plenty this time as a type of overlay—"The hare in pastures or in plains is found, / Emblem of human life, who runs the round."[30] Or again, in this same spirit but with reference once more to the scale of history rather than the span of life, Dryden remarks upon the shock of recognition with which we respond to Chaucer's cast of characters and then adds that "mankind is ever the same, and nothing is lost out of nature, though every thing is altered" (II, 285).

This is not a high Aristotelian physics but a kind of chemistry, a Dryden's law of psychodynamics that strikes me, at least, as being a more truly "organic" figure than anything in the *Poetics*. The stress in "every thing" falls on "thing," revealing the mobility of Dryden's phenomenal consciousness. Such a view of nature is very different from the radically ahistorical, uniformitarian view of his rival Thomas Rymer, who argued that in Athens and London, "*nature* is the same, and *man* is the same."[31] As in a kaleidoscope, everything in Dryden's concept of nature changes yet stays within the whirl of the essential, which consists, I would suggest, in the primary instincts. Here is a possible meeting place of Dryden's psychology, his understanding of nature, and his theory of composition. There is a clue, as usual, to be found in Montaigne, who offers this further apology for his casual approach to writing: "Let me begin with whatever subject I please, for all subjects are linked with one another" (II, 5). But the most significant source is nearer home; Dryden identifies it outright in what I take to be the key passage in the "Preface." It is carelessly planted near the beginning to justify one of Dryden's first digressions: "In the mean time, to follow the thrid of my discourse (as thoughts, according to Mr. Hobbs, have always some connexion) so from Chaucer I was led to think on Boccace. . . ."[32]

I have quoted this passage from an unmodernized text in order to call attention to a mistranscription in Watson's modern edition which from my standpoint is quite important. Dryden's spelling is "thrid," showing that his one earlier use of this phrase ("I resume the thrid of my discourse," he says again in the "Preface" [ibid., I, xvii]) should not read "where you break off the *third* of your discourse," and so on (II, 55). This expression occurs in a postscript to Dryden's 1691 letter to William Walsh on Walsh's verses: "Your apostrophes to your mistress," writes Dryden there, "where you break off the [thrid] of your discourse, and address yourself to her, are in my opinion as fine turns of gallantry as I have met with anywhere." Only nine years before the "Preface," then, Dryden still understands digression to be a formal matter, a *parecbasis*: one sort of figure in this instance is cleanly interrupted by another, apostrophe. Thus in the letter to Walsh, the "parts" of poetry need not be uniform but their disparity, like the relation of a proper subplot to a main plot, has rules of its own. Even in Dryden's second descent to the Labyrinth in the "Preface" ("I *resume* the thread") there is a relapse back to this more mechanistic understanding of composition. But the passage referring to Hobbes places Dryden the critical theorist on new ground altogether.[33]

In the section of *Leviathan* to which Dryden refers, "Of the Consequence or TRAYNE of Imaginations," Hobbes distinguishes two kinds of association, the first *"Unguided, without Designe,* and inconstant," and the second *"regulated* by some desire, and designe."[34] At first Dryden may seem to be mistaken (though inspired) to have inferred from this conventional-seeming analysis that one's thoughts are *always* connected. Another look at Hobbes's "unguided" associations will show, however, that in his view also the mind always harbors a network of connections from which, as Dryden would say, "nothing is lost." In unregulated thinking, says Hobbes, the thoughts *"seem* impertinent one to another, as in a Dream" (italics mine), and he allows further that "in this wild ranging of the mind, a man may oft-times perceive the way of it, and the dependence of one thought upon another" (ibid.).

These passages constitute the origin of systematic modern Associationism (Aristotle's psychology had also been based on association, but that aspect of his thought was not to prove influential), a doctrine which in its essentials has continued to dominate psychological thinking to this day and remains nearly impervious to the succeeding waves of metaphysically grounded revisionism, like that of Coleridge in the *Biographia*,[35] which arise to challenge it. It is obvious that *both* "traynes" in Hobbes are in fact motivated, or determined, to the same extent. Only an inattentive use of idiom causes him to mention the "way" of free association and yet still to reserve the notion of purpose for the regulated kind.

Whether one thinks of Dryden's "thrid," David Hartley's "vibratiuncles," or Freud's "neurones," there has always been plenty of determination beneath the surface. Scarcely anyone in Dryden's day paid any attention to it, however. Taking advantage of the almost universal belief that there is no rhyme or reason to most vagaries of the mind, Dryden frequently hints at the opposite of what he purports to mean without fear of being caught. Having labored to flesh out his eulogies of patrons all his life, Dryden in the end has ironic recourse to terms we have already discussed in his "Dedication" of the *Fables* to the Duke of Ormond: "I have sometimes been forc'd to amplifie on others; but here, where the subject is so fruitful, that the harvest overcomes the reaper, I am shorten'd by my chain, and can only see what is forbidden me [by the Duke's modesty] to reach."[36] Tantalizingly close to open ridicule, this is the Dryden who elsewhere speaks, most uncharacteristically for his time, of ideas to be developed in translation that are "secretly in the poet" (II, 19). So where Chaucer writes in the "Nun's Priest's Tale,"

> This gentil cok hadde in his governaunce
> Sevene hennes, for to doon al his plesaunce,
> Which were his sustres and his paramours,
> And wonder lyk to him, as of colours,

Dryden's translation elicits the following:

> This gentle cock for solace of his life,
> Six misses had besides his lawful wife;
> Scandal that spares no King, tho' ne'er so good,
> Says, they were all of his own flesh and blood:
> His sisters both by sire, and mother's side,
> And sure their likeness show'd them near ally'd. (*Fables*,
> II, 5)[37]

The jibe at King William is not gratuitous; for Dryden, it emerges from the secret meaning of *governaunce*, and surely his interpretation is valid. Chaunticleer *is* a foolish king who is led astray by eloquence, like Alexander in "Alexander's Feast," which Dryden reprinted in the *Fables*.

Because Dryden's underworld is unusually labyrinthine, he needs to provide both himself and his reader with a "thrid" from which there is no danger of separation no matter where it leads. Although I have had to do in these last paragraphs with deliberately filiated covert allusions of the kind that Dryden and his successors in satire perfected, I have also tried to show that Dryden's own philosophy of composition would encourage the discovery of meanings that are less calculated than these. For this reason it is difficult to accept T. S. Eliot's declaration that "it would scarcely have occurred to him that there was anything *irrational* in poetic imagination."[38] In fact, unless we are content to let the "thrid" drop as an insignificant figure of speech—but where could it have come from?—the logic of the Hobbesian position must be pursued yet further, with the continued sanction, though, of Hobbes himself. Like Hobbes, though rather more cheerfully so, Dryden was on most occasions a determinist. In 1664 he was already writing of "the rational creatures of the Almighty Poet, who walk at liberty, in their own opinion, because their fetters are invisible" (I, 4). It is a creature of this sort who seems so much taken aback by the spontaneous growth of his house in the first paragraph of the "Preface to *Fables*," and who then writes very accurately in the passage referring to Hobbes with which we have been concerned: "From Chaucer I was led to think on Boccace"—led, no doubt, by the Almighty Poet who wrote them all.

V

There is more to say about the consequences of Dryden's determinism, especially for his theory of translation. But first one needs to understand the concept of "nature" against the backdrop of which his invisibly shackled creature appears. There are those who take it for granted that the Association of Ideas (the phrase was first used by Locke) is a mechanistic theory; Father Ong in particular has interpreted the Lockeian model of mind to be "quantitative," even "geometric."[39] Indeed, within the clear and distinct intellectual horizons of what was once called the Age of Reason, this psychology could be shown to have accompanied the rise of Newton's mechanics and of Deism with its Divine Watchmaker. But we have just now seen Dryden, for one, writing of an Almighty *Poet,* not a technician. If it be argued, as it sometimes is, that it is just the function of the Divine Analogy to reduce poets to technicians, the sufficiently cautious assertion of E. L. Tuveson may be offered in answer: "The schoolmen had assumed that, since man is the center and the object of nature, the universe must present an analogy to the structure of the human mind and personality.

Hobbes assumed just the opposite: the mind must be patterned after the physical universe. Particles of matter impinging on the organism give rise to modifications in the body which constitute the very substance of thought. Connections of these modifications, occurring in accidental sequences, in some way give rise to all our notions of relations."[40] Hobbes's view, I take it, is materialistic but not mechanistic—and while it is true that mechanism has always been considered an outgrowth of materialism, the former term was not applied in biology, according to the *OED,* until the nineteenth century.

What I have been trying to demonstrate is that the "Preface to *Fables,*" with its parts not laid out in sequence but threaded back upon themselves until they are tangled too densely to be sorted out again, furnishes strong proof by example that Dryden's poetics of composition cannot be accounted for by a mechanistic explanation. For Dryden, although the self is unwittingly deployed by a prior force, it is not thereby simplified or reduced. In the *Essay,* Dryden-Neander utters a commonplace in the course of praising Shakespeare which yet looks forward to later stages in the history of criticism: "He needed not the spectacles of books to read Nature; he looked inwards and found her there" (I, 67). If Dryden had truly wished in this case to be a "supreme conformist," as he has been called, he might better have said that Shakespeare looked outward. As it is, he subjects Shakespeare's "nature" to a secondary complication by confining it within the memory, the faculty that Hobbes had characterized as "decaying sense." Thus in Dryden's stock contrast between the imitation of books and the imitation of nature, which in itself would have passed current with any of his contemporaries, he nevertheless manages to commit Shakespeare to a measure of inwardness that is quite new. Dryden scholars who depict their author as a purveyor of elegant commonplaces[41] will point out that nearly everyone in Dryden's day praised the genius of Homer and Shakespeare. That is true: but even in 1665 Dryden is trying to get at something a little more interesting, namely, the "nature" of genius.

The concept of a reproducible nature that is inward or psychological differs markedly from the "nature" that Pope was to equate simultaneously with "Homer" and the objective world. It was not possible for Pope to enforce the analogy between inner and outer without glaring catachreses. Addison's associationist division of the pleasures of imagination between the primary (sense) and the secondary (the comparison and contrast of sense with memory) is somewhat more circumspect because it shows, by a turn of thought that consorts wholly with Dryden's, that the genius even of a Shakespeare is already a secondary process, more complex and in some ways superior to the primary pleasures of imagination but too much altered for analogies to be of much use in accounting for it. Hence it will appear that the "nature that is always the same" for Dryden is not that of the external world but instead that of the mind in its inmost workings. It is on these grounds that he responds to Rymer's notion that nature in Athens and London is the same in the unpublished notes called "Heads of an Answer to Mr. Rymer": "Tho' nature, as he objects, is the same in all places, and reason too the same, yet the climate, the age, the dispositions of the people to whom a poet writes," and so forth, are all different (I, 214). "Climate" and "the age" were in the air, as the French critics had begun to export some rudiments of historical relativism; but the word *dispositions,* even if it only means something like "habits," is still so sweeping that it threatens the measure of stability that even Dryden claims for *nature* and *reason.*

Dryden's earliest and most startling discussion of nature is woven in and out of the *Essay,* beginning with Crites on the overthrow of Thomism: "Is it not evident in these last hundred years . . . that almost a new nature has been revealed to us?" (I, 26). Even if we suppose this new nature to be the one that is and all along has covertly been "always the same," the novelty of its bearing on knowledge must still discredit any appeal to fixed rules of representation. As Eugenius is quick to point out later (I, 32), Crites can never defend the *mimesis* of the ancients once he has referred to ancient times, beginning with Aristotle, as "credulous and doting ages" (I, 26). The nature that now stands almost revealed remains somewhat wooden as a concept, as we shall see in a moment, but it is still too vital and variable to be represented adequately within any of the then-current literary formulas.

With the "new nature" to support him, Neander can proceed to defend the "tragi-comic" mixture; unlike Aristotle or Sidney, he recognizes that in the "variety and copiousness" of a plot dominant themes can be restated in different keys: "If contrary motions may be found in nature to agree, if a planet can go east and west at the same time, one way by viture of his own motion, the other by the force of the First Mover, it will not be difficult to imagine how the under-plot, which is only different, not contrary to the great design, may naturally be conducted along with it" (I, 59).[42] Again the Almighty Poet appears behind a similitude in Dryden. Whereas in Aristotle, whose terminology Neander borrows in this passage only to subvert it, "art" is an external movement guiding that which lacks its own principle of movement, in Dryden the design of nature is twofold, not exactly a conflict between superimposed and inwardly dynamic forms but nearly that. The entire creative movement that Dryden has in mind reconciles the reasoned perambulation of a creature with the divine fetters that hold the creature back. It is very difficult to conceive of this reconciliation as a mechanical one, as the formalism of the *Essay* is, again, nearly imperceptible. Even during his defense of rhyme Neander admits that the formality of heroic couplets may be a hindrance, adding that breaks in the hemistich will make rhyme "as loose and free as nature" (I, 84).

Crites and his companions may possibly have believed that a perfect knowledge of nature was almost at hand. By the time of the "Preface to *Fables*," however, Dryden is likely to have arrived at the more uncertain feeling that truth in science "was farther off from possession, by being so near" (II, 279). He had become, in any case, the sort of critic who was known in the time of Horace as an "anomalist" with respect to words, one who believes, that is, that because there is no fixed analogy between words and things there is no warrant for the codification of a language:[43] "Another poet, in another age, may take the same liberty with my writings," Dryden says, that he, Dryden, has taken with Chaucer's (II, 287). Whether nature in its actuality remains the same or not, in any case, it cannot be expected to remain the same throughout the history of consciousness, and therefore the referents of words and the allegedly mimetic element in formal structures can no longer claim the authority of fixed objects. As the "new nature" becomes looser and freer, more various and atomistic, the individual comes into focus and the class, or species, becomes increasingly blurred at the edges. Nature ceases to be nature *(phusis)* and becomes reality *(natura:* the swerving atoms of Lucretius). Even in the *Essay,* the fragile formalism of Neander's defense of rhyme and his sense that "A play . . ., to be like Nature, is to be set above it" (I, 88) should not prevent one from seeing what has already happened. A "play," according to Lisideius, who does not even find generic distinctions interesting enough to speak of "tragedy" or "comedy," is *"a just and lively image of human nature,"* and so on. What Aristotle had called the "soul of tragedy," the *muthos* or archetypal representation of action, is mentioned only in passing toward the end of this definition.[44]

From time to time later in his career, and in certain passages even in the "Preface to *Fables*," Dryden will try to resurrect "invention," and he will never cease to rate the power of invention first among the attributes of the authors he discusses. This is the sort of evidence that is carefully documented by his neo-Aristotelian commentators,[45] but neither they nor Dryden himself can explain *why* he revives the "invention" topic, in which, manifestly, he has little or no interest as a practical critic. He rarely discusses the architectonic aspects of literature. On the contrary, his main concern, early and late, is with character, both the characters in plays and the character of authors. Beginning in the *Essay,* this interest may be said to have carried Dryden in two opposite directions. One of these, which led to his conception of the larger-than-life "heroic drama," did not prove fruitful. It is misleading to assume, however, with the authors of *The Rehearsal,* that even this tendency is wholly opposed to the spirit of realism.[46] When Neander says, "A play, to be like nature, is to be set above it," it is much likelier that he has in mind the verisimilar illusion created by exaggerated perspective in the visual arts (hence the ensuing comparison with sculpture) than the idealized "nature" of Neo-platonism.

The second direction in which his interest in character leads Dryden is the more openly realistic course he was to pursue to the end. It will be found in his somewhat novel alertness to nuance and detail and also in his individualism, which is what essentially distinguishes him from the Court Wits. The simplicity of Rochester's "Satyr Against Mankind," with its exuberantly cynical reductions, is unavailable to Dryden, who is schooled rather by honest Montaigne, author of "De l'inconstance de nos actions" (II, 1). Owing to the intervening influence of Hobbes, however, Dryden differed from Montaigne on human inconstancy without perhaps knowing it. Whereas it is the purpose of Montaigne's essay to maintain that there is no underlying principle guiding our behavior, Dryden recalls Montaigne specifically in order to defend the *unity* of a characterization in one of his own plays. The critics, he says in the late "Preface to *Don Sebastian*" (1690), "maintain that the character of Dorax is not only unnatural but inconsistent in itself; let them read the play and think again, and if they are not satisfied, cast their eyes on that chapter of the wīse Montaigne which is intituled 'De l'inconstance de nos actions humaines' " (II, 50). In Dorax, in other words, there is a Hobbesian "thrid" everywhere to be followed. This is the theory of characterization that was to continue unchallenged in literature until the "decentering of the human subject" began to preoccupy the New Wave novelists in France.

VI

What I am here calling Dryden's "individualism" is not a late development; it makes an important appearance in the *Essay* when Neander programmatically revises the psychology of humors that the English had taken over from Roman comedy. As Neander complains, such a psychology can accommodate "only the general characters of men and manners" (I, 73). In reaction to this generality the New Man undertakes to match his own identity with the New Nature. He discovers "humour" in that quality (or those qualities, in the case of Falstaff) "wherein one man differs from all others" (I, 72). In practice, Dryden succeeded little better than the humor-fanatic Shadwell[47] in freeing himself from the principle of the "ruling passion," which lent itself to extravagances of portraiture and fostered its own sort of rigidity. If Jonson's Morose hates noise, there is little that he can be permitted to say on any other theme. In theory, however, this concept opens out upon that novelistic fullness of presentation that was later to be called the comédie humaine, and leads directly to the appreciation of Ovid and Chaucer in the "Preface":[48] "Both of them understood the manners; under which name I comprehend the passions and, in a larger sense, the descriptions of persons, and their very habits" (II, 278; *very* means that which belongs to the individual[49] and *habits* means bearing or outward appearance). It is the "plenty" in Chaucer's characterizations that finally earns Dryden's famous benediction, and while it is true that he took much of the material in his appreciative roll call from the elder Francis Beaumont,[50] the precision of his individualism goes far beyond any earlier Chaucer criticism. What is new and admirable is his conviction—the same conviction that Johnson was to query in Pope's judgment of Shakespeare—that no voices in Chaucer are quite interchangeable: "Even the grave and serious characters are distinguished by their several sorts of gravity. . . . Even the ribaldry of the low characters is different" (II, 284).

The "Preface to *All for Love*" is the response of a professional writer to the condescension of aristocratic dilletantes; this conflict also appears in the contrast between Neander's evidently recent standing and the established character of the Court Wits in the *Essay*. A recent writer on the affective qualities of Dryden's prose has shown how much his style varies with the degree of subservience in his address.[51] Dryden's was a landed family, and I do not mean to suggest that his individualism and his sense of being self-made reveal him to have been, as it were, a suburban writer—or a "City Bard" like Blackmore. All the same, would Buckingham or Rochester, adding to their palaces, keep wishing for "one convenience more" (II, 269)? Dryden's rank is essentially that of those who have most admired the fitness and naturalness of his prose, from Johnson ("every word . . . falls into its proper place") to Eliot ("every blow delivered with exactly the right force") to most of his admirers in the universities today.

Middle-class criticism invented and first exemplified the notion of the verisimilar (the completely unreal "nature" of the patrician Sidney can be alleged in contrast), and it also pioneered the idea that a responsive criticism should be flexible. More than the upper class with its spontaneous code of belonging and the oppressed classes with their spontaneous calculus of need—neither of these being structures of consciousness that can be deliberately "learned"—the middle-class tends, comparatively speaking, to improvise its values according to every socioeconomic trend, veering, for instance, between hedonism and austerity. Classical Marxist analysis may be wrong to confine its critique of reflexive ideology chiefly to the middle class, in which behavior is not "free," to be sure, but is more subtly mediated by a sense of alternative than it is in the upper and lower classes. This idea is implicit in the writing of a recent snobbish reviewer of Evelyn Waugh's letters: "[Waugh] thought more of aristocrats than of artists. This viewpoint had its limitations but at least it saved him from the folly of imagining that behavior could be much influenced by intellectual fashions."[52]

The con man, the bricoleur, the tricky slave (paradoxically), the literary hireling, the "Renaissance Man" (paradoxically: but it was not a fully recognized type until burghers like Franklin signaled the end of the breed), and Keats's brilliantly conceived "chameleon poet": all these characters are bourgeois self-conceptions made possible in the democratic atmosphere so much deplored by the virtuous philosopher Plato, whose "one man, one job" is possibly the most important root idea of the *Republic*. In Dryden's time, however, it is not surprising that "virtue" would seem to belong to another sort of sensibility, to be invested by a "new man" in the new class that had discovered a "new nature" in which that class could see itself reflected quite apart from the monotonously inflexible nature of the debauched court. So in the "Preface to *Fables*" Dryden pauses over *The Wife of Bath's Tale* to concentrate on the old crone's nuptial oration against "the silly pride of ancestry and titles without inherent virtue, which is the true nobility," and it is to this theme that Dryden's sly forgetfulness quickly returns him: "When I took up Boccace, unawares I fell on the same argument of preferring virtue to nobility of blood and titles" (II, 290)—so revealing is the "thrid" of thought.

In the context of this discussion it should be clear that Lisideius's "definition of a play" (I, 25) revises Aristotle's definition from an essentially social standpoint. (As I have noted, Dryden's experiments with "heroic plays" in the next decade represent a separate tendency in his thinking, one that is not dominant in the first and last phases of his career.) The only trace of "action" in Lisideius's definition is the belatedly mentioned "changes of fortune"—into which phrase there has crept a decidedly commercial flavor. Since the time of the *Mirror for Magistrates* the wheel of fortune had come to turn most conspicuously for the merchant-princes, and in the time of Dryden the middle-class dramas of Lillo and Lessing in the next century were already theoretically possible. Even during Dryden's period of involvement with heroic plays there is evidence of apostasy from the focus on "action." "The story," he says in the 1671 "Preface to *An Evening's Love*," "is the least part" of the poet's artistic investment (I, 154), and he declares again in the newly Longininian "Preface to *The State of Innocence*" (1677) that "the fable is not the greatest masterpiece of a tragedy, tho' it be the foundation of it" (I, 211). Such opinions as these are profoundly anti-Aristotelian.

VII

One begins to see how Dryden could adjust to his final vocation as a translator. Once *inventio* has been taken down from its pedestal, there must be a reconsideration of the basis upon which poets can lay claim to originality. (Note that originality is not entailed in what I have been calling "individuality," a concept which arises, perhaps, only in homogeneous cultures where there is an eye for small differences and atomistic variations.) Both Ovid and Chaucer "built on the inventions of other men" (II, 278), says Dryden, but it must come as a surprise, given his critical milieu, that he does not hold this shortcoming to be important. The vocational pride of Dryden himself is at stake, and he protects it by shifting his attention and praise away from the Sidneyan "fore-conceit" toward the more palpably verbal elements of composition. In the passage quoted above, the poet rests content to use someone else's "story" or "fable," trusting in his ability to work up the material better. In this attitude it is evident that the high calling of mimesis has already been forsaken; soon enough it will seem sufficient simply to repeat, with modernized eloquence, the works of the past.

As Earl Miner has shown, there is a play on the term *translatio* in those "progress poems" by Dryden that are based on the Humanist theme of the *translatio studii*. Translation clearly has a very broad meaning, for instance, in Dryden's poem (1684) in praise of Roscommon's *Essay on Translated Verse:*

> 'Tis sure the noble plant, translated first,
> Advanced its head in Grecian gardens nursed
> . . .
> Nor stopped translation here.
>
> (II, 14)[53]

If the evidence of his criticism can be credited, Dryden began to assess the presence of the past in the work of current poets only after he took up translation. From the standpoint of the translator, the "Almighty Poet" who controls his actions is the poetic tradition itself. Having resigned himself to speak the thoughts of others, the translator carries out his task like the medium at a séance, solicited by the mighty dead: Dryden "could not balk" the speeches of "Ajax and Ulysses," and he is "taken with" a passage in Ovid (II, 270).

However, the translator's labor is no less a "pleasing task" (ibid.) for being indentured, and in fact there are certain consolations available to him. If he adopts Dryden's technique of "paraphrase" (which is midway between a closely rendered "metaphrase" and a loosely adapted "imitation" [see the "Preface to *Ovid's Epistles,*" I, 268]), the translator can improve the authors who importune him, not only by refining their diction but also by smoothing out their argument: "I have . . . added somewhat of my own where I thought my author was deficient, and had not given his thoughts their true lustre, for want of words in the beginning of our language" (II, 287). The business of a translator is to realize what is latent or evasive in his author. The authority of the master is absolute, but the servant is a good steward and knows the master's business better than the master does. This is possible, of course, only when a rare clairvoyance exists between author and translator; hence in Dryden, as so often in Longinus, what is happiest in discourse comes from being haunted by an alien voice. What Longinus calls a flooding, or "effluence," Dryden with equal vividness describes "in all transfusion, that is, in all translations" (II, 288).

These terms of transmission can be applied to the idea of literary tradition quite apart from the relationship between authors and translators. A curious effect of uneasy conscience in having diminished the importance of *inventio* is the tendency Dryden shares with many others in his century, from Jonson to his own contemporaries in France, to assume that every author has his source. In the "Preface to the *Aeneis*," in which he promotes Virgil in every way he can think of, Dryden echoes the widespread opinion that Homer himself had as many sources (now lost to the world) as Virgil had. Similarly in the "Preface to *Fables*," he avoids saying that Chaucer had no source for *The Knight's Tale* although he, Dryden, has no evidence to the contrary. What he says is that the source must be lost and that the service Chaucer performed for it must have been the same service, neither greater nor less, that Dryden's translations perform in the present volume: "The name of [the author of *Palamon and Arcite*] being wholly lost, Chaucer is now become an original; and I question not but the poem has received many beauties by passing through his noble hands" (II, 291).

Apparently the spirit of literature, like the sublime in Longinus, is a quality that gets translated from source-text to source-text. For the integrity of this idea, which implicitly denies the autonomy of the *cogito,* one can look again toward Hobbes, who insisted that the imagination is as closely bound to experience—to the past—as any other faculty. Imagination is furnished solely by the "decaying sense" of memory.[54] Thus the imagination posits its originality in the moment of forgetting the past by which it is constituted. In common with some of his contemporaries, as we have seen, Dryden calls translation "transfusion" in the "Preface to *Fables*." This word also appears in an earlier passage: "Milton was the poetical son of Spenser, and Mr. Waller of Fairfax; for we have our lineal descents and clans as well as other families: Spenser more than once insinuates that the soul of Chaucer was transfused into his body; and that he was begotten by him two hundred years after his decease" (II, 270).[55] Dryden here returns to an idea he had already expressed in the "Ode on Mrs. Killigrew" (1685), where yet another word for translation marks one of the moments when the lady is praised less fulsomely than she seems to be:

> If by traduction came thy mind
> Our wonder is the less to find
> A soul so charming from a stock so good.[56]

Dryden of course continues to distinguish between translation and original composition. But still, the outlook of Hobbes, with its reduction of the distance between originality and reproduction, must greatly benefit the self-esteem of a writer who is no longer free to do as he pleases. Perhaps recognizing a closer kinship with Hobbes than he cares to acknowledge, Dryden uncharacteristically chides the philosopher for his apparent neglect, in *his* preface to a translation written in old age, of original invention as the foremost among poetic values: "He tells us that the first beauty of an epic poem consists in diction," whereas "the design, the disposition, the manners, and the thoughts are all before it" (II, 275).[57] But the passage on "lineal descent" is more representative of the late Dryden. Not only does it sketch a theory of authorial transfusion, but it also calls attention to itself in a special way simply in seeming to be the least motivated of all the digressions in the "Preface." Other than by the circuitous route I have just followed, the reader will be hard put to make the transition between Dryden's praise of himself as a translator who can capture the spirit of his original—"and this, I may say, without vanity, is not the talent of every poet" (II, 270)—and the passage on the ancestry of great poets, which concludes in its turn with the subject of actual translations: Waller learned "the harmony of his numbers from *Godfrey of Bulloign,* which was turned into English by Mr. Fairfax" (II, 271). Only with reference to Hobbes can one find the thread of Dryden's discourse. The decision to begin with "diction" indulged by an old man in a new vocation (translating Homer) is just the decision to which, for the most part, Dryden himself had come to be committed.

Although he refuses to identify himself with Hobbes, Dryden takes every opportunity to compare himself with the authors he has translated, perhaps in order to show that the process of "transfusion" is reciprocal. Deservedly, Dryden's power of empathy is the quality for which the "Preface" is best remembered. Not only is Chaucer Dryden's "predecessor in the laurel" (II, 271), but it was Chaucer's peculiar strength as a poet to be able to transport his reader—or translator—into his own place and time. Owing to this gift, which resembles the power of "visualization" in Longinus, Dryden knows the Canterbury pilgrims "as distinctly as if I had supped with them at the Tabard in Southwark" (II, 278). In this convivial reaction Dryden finds a way of transcending time that resembles the First Circle of Dante or the symposium of the dead in other writers. At the Tabard the pleasure of the banquet consists in its "plenty," a collation shared by elected souls which are each in themselves storehouses of plenty, like Shakespeare's "largest and most comprehensive soul" in the *Essay* (I, 67). "I found I had a soul congenial to his," says Dryden of Chaucer (II, 287), having already announced that he finds translating Homer "more suitable to my temper" than translating Virgil (II, 276). In seating himself at this banquet of souls, Dryden recoups whatever loss of pride he may feel as their translator. In the company of such writers, the excellence of whom his audience either knows or can be taught to perceive (to this latter end, he devotes most of his attention to Chaucer), Dryden can defy his petty detractors, again like Dante in the First Circle, as though he too were already canonized by posterity.

For the reader who knows both authors, an affinity between Dryden's "Preface" and *The Pleasure of the Text* by Roland Barthes should be evident. Of all the authors in his day who were willing to accept *prodesse ut delectare* for their mandate, Dryden keeps pleasure most in view. As he admitted long before the "Preface," "to my shame . . . I never read any thing but for pleasure" ("The Life of Plutarch," II, 4).[58] Soon enough the formality of shame will be abandoned and pleasure will be its own excuse; it had always been his contention that whatever the purpose of tragedy may be, the purpose of comedy "is divertisement and delight" (I, 152). This heretical assertion was avidly seized upon by Collier in his *Short View*,[59] as Dryden doubtless remembers in the "Preface" when he alleges as reason sufficient that he has found in Homer a "more pleasing task" than translating Virgil (II, 274), and then repeats his pleasure almost verbatim under the cloak of forgetfulness: "I have translated his first book with greater pleasure than any part of Virgil" (II, 276). What strikes one as Barthesian is the presentation of this task as an erotics, an Aretine for the Aging: "It was not a pleasure without pains: the continual agitation of the spirits must needs be the weakening of any constitution, especially in age; and many pauses are required for refreshment betwixt the heats" (II, 276–77).

There is undoubtedly an aristocratic literary hedonism, though often it is a bourgeois projection like the one lavished on pedigreed detectives in fiction. But that sort of "taste" is in any case not at issue here. The savoring of first editions and crusty port is a ritual of exclusion and not a celebration of plenitude like that of Dryden. This is an important distinction, I think, which should qualify the implicitly Marxist austerity of writers who complain, with Frank Lentricchia, that some contemporary criticism recommends "a new hedonism."[60] That is true enough, but the recommendation is in fact perfectly democratic. The best remembrancers of Dryden's pleasure are the pleasure of Barthes and the ironically self-excluding apostrophe of Walter Benjamin while unpacking his library: "O bliss of the collector, bliss of the man of leisure!"[61] Perhaps Freud's alertness to the eroticization of writing belongs here as well.[62] There is not a little of the homme moyen sensuel in Dryden's pleasure, and in the pleasure of those I have just mentioned, in that it seems so indifferent to Platonic or puritan objections.[63] When Dryden at first feels called upon to defend himself in 1685 for "the englishing of the *Nature of Love,* from the fourth book of Lucretius," he soon quite simply decides that no defense is necessary: "Without the least formality of an excuse, I own it pleased me: and let my enemies make the worst they can of this confession" ("Preface to *Sylvae*," II, 27).

VIII

Not until Keats, Hazlitt, and De Quincey will any writers about books evince the literary hedonism of Dryden. It is no great paradox, despite this unusual element in his criticism, that Dryden especially enjoys *purity* of style.[64] Everywhere in his work, and most of all in his occasional outbursts of grammatical or tropical nicety, Dryden revels in the mastery of composition. In this pleasure, the pleasurable pride of *having learned* to write—so obvious is it that his friends, Howard and Walsh, and the neighborhood bully, Elkanah Settle, do not yet know how[65]—there is a childishness which is not unattractive. In writing and the judgment of writing Dryden expresses the pleasure of retention and control. Perhaps the awareness of this sophisticated regressiveness in himself is what makes him more than usually attentive to the childhood of man and of culture.

As a creature of his age he of course takes a condescending view of everything childish, as when he calls Ovid's rhetorical extravagances "boyisms" (II, 279); but Dryden returns more frequently to those things that are crude, archaic, or unmastered than is usual in his era, and his attitude toward them is actually ambivalent. Although he can say, sententiously enough, "We must be children before we can grow men" (II, 281), the subject is never quite closed. His most predictably negative opinions about the past will be found to issue from the critically unprofitable period of the 1670s, when he was attempting to raise his contemporaries above the Elizabethans. It is at this time that he anticipates the apology of Johnson's "Preface to Shakespeare," viz., that "the times were ignorant in which they lived," and follows that assertion by transposing the attributes of the two periods so unwarrantably that I suspect not even Rymer could have agreed with him: "Poetry was then, if not in its infancy among us, at least not arrived to its full *vigour* and maturity" ("Defence of the Epilogue," I, 172; italics mine). This way of putting the contrast is so clearly tendentious that it betrays uncertainty, the same uncertainty that appears in Dryden's first published reference to Chaucer as "our English Ennius" ("Postscript to the *Aeneis*," II, 259).[66]

One could draw a rough parallel between Dryden's alleged formalism and his alleged belief in progress. In both cases to some extent the characterization is undeniable. Dryden is certainly at home with all the dramatic and other generic prescriptions and invokes them on cue for arguments of all kinds, and by the same token he is constant in his praise of the refinement of modern poetry; he is chiefly responsible for the overpraise of Denham and Waller that was to echo throughout the next century. It could be said, in sum, that Dryden was a formalist and a Modern by design, but an impressionist and an Ancient by instinct. I do not mean to say that he was an Ancient like Crites in the *Essay,* who by a sleight of argument substitutes the *Poetics* for the Greek dramas themselves and is able to conclude on that basis that the Ancients are not only more civilized than the Moderns but also better formalists. Dryden's tendency to prefer old things to new has rather to do with his having recognized the intrinsic value of imperfection. Thus Chaucer's versification, of which Dryden of course knew nothing, has "the rude sweetness of a Scotch tune in it, which is natural and pleasing, though not perfect" (II, 281).[67]

In this typically casual observation, which may have provided Addison with the precedent he needed for his appreciation of "The Ballad of Chevy Chase," there stands embodied an aesthetic of the primitive which has far-reaching implications and constitutes yet another challenge to the hegemony of established norms and forms. It is also closely allied to the nostalgic linquistics of the primitive that was to be developed in all the treatises on the origin of language and metaphor in the next century. This view of language is anticipated almost by accident in Sprat's *History of the Royal Society.* Even though in the previous chapter Sprat has argued that in every culture language reached perfection when civilization was at its height (the standard assumption in Dryden's milieu), Sprat then becomes so incensed at the "specious Tropes and Figures" of modern usage that he announces, as the program of the Royal Society, a "return back to the primitive purity and shortness, when men deliver'd so many *things* almost in an equal number of *words.*"[68] This extreme of thought, which was soon to be put into practice in Swift's Academy of Lagado, represents another part of Hobbes's legacy. The Hobbesian outlook holds good for either of two complementary worlds which are indistinguishable in experience: an altogether material world in which mind itself and its symbols are atomistic and words are really objects; or else a world that is no different in structure from the other one, a world in which each phenomenal thing is a sign—an index, a symptom, or a cipher of some thing other than itself—but in which words are still understood to belong in the same medium with, say, sticks and stones. Thinking that is at home in either of these worlds remains steadily on the border between nature and its representation; having already called it Longinian thinking, I will show in the next chapter that it is also present, though approached from the transcendental rather than the material side of the balance, in Shelley's *Defence of Poetry.*

One happy consequence of this habit of thought is that it instantly shows up the inadequacy of the primitive-vs.-modern formula as a scale of aesthetic value—whether the formula be typically stated by Puttenham in his contrast between "monstrous . . . conceits" and the civilized virtue of a mind that is "very formall, and in his much multiformitie *uniforme,*"[69] or less typically by Wordsworth in his evaluatively opposed contrast between language "derived from the best objects" and the "arbitrary and capricious habits of expression" fostered by advanced cultures. For the most part, in both precept and practice, Dryden is undecided between these versions of the formula because he seems to see the futility of the double standard on which both are founded. In order to defend this assertion, I turn now to consider several other aspects of Dryden's casual but telling evasion of dualistic thought.

We have seen how regularly Dryden affirms a festal communion between himself and the authors he admires, loosely translating them as if to imagine, as Longinus would have it, that he himself has written what they wrote. He collapses other conventional distinctions as well. Just as the authors Dryden translates are the heroes of his "Preface" and resemble him, so in turn "The very heroes show their authors" (II, 276). Here follows the well-known passage about hot Achilles and patient Aeneas.[70] Of a piece with his readiness to admire self-portraiture in fiction is Dryden's earlier contribution to the theatrical dispute between "wit" and "humor" in comedy. Proponents of humor-comedies insisted that there be a strict demarcation between authors—guarding their impersonality—and their objectivity conceived eccentrics. Dryden saw that characterizations of this sort would have to be "forced" (I, 146) and would scarcely be recognizable in an educated society with more or less uniform manners. He preferred that the whole fabric of dialogue in a comedy be suffused, instead, with the "wit" of the author. Such unconcealed evidence of the dyer's hand, recalling the "confederacy" between antagonists effected by rhyme in the *Essay,* parallels the tendency of epic authors to write themselves into their heroes. Herein Dryden differs notably from the major critic who perhaps most resembles him, Hazlitt, who loved Shakespeare's impersonality and deplored the loss of the "distinguishing peculiarities of men and manners" that makes a "modern comedy," as he believed, impossible.[71] It remained for Wilde and Shaw to prove Hazlitt wrong and Dryden right. As a basis on which criticism can proceed without being forced on the rack of presupposition, I think that in general Dryden's view is far preferable, together with nearly all pre-Kantian criticism in this respect, because it avoids the fallacy of autotelic form.

For reasons similar to these, Dryden shares with Longinus the tendency to let his criticism merge with its object—writing an essay on drama, for example, in dialogue. In the "Preface to *Fables,*" Dryden writes a fable about a banished, diversely maligned but supremely insouciant poet who is forced to "build" anew and lives to consecrate his monument.[72] (Having come so cheerfully to terms with his "lineal descent," Dryden not surprisingly appears, with Longinus, at the Colonus phase of the oedipal progress.) Arguably there is some trace of imitative form in everything he wrote, and a corresponding lack of attention to the requirements of the traditional, impersonally constituted genres. This Longinian blending of forms accompanies the relativism of Dryden's thinking generally. To be sure, much of his criticism goes forward by appealing to principles of genre and decorum. At the same time, however, as Irvin Ehrenpreis has argued, Dryden tests the edges of genres, mixing and "coruscating" their surfaces.[73]

If Dryden's epistemological categories are provisional, his judgments are even more so. Neither the designer of a work nor the judge of its merits can be "very exact" except "as he supposes" (II, 269). Even with a carefully constructed groundwork all comparisons must be tentative: "By this means, both the poets being set in the same light and dressed in the same

English habit, story to be compared with story, a certain judgment may be made betwixt them"—not by the translator himself, even under such careful controls, but only "by the reader" (II, 271). To form any kind of judgment at all, one needs some standard of comparison; ex cathedra principles like those of Rymer are simply unavailable. Dryden typically apportions values between two objects.[74] This technique is not at all new; and the majority of the insights Dryden gains from it are not new either. His comparison of Homer and Virgil is for the most part commonplace, and its values are distressingly unstable, as the reader of the parallel but evaluatively inverted comparison in the "Preface to the *Aeneis*" will discover. However, although such considerations as these certainly undermine the notion that Dryden was "the father of comparative literature," they should not obscure what remains unusual in his handling of comparisons in the "Preface to *Fables*." For one thing, no literary essay had ever before arrived at its judgments *exclusively* by means of comparison, and this innovation actually reflects a major epistemological shift. For the first time comparison is no longer an alternative form of judgment brought in to reinforce positive certainty; it has become the only form of judgment and seems in fact to have acquired the function of challenging autocratic pronouncements. The modification of judgment by comparison brings with it a new diffidence; the poet's boast that his soul is more congenial to some authors than to others is also the critic's modest admission, at every turn, that he is probably biased.

Another unusual aspect of Dryden's comparisons is his fascinating use of syncretistic reduction to create a kind of myth-criticism in which, for provisional purposes, all texts are similar. Here is the one facet of "invention" as a critical topic that seems to interest him, at least when he is not trying to minimize similarities. "I say not this in derogation of Virgil," he assures us in the "Preface," "neither do I contradict any thing I have formerly said in his just praise" (II, 275); perhaps not, but what he *had* formerly said and now seems to deny is that "the designs of the two poets were as different as the courses of their heroes."[75] What he seems newly to appreciate in 1700 is the degree to which inventions repeat themselves: "The adventures of Ulysses in the *Odysseis* are imitated in the first six books of Virgil's *Aeneis*; . . . the seas were the same in which both heroes wandered; and Dido cannot be denied to be the poetical daughter of Calypso. The six latter books of Virgil's poem are the four-and-twenty *Iliads* contracted: a quarrel occasioned by a lady, a single combat, battles fought, and a town besieged" (II, 275).

Much of this too had been said by earlier commentators, but it was the sort of material that had always been invoked solely for the purpose of vindicating the character of one poet or another.[76] Dryden is conventional enough to write his comparison in that same context, but it is not fanciful, I think, to detect in him a delight in the comparison undertaken as its own reward. To say that Dido is the "poetical daughter" of Calypso is much the same as to say that Milton is the poetical son of Spenser; authors and characters merge once again, this time not only to confirm the priority of the past but also, without contradiction, to intimate the uniformity of all invention in the timeless narrative present which transcends chronicles of "lineal descent." "The seas are the same": there is but one oceanic stage on which the story of *Totem and Taboo,* or some rough equivalent, is endlessly enacted—a dispute over a lady in the primal horde resulting in the foundation of society. "Invention" appeals to Dryden in this context precisely because it is no longer an object of dissimilative, or categorical, thought. As a single "fable" inevitably to be repeated, that which is invented stands at the opposite extreme from the affection for the self-identity of things which likewise discourages—though it cannot prevent—the formation of categories. Dryden's critical interest, then, like that of Longinus, is most active at just those liminal regions of significance in a text that escape the attention of Aristotle.

IX

The microcosmic extreme includes diction and words generally. On this topic especially Dryden supposes himself to have orthodox opinions. Eliot approvingly quotes a passage from the early "Preface to *Annus Mirabilis*" (1667) which is certainly conventional but is not in fact typical of Dryden. Here is part of the passage: "The first happiness of the poet's imagination is properly invention, or the finding of the thought: the second is fancy, or the variation, deriving, or moulding of that thought . . .; the third is elocution, or the art of clothing and adorning the thought."[77] In the long run, Dryden proves to be dissatisfied with this settled dichotomy of thought and words, which he expresses, like most other writers, in metaphors of clothing. As long as the image of outer-wear seems adequate for it, language will certainly remain less important than whatever it is one supposes thought to be. But at some time the question will arise, as it did more insistently for the New Critics: Where is thought located and how can it be identified apart from words? As Lévi-Strauss definitively reminded the present generation, the "myth" to which its descriptions refer is another description.[78] While Dryden cannot be said to have deliberately entertained this idea, he does appear to have found the notion of words as dress a little threadbare. In the "Preface to *All for Love,*" again, he reserves that trope for the specifically satiric purpose of exposing Rochester: "Expressions therefore are a modest clothing of our thoughts, as breeches and petticoats are of our bodies" (I, 223).

In the "Preface to *Fables*" there is another passage in which invention is given precedence over language, but with obvious misgivings. Dryden has just criticized Hobbes, as we noted, for putting words before invention, which is "the first virtue of an epic poet." Still in disparagement of words, he continues as follows: "Now the words are the colouring of the work, which, in the order of nature, is last to be considered. . . . Words, indeed, like glaring colours, are the first beauties that arise and strike the sight; but if the draught be false or lame, the figures ill disposed, the manners obscure or inconsistent, or the thoughts unnatural, then the finest colours are but daubing, and the piece is a beautiful monster at best." Dryden still strains toward the Aristotelian outlook in this passage, or more specifically the Horatian one, but the strain is apparent. Colors are not as easily removed as clothes. *Colouring* remains primarily a rhetorical term for Dryden (the tropes and figures were traditionally "colors"), but it already looks forward to its crucially important position in the theoretical works of Wordsworth and Shelley. How can the "work," or even the "draught," be imagined apart from its coloring? The latter distinction is conceivable in the case, say, of an architect's plan, but plans, as the first paragraph of the "Preface" demonstrates, are irrelevant to the growth of forms. The example of an artist's cartoon would be even less apropos for one who has already said that the "first part" of his preface, before which there was nothing, is simultaneously comprised of a "draught" and of the "dead-colouring of the whole," as in a sepia wash (II, 273). By Dryden's reckoning, then, an artist's first lines and first colors come into being interdependently, and his own "Preface" is a beautiful monster.

Because translation is chiefly a matter of choosing words, Dryden in his late prefaces may have had an especially difficult time keeping words from usurping the whole domain of "thought," or of his own thought in any case. He had always had an almost unseemly regard for verbal surfaces—quite apart, that is, from his indulgence in the respectable form of sneering known as "verbal criticism."[79] In the unpublished "Heads of an Answer to Rymer," which is certainly his least Aristotelian essay, Dryden argues quite unusually as follows: "Amongst us, who have a stronger genius for writing, the operations from the writing are much stronger: for the raising of Shakespeare's passions are more from the excellency of the words and thoughts than the justness of the occasion" (I, 216–217). "Words and thoughts" are here nearly appositive, like Wordsworth's "rocks and stones": there may be a difference, but we are not sure what it is. The closeness of these conventionally opposed terms in such phrases may suggest that there is a noncommittal, even evasive element in Dryden's well-known definition of wit as "a propriety of thoughts and words" (I, 207).

Although he never cancels the distance between thoughts and words altogether, it remains an extremely narrow distance which can be gauged with some accuracy in the following passage on the efficacy of translation: "I grant that something must be lost in all transfusion, that is, in all translations; but the sense will remain, which would otherwise be lost, or at least maimed, when it is scarce intelligible, and that but to few" (II, 288). This passage appears at first to turn on an implicit distinction between words and "sense": words change, while sense, like nature, stays always the same. But if that is so, if sense being always the same can never change, it must be something *verbal* that is "lost" in translation, as of course it is. But if what is lost is verbal, then it must also be the sense, which is said to be lost or maimed altogether where no words are used—and is not a fixed entity in that case after all. On Dryden's own showing, in short, sense and language are not differential but interchangeable terms.

Nevertheless, if we fall back on the meaning of this passage that was no doubt intended, an opposition does remain between sense, which is permanently given, and words, by which sense is new-made. Dryden is neither an Ancient nor a Modern, finally, because his belief in the priority of sense to language—of Homer's having exhausted invention, for example—is more or less evenly balanced by his unswerving faith in the progress or "refinement" of language, with the help of which he has "improved" Chaucer.[80] It is too readily assumed that all Dryden's contemporaries shared his belief in the continued progress of language. Dryden himself admits that they did not: "Many are of a contrary opinion, that the English tongue [in Jonson's time] was in the height of its perfection" ("Defence of the Epilogue," I, 171). It may well be asked, then, why it is so important for Dryden to insist that English is improving, that Denham and Waller are new benchmarks, and so on.

These opinions constitute Dryden's last formalism and serve, like the formality with which the *Essay* was composed, to salvage the self-respect of the author and his contemporaries. The equilibrium between the vigor of the past and the refinement of the present is actually very precarious. Dryden reveals the weakness of his case in the difficulty he has maintaining it. He insists, for example, that Chaucer will not scan (II, 281), despite Speght's warning in the 1602 edition that probably Chaucer would scan if only we understood his system. By expressing this conviction, Dryden commits himself to the lame idea that a person whom he credits with the highest intelligence and with proficiency in all the arts and sciences (II, 277, 287) is unable to count feet or to invent a means of doing so. Dryden has no choice but to find Chaucer wanting in this respect; otherwise there would be nothing left to say for modernity, and in that case the reciprocity of benefit between past and present souls, on the strength of which Dryden justifies his own election to the symposium of his "Preface," could no longer be demonstrated. Thus the assertion that "our numbers were in their nonage" until Waller and Denham appeared (II, 281) must be made by any handy means to seem stronger and more conclusive than it is.

It is not only a matter of saving some few scraps of honor for the Moderns, but of affirming what the Hobbesian Dryden had always helplessly denied: the freedom of the will. Having yielded priority in invention, characterization, and copiousness of thought—all draughts of dead-coloring that can only be retouched once they are laid down—Dryden then retrenches and maintains that his own authority, his originative exercise of will, is directed toward the refinement of the heroic couplet. But if this refinement is a worthwhile accomplishment, why not praise other sorts of refinement as well? Dryden boasts of having improved a system of versification, yet disparages Virgil for having *merely* improved Homer's plot. In every respect—and there would be no harm in this if the stakes were lower—the secondariness of the Moderns is elaborative, interpretive in nature. It is an art of variation within limits prescribed, not prescribed in this case by an Almighty Poet but by the poetic tradition, a "thrid" of yet another kind that keeps one from going astray even when one hopes to do so.

In the "Preface to *Fables*" Dryden relaxes. Forsaking or modifying nearly all the categories of his age and of his own earlier thought, he is an exemplar, in this one essay, of criticism without the ballast of "methodology." Only two categories remain, concerning the need for which we might expect Dryden to remain adamant, namely, the categories of poetry and prose. After all, Dryden stakes his whole claim to originality upon the very feature, versification, which defined *poetry* for his contemporaries. Thus the young Addison would insist, in his "Essay" prefixed to Dryden's *Georgics* (1697), that "to choose the pleasantest [way of conveying truth] is that which chiefly distinguishes poetry from prose."[81] Here in vague outline is the formalist doctrine of the "poetic function," so worded that it may surely appeal to the literary hedonist in Dryden. Nevertheless, in the "Preface to *Fables*," Dryden seems to treat even this distinction very casually. Chaucer wrote "novels in prose, and many works in verse" (II, 271), it hardly seems to matter which. Nor does it matter any longer in Dryden's own practice, which he describes in the next paragraph: "Thoughts, such as they are, come crowding in so fast upon me that my only difficulty is to choose or to reject, to run them into verse or to give them the other harmony of prose" (II, 272).

For Dryden at the end of his life, fully in the habit of alternating translations with prefaces, verse and prose have come to be more similar, as habits, than any formal distinction can suggest.[82] As early as the "Prologue to *Oedipus*" (1679), Dryden seems not to feel the need for a distinction:

> Then Sophocles with Socrates did sit,
> Supreme in wisdom one, and one in wit:
> And wit from wisdom differed not in those,
> But 'twas sung in verse, or said in prose.

(I, 235)

It cannot be supposed that Dryden late in his career, if anything more securely in possession of the critical laurel than the poetic one, would endorse the separate and inferior status we assign to our critical prosings today, although he would know that they must always be secondary and elaborative. The "Preface" offers pleasures and complications very near those of verse and is certainly, itself, one of the more important fables. It is a late variant on the plots of Homer and Virgil: all at sea at first, the author settles down to quarrel over the effects of literature on the "beaux and ladies of pleasure in the town" (II, 285), engages in single combat with Collier, extends the combat to encompass all his enemies, and all the while defends the fortress of his art.

FOUR

Shelley's "Defence of Poetry" in Our Time

There is no evidence that any of the major Romantics read Longinus at all carefully. Coleridge appears to have known him best, but even his judgment is perfunctory. Shelley's lone reference to Longinus vaguely supposes him to be hostile—like any other reviewer—to the free enterprise of poetry: "Poetry and the art which professes to regulate and limit its powers cannot subsist together. Longinus could not have been the contemporary of Homer, nor Boileau of Horace [i.e., Horace the writer of lyric poems]."[1] It is hard to decide, on the evidence of this passage, whether Shelley read Longinus or not, but it is plain that he did not read him carefully. Whatever the case may be, however, Shelley is closest in spirit to Longinus of all the Romantic critics, including Coleridge.

One might say that Shelley was *at liberty* to be more Longinian than Coleridge—less given to formalization, that is—because Shelley was never much affected by the holistic aesthetics of Kant.[2] There is little evidence in his critical thinking of the plastic "multëity in unity" that appears everywhere in Coleridge. There are times when Shelley too supposes that form must be the standard of art, but whenever he does so he finds the conventional notions of decorum and internal consistency to be quite sufficient. In this vein of commonplace Shelley describes what is "harmonious and perfect" in Greek art as "a whole, consistent with itself" (*Prose*, 218), while in the *Defence of Poetry* he observes that the Athenian drama was practiced most "according to the philosophy of it" and preserved "a beautiful proportion and unity."[3]

In this and a few other particulars, the influence of Aristotle can be found in Shelley[4]—whose approach to poetry, however, is fundamentally very different. As Shelley's critics have always pointed out, there is little or nothing of a specifically aesthetic nature in his writing.[5] He frequently adverts to the idea of unity and harmony in the universe or in the "great mind" that animates the universe, but that sort of unity can only be approximated, as he also says, in the domain of physical objects and works of art. What is most typically "poetical" for Shelley is the fragment, or moment. Even the most perfectly sustained compositions are best viewed as fragments of a "cyclic poem" (Jordan, 30). To this "poem" alone Shelley's concept of unity can be applied, as we shall see. His emphasis similarly falls on discontinuity in the relationship between part and whole: "The parts of a composition may be poetical, without the composition as a whole being a poem. A single sentence may be considered *as a* whole, though it be found in a series of unassimilated portions; a single word even may be found in a series of unassimilated portions; a single word even may be the spark of inextinguishable thought" (pp. 36–37). Everywhere in Shelley there recurs the idea, in itself naive and undisciplined by dialectic, that essences are liberating while forms are oppressive: hence the conflict between freedom and institutional restraint in politics or between impulse and ceremony in morals. In his poetics this contrast is fortunately more complicated but it remains instrumental.

Just as the sublime was transmitted from soul to soul in Longinus, so it is, in Shelley, with the poetic "spark." In the early days of electricity and galvanism literary sparks flew freely. Byron's poetry is full of them. Most of all in Shelley, though, in such passages as this one from the *Defence,* they resemble the oratorical thunderbolt of Longinus: "Poetry is a sword of lightning, ever unsheathed, which consumes the scabbard that would contain it" (Jordan, 47). Volatility thus heatedly imagined defies form, as when the "strain" of a poetic mind like that of Bacon "distends, and then bursts the circumference of the hearer's mind" (p. 35).[6] Because Shelley was inclined to believe that light is a fluid and not a particle,[7] his mind could move easily from the thrust of lightning to its devastation without distinguishing cause and effect; lightning itself is the overflow, as from a fountain, that it causes. Thus because Dante was the "Lucifer" of a "starry flock" in Republican Italy, each of whose words is "a spark, a burning atom . . . pregnant with a lightning which has yet found no conductor," it follows that a "great poem" like the *Commedia* "is a fountain that will shed—with the help of a conductor—"its divine effluence" on the auditor (pp. 62–63).[8] The sliding of these figures from stars to lightning to streams to conduits closely resembles Longinus's rendering of the "vapours" that are transmitted from "the men of old" to "the souls of those who emulate them," vapors that "we may describe as *effluences.*"

The result of this flooding, Shelley says, is that we become "a portion of that beauty which we contemplate."[9] Just so, the effect of this experience on the auditor in Longinus is the pleasing illusion that the soul "had itself produced what it has heard." Both writers imagine a conductor, then, through which the poetic spark can be passed to many persons in turn, each in turn fancying himself to be its originator. So Shelley writes: "The pleasure resulting from the manner in which [poets] express the influence of society or nature upon their own minds, communicates itself to others, and gathers a sort of *reduplication* from the community" (Jordan, 29). The word I have italicized suggests the production of a facsimile as well as increase in general. For Shelley as well as for Longinus, surprisingly enough when one considers how vague the ideas of both of them appear to be, the function of inspiration is, quite precisely, to reproduce itself. I shall discuss this point in more detail elsewhere.

So much, then, for the affinities of Shelley and Longinus. A much broader and more generalized comparison is obviously possible: I have only wanted to stress one or two of the issues that have been recurrent themes in this book. To turn now to a more unlikely pairing, Shelley and Dryden. They have been contrasted as the very antipodes of poetry in famous essays by T. S. Eliot and C. S. Lewis,[10] and certainly in most respects their sensibilities and talents have nothing in common. Shelley loathed "the reign of Charles II" (Jordan, 48). Because he took it for granted, with Longinus, that political and sensual tyranny always coexist, Shelley could never have sympathized with Dryden, whose personality was, for the most part, that of his age. Here Shelley differs markedly from Hazlitt—and from Keats, who studied Dryden carefully in 1819 and in whose casual criticism there is more of the chameleon poet than the virtuous philosopher. And yet, with all this said, Shelley and the Dryden of the "Preface to *Fables*" still share important ideas. What I want to emphasize, in this case also, is the similarity of their attitudes toward the flow of inspiration.

Dryden more than once wrote of the "Almighty Poet" who determines our actions whether we know it or not, much as a narrator determines the actions of a character. Part of what determines us, especially if we are poets, is this Poet's preexisting language; in writing of the "lineal descent" of poets and the "transfusion" of translation, Dryden indicates that every poem is dictated by the language that comes before it. Shelley nearly always stresses the contrast between creation and translation—as when he tells Leigh Hunt that he, Hunt, was "formed to be a living fountain and not a canal however clear"[11]—but at bottom his view of originality in fact resembles Dryden's. His version of Dryden's "lineal descent" is, again, the "great cyclic poem," the first chaotic fragments of which anticipate everything to come. In the characteristic phrasing of both Longinus and Dryden the difference between inspiration and inspiring language is very slight, and this is true also in Shelley. His cyclic poem is closely equivalent to, and sometimes identical with, the concepts of "Power" and "Mind" that would be complementary to a poem of any kind in normal usage. These matters will receive a large share of attention in the present chapter.

Dryden and Shelley also take similar views of poetic craft. Dryden appears to have decided by 1700, following Hobbes, that "thoughts . . . have always some connexion" and therefore need not, perhaps cannot, be composed with exhaustive care. Shelley too, in a draft of the first paragraph of the *Defence,* defined the imagination as a force that promotes associations (Jordan, 25n.).[12] In his published revision Shelley avoided the mechanistic overtones of this definition, but I think that his changed wording makes little or no practical difference. Throughout the *Defence* the imagination, dictating unpremeditated verse, remains inseparable from the Muse. The "birth and recurrence" of poetry have "no necessary connexion with consciousness or will" (pp. 76–77). Here again Shelley differs substantially from Coleridge, whose Secondary Imagination coexists "with the conscious will."

Both Shelley and the later Dryden oppose systematic thinking about literature. (Herein Shelley most resembles Byron, who declared that "when a man talks of system, his case is hopeless.") Indeed, Shelley mistrusted complex theories in any field (religion, say, or "political economy") as defects of feeling. He read the literary journals but remained aloof, until he read Peacock, from any and all controversies that had no direct bearing on politics. He never mentioned Hazlitt's critical ideas, perhaps because he disliked him in person and as a journalist; he thought of Jeffrey, Gifford, Wilson, Southey, and the rest solely as creatures of party faction; and to Byron's feud with Bowles over Pope his first reaction was simply indifference.[13] He read and borrowed from Wordsworth's "Preface" and from Coleridge, especially the *Biographia* and *The Statesman's Manual,* but he nearly always severed what he borrowed from its original close-knit context. Unlike Coleridge, Shelley lacked patience to develop qualified viewpoints. His taste in philosophy ran to the simplicity of extremes, whether of materialism or idealism, and he was inclined, as M. H. Abrams has remarked disapprovingly, to encourage "a general annulment of distinctions."[14] It is just this tendency, though, that I find myself admiring and wishing to defend in *A Defence of Poetry,* which Yeats declared, largely in tribute to its unqualified stance, to be "the profoundest essay on the foundations of poetry in English."[15]

I

In late February 1821 Shelley wrote his publisher that in his *Defence* he would "expose the inmost idol of [Peacock's] error" (*Letters,* II, 269). But in the first half-paragraph of his *Defence,* and from time to time later, Shelley himself comes close to sharing the error. For the next few pages I shall hover around that first half-paragraph with the purpose of identifying this error fully. Having done that, I will be able to show just where Shelley actually follows Peacock and where, in turning against him, he makes his most important contribution to poetics.

Two of the "poets" most conspicuously celebrated in the *Defence* are Plato, whose *eidola,* or false images in a cave, are said to be the poet's only materials in the *Republic,* and Bacon, another disparager of poetry and of the "idols of the cave." So, in harboring an "inmost idol," according to

Shelley's witty expression, Peacock has been taken in by appearances and thus joins company with the poets he abuses. But he also joins the philosophers whose views he shares: it is at once Shelley's compliment to Peacock and the essence of his refutation that by allusion he unites his friend with other writers whose vigorous imaginations belie their complicity with the image-makers.[16] But just how far is Shelley himself, prior to the *Defence* and even within it, taken in by the idol he exposes in Peacock? Quite far, apparently, if he chooses to begin his essay by assigning special but only limited tasks to that rather petty faculty, the image-ination, over which Peacock has triumphed. To speak of image-making is to suppose the accessibility of some reality that will be obscured by images. The attacks of Peacock and Plato and Bacon all depend on their enforcement of this contrast, which appears to be upheld, in turn, by Shelley's first remarks on the imagination and the reason.

"Poetry," Peacock had written memorably in "The Four Ages of Poetry," "is the mental rattle that awakened the attention of intellect in the infancy of society" (Jordan, 18). In other words, by fostering the savage's eye for resemblances, poetry helped him to begin organizing his experience. Because all their neighbors were engrossed in "robbing and fighting" (p. 5), the poets were at first the sole makers and guardians of their culture, "not only historians but theologians, moralists, and"—as Shelley noted in particular—"legislators" (p. 6). Imagination, in short—and this is the key point to have in mind—precedes reason in the evolution of the human faculties, but then with the perfecting of reason the imagination becomes vestigial and should properly fall into disuse. Reason and only reason contributes to scientific progress. It affords "the philosophic mental tranquillity which looks round with an equal eye on all external things, collects a store of ideas, discriminates their relative value, assigns to all their proper place," and in general subserves "the real business of life" (p. 17; Shelley could have capitalized on all these untimely allusions to Wordsworth). "Poetry," by contrast, "cannot travel out of the regions of its birth, the uncultivated lands of semi-civilized men" (p. 15). Because it is necessarily figurative and twisted into meter ("language on the rack of Procrustes" [p. 19]), poetry is unfit for "pure reason and dispassionte truth. . . , as we may judge by versifying one of Euclid's equations" (p. 9). Poetry "can never make a philosopher, nor a statesman, nor in any class of life an useful or rational man" (p. 18).

Unquestionably Peacock somewhat exaggerates his position for effect. Although it is difficult to agree with his early editor that his attitude toward scientific rationalism is actually "ironic,"[17] he undoubtedly did believe, being a writer himself, that literature has its place. Thus he probably agreed in advance, at least to some small extent, with Shelley. And Shelley, on the other hand, although he believed that his friend was "a nursling of the exact and superficial school of poetry" and thus far in league with those reviewers who were real enemies (*Letters,* II, 126), could still agree with Peacock in some ways. Peacock's point of view, however cavalierly expressed, was in many respects that of Plato,[18] and it also coincided with Shelley's own favorable attitude toward experimental science[19] and progressive politics. Nevertheless, Peacock's *Four Ages* had to be answered. There was still that "inmost idol" to be exposed.

When Peacock writes that "the savage . . . lisps in numbers" (Jordan, 4), Shelley agrees in response that "the savage (for the savage is to ages what the child is to years) is naturally a poet" (p. 27). This opinion they both inherit from nearly all the Enlightenment theorists of the origin of language.[20] By and large, however, these writers (who include Rousseau, Herder, and Monboddo) anticipate Peacock rather than Shelley in arguing that for better or worse society has outgrown the kind of knowledge that depends on figures of speech. On this significant point Shelley parts company with practically everyone: He agrees that imagination precedes reason in the development of thought, but he goes on to insist that the imagination has not therefore been left behind by the grand march of intellect. On the contrary, imagination must pave the way for the reason in every new venture of thought or else the mind will atrophy and fail to keep pace with the need for change in society. Moreover, reason has no useful function that is independent of, or different from, the function of the imagination. Insofar as it is valuable, reason "in her most exalted mood" (1850 *Prelude,* XIV, 189) simply *is* the imagination. Hence for any praise-worthy human endeavor there is only one faculty, not two of them dividing the labor.

This is Shelley's most radical and effective position.[21] We have noted, though, that the opening sentences of the *Defence* promise nothing so extreme. There Shelley discriminates between reason and imagination as though they were equal in value, and he does so in terms that would almost have satisfied Peacock. Shelley's first definition of reason, "mind contemplating the relations borne by one thought to another, however produced," seems roughly the same as the description by Peacock of the rational philosophic mind that I have already quoted. And imagination viewed as "mind acting on those thoughts so as to colour them with its own light" (Jordan, 25) seems to be just the sort of subjectivity, ornamental at best and a distortion of accurate thought at worst, that the scientific approach to the world is said to have outmoded. So far there are really no grounds for challenging Peacock. These first sentences themselves are so cumbrously pseudoscientific in manner that they seem an unconscious parody of Coleridge in certain registers and of Shelley's own tractarian prose.[22] From this point on, in both argument and tone, Shelley's personal view will begin to take over, but for the moment he seems to be invoking his own earlier philosophy of mind, the philosophy he still held when he last spoke with Peacock in England.

As an apprentice Godwinian and admirer of Paine's *Age of Reason,* Shelley had believed that reason would prevail in the world. That was his faith—although "faith" itself he held in distaste as superstition, as a product of imagination to which the mind obstinately clings. Reason was then, to him, "a thing independent and inflexible [i.e., incorruptible]" (*Letters,* I, 101). The imagination, by contrast, is enamored of unrealities. In a fragment on religion of 1814 Shelley calls the belief in miracles "a creative activity of imagination" (*Prose,* 142), and in the "Fragment on Miracles" of the same period he declares that "logic and dialectics" are better than the imaginative adherence to "a doctrine pretending to be true" (ibid., 144). There is no difference between these opinions and Peacock's contrast between rational enlightenment and the poet's reliance on "the superstitions which are the creed of his age" (Jordan, 4–5). In Peacock's view, and the earlier Shelley's, imagination is a backward faculty that is ranged against innovation; it consists merely in "a crude congeries of traditional phantasies" (p. 5).

Even as late as 1819 (in the *Philosophical View of Reform*), when Shelley no longer idolized the Reason of the Enlightenment, he still evidently thought that although neither faculty was obsolete, "the cultivation of the imagination and the cultivation of scientific truth" were separate but equal enterprises (*Prose,* 259). The position implied here is the one that anyone not given to extremes will be likely to take: Poetry and science each have their sphere, and each has a useful cultural function as long as it is not considered to be a substitute for the other. This is the position of I. A. Richards, for example, who maintains that our "intellectual beliefs" and "emotional beliefs" depend on efficient communications issuing from the reason and the imagination, respectively. But in Richards's designation of poetry as "pseudo-statement" there still appears the bias that marks the attitude of a Peacock. In thinking of this kind, however evenhanded it may seem, rhetoric is viewed as a special kind of language that is the natural enemy of logic. Figural language that is not candidly fictive in its designs upon us will try to pass itself off as the "literal" language of science. At one time this was the earnestly held opinion of Shelley himself. Writing—as it happens—of the poetry of Peacock in 1812, the young Shelley warns himself against its siren call: "I have rigidly accustomed myself not to be seduced by the loveliest eloquence or the sweetest strains" (*Letters,* I, 325).

Probably as long as one accepts the validity of the distinction between the figural and the literal, one is likely to be wary lest poetry exceed its bounds and poach in the preserves of prose: "The best way, on topics similar to these, is to tell the plain truth, without the confusion and ornament of metaphor." That is Shelley addressing the Irish in 1812, complaining of what he was later to describe, in his *Treatise on Morals,* as "the abuse of a metaphorical expression to a literal purpose" (*Prose*, 65, 188).[23] Now, one cannot be brought to reconsider this invidious contrast without first coming to question whether the notion of "metaphor," or transfer of sense, is indeed only intelligible, as it has been said to be,[24] in opposition to the "literal," or proper sense. Two different ideas are commonly proposed as to what the literal might be. According to the first and etymologically legitimate idea, a word is used literally if it corresponds to its accepted definition. The second concerns a word that is used in accordance with its normative connection to an object. It is this latter, less cautious sense of the "literal" that Shelley contrasts with metaphor in his *Treatise on Morals*.

In so doing he parallels the contrast he makes elsewhere in the same essay between two fundamental types of philosophy, one of which deals with fact and the other with words (called "logic" here but surely including the philosophies of rhetoric and grammar): "Metaphysics may be defined as the science of all that we know, feel, remember, and believe inasmuch as our knowledge, sensations, memory, and faith constitute the universe considered relatively to human identity. Logic, or the science of words, must no longer be confounded with metaphysics or the science of facts. Words are the instruments of mind whose capacities it becomes the metaphysician to know, but they are not mind, nor are they portions of mind" (*Prose*, 185). It will be noticed that although Shelley may insist that "the science of things is superior to the science of words" (*Letters*, I, 318), he takes it for granted almost from the beginning that "things" are *mental*.[25] This idea gains in importance in his later work, but it is there very early. "Nothing exists but as it is perceived" (*Prose*, 174) is Shelley's Berkeleyan dictum in "On Life" and elsewhere; hence his "facts" should not be confused with things in themselves. He will often write "things" when he means "thoughts" (in the opening sentences of the *Defence* there are two manuscript changes from "things" to "thoughts"), but that is simply because the nominalist habit of expression is difficult to get over and too handy to do without.

The subtler distinction, with which for a long time Shelley continues to sustain the conventional contrasts of science and poetry or reason and imagination, is the distinction between thought and words. Although even in the *Defence* he glances in passing at "those who cannot distinguish words from thoughts" (Jordan, 55), this distinction too is more typical, I think, of an earlier period. It is most frequently and polemically urged in the disputatious prose of 1812, when he says, for example, that "words are only signs for ideas" (*Letters*, I, 215, 317). To come to an end of this survey of Shelley's early thinking about the idols of the cave, my point is that in the *Defence* almost for the first time Shelley went some way toward giving up the idol of the idols—the notion that appearances make up half of a pair, the other half being fact, or reality—in order to succeed in exposing the "inmost idol" of Peacock's "error." In the "Four Ages" Peacock had written that "the reason and the understanding are best addressed in the simplest and most unvarnished prose" (Jordan, 9). This had been Shelley's own opinion, and it seems to survive, in both style and theme, in the first sentences of the *Defence*.

II

The business of the imagination, Shelley adds to these sentences, is "to colour [thoughts] with its own light, . . . composing from them, as from elements, other thoughts, each containing within itself the principle of its own integrity" (Jordan, 25). The "thoughts" that are thus colored, the same thoughts that are also contemplated by the reason, are what the philosophers of the Empirical tradition called "impressions"; they are given to the mind, either by sense or by unknown causes. Empiricists like Hume contrast thoughts such as these with the compound thoughts, or "ideas," that are forged exclusively by the imagination, because there is no demonstrable basis in reality for the arrangement of impressions in a connecting pattern. "Reason alone," writes Hume in the *Treatise of Human Nature,* "can never give rise to any original idea."[26] Shelley follows Hume very closely but he does not normally consider impressions, understood as sense-data, to be "thoughts." His normal attitude is expressed most clearly in his *Treatise on Morals:* "The most astonishing combinations of poetry, the subtlest deductions of logic and mathematics are no other than combinations which the intellect makes of sensations according to its own laws" (*Prose,* 182). Thus, since the function of combining is performed solely by the imagination, it must be concluded that *all* thoughts, including those contemplated by the reason, are furnished by the imagination, which alone is independent from the contingency of the real. In other words, science does not offer unmediated representations of the world; like poetry, science is mind obeying "its own laws."

Most broadly considered, the coloring of imagination is the filter of self that veils perception. It is what causes Sir William Drummond, the disciple of Hume and Berkeley whom Shelley admired, to speak of "the painted field of my vision."[27] Shelley rather curiously describes this distortion as an anthropomorphosis: "We see trees, houses, fields, living beings in our own shape, and in shapes more or less analogous to our own" (*Prose,* 184). This is eccentric; even solipsism and psychosis, we assume, will project themselves in images that partly disguise the self. But the general meaning is clear. With perhaps only slight exaggeration, a recent commentator on the *Defence* has written that Shelley regards "the world as a mind-made poem in which metaphor is tantamount to metamorphosis and imagination is the agent of transformation in human nature."[28] Reason, on the other hand, is inert and lacks any vital principle of its own. Calculating machine that it is, it lacks the self-consciousness it would need even to be aware of its own achievement or to perceive the significance of its information: "We want the creative faculty to imagine that which we know" (Jordan, 68–69). By the time Shelley has said this, the gathering force of his argument has long since driven reason from the field. At the end of the first paragraph, after it had seemed that the two faculties would divide the useful arts equally between themselves, Shelley violently tilts the bias in his series of contrasting definitions: "Reason is the enumeration of quantities already known; imagination is the perception of the value of those quantities, both separately and as a whole. Reason respects the differences, and imagination the similitudes of things. Reason is to the imagination as the instrument to the agent, as the body to the spirit, as the shadow to the substance" (p. 26).

In this passage reason is most drastically curtailed as the "instrument to the agent." It is a tool with operations that have no independence from the force that puts it to work. It repeats the gestures of what wields it just as a hammer extends the movement of an arm. Thus, Shelley's victory over Peacock comes about not simply from his having asserted the inferiority of reason but from his having first insinuated and then asserted that reason is not really a separate faculty at all, but only the echo, or ape, of imagination, mechanically reproducing acts of mind that were once, and only once, creative. This assertion is reflected in the symbols Shelley uses to describe the relationship of the two faculties in the second draft of the letter to his publisher that was to have been the *Defence:* "[Peacock] would extinguish Imagination which is the Sun of life, & grope his way by the cold & uncertain & borrowed light of . . . the Moon he calls Reason,—. . . the watery [*light*] orb which is the Queen of his [*cold*] pale Heaven" (*Letters,* II, 275).[29] Readers of Nabokov's *Pale Fire,* if not of *Timon of Athens,* will recognize Shelley's source, which provides these metaphors with some of their polemical strength: "The moon's an arrant thief, / And her pale fire she snatches from the sun" (IV, iv, 439–40; Timon has just said that the sun is also a thief—of which more below). Shelley's conceit is the more pointed in that traditionally, and most notably in Shakespeare, it is the imagination that was compared with the moon. For Shelley the imagination becomes a sun that creates its world by making it visible. Heating up the cool terminology of Hume, Shelley in such passages becomes a hierophant of "the Magian worship of the sun as the creator and preserver of the world" (*Prose,* 272).[30]

With this main point established, Shelley can then devise still more daring expressions that reach out to encompass the old and lesser idea of imagination as well as his new one. Wordsworth in the "Preface" says finely that poetry is "the breath and finer spirit of all things," but then seems content for it to serve the scientist merely as an ornament or a means of popularization, better perhaps than the poetry of Erasmus Darwin but not fundamentally different from it.[31] Shelley is bolder. He insists that imagination—"poetry"—presides over both the humanization *and* the conceptual groundwork of science. Thus it is both "the root and blossom of all other systems of thought; it is that from which all spring, and that which adorns all" (Jordan, 70). It governs every phase of the scientific method, from the inmost bulwark of deduction to the furthest horizon of speculation, being "the center and circumference of knowledge; . . . that which comprehends all science, and that to which all science must be referred" (ibid.).

All this is more carefully thought through than may appear. Even for the scientist, Shelley's hyperboles in defense of mythopoeic knowledge do not overstep the bounds of the plausible. In thinking of science, Shelley is likely to have had in mind the laws of "natural science" and the principles of moral and political utility. Setting the latter aside for the moment, one can speak, not very fancifully, of the poetic origins of the laws of physical science. *Gravity,* a word Shelley himself often uses metaphorically for "attraction," was intuited first by the poets. The author of *The Witch of Atlas* could point to Aristophanes' myth of the hermaphrodites in the *Symposium;* he would have known, in any case, of the elder Darwin's opinion that life in its infancy passed through a hermaphroditic stage.[32] Or, citing a more narrowly gravitational principle, "Everything that rises must fall," one could argue that this idea was first conceived imaginatively as the Elizabethan Wheel of Fortune. Yet further, as Douglas Bush notes somewhat disapprovingly, there is Shelley's own "linking of love with electricity in a thought-created world."[33] There are likewise poetic anticipations of the Conservation of Energy, e.g., Milton's account of creation from Chaos, the balance of destruction and preservation mirrored forth in the Hindu zodiac,[34] and many others. These examples do not resemble "the versifying of one of Euclid's equations," but they will serve to explain what Shelley means. Geometry itself, in any case, does not offer an escape from subjectivity. As Hilary Putnam writes, "The overthrow of Euclidean geometry was not *just* an overthrow of a theory of space. Euclidean geometry was the paradigm of certainty, attained through a priori reasoning, and more than that, the paradigm held up to the moral philosopher by Plato as well as by Spinoza."[35] Even at this extreme, then, it is not the hyperbolic Shelley but the scientific Peacock who is involved in a fallacy.

The greatest apparent weakness of Shelley's position concerning science is the fact that even the most prescient of intuitions cannot in themselves prove anything. If the imagination does supply the reason with hypotheses, it is left for the reason to devise the experiments that will verify them. But verification and proof are not the same thing. Verification, the strict ascertainment of what is true, is generally thought to be impossible; even the most retrenched objectivists believe that what is true must be determined negatively, i.e., by the falsification of alternatives. Proof, a more practical affair that certainly is possible, can be established only with respect to more or less changeable and relative contexts. The principles that dictate an experiment subtly anticipate its success or failure. Far more than Bacon, for one, supposed, what Thomas Kuhn has called "paradigms" of thought shape and determine each experimental phase in the history of science until new paradigms arise, making what had hitherto been proved newly limited in its application or even irrelevant to the new aims of science. (I only refer here to the strongest results of science, to what really has in one sense or another been proved, and not to such phantoms temporarily sustained by experiment as phlogiston, atmospheric ether, and the like.)

This idea of science is the one supported by Shelley: the operations of reason do not differ in kind from those of imagination but only repeat them in ever narrower applications because the horizons of reason are governed by general conceptions that are not its own. Our tendency to forget that the facts in our possession have been preselected by our attitudes is fully accounted for in Shelley's observation that "the poetry in [utilitarian thought] is concealed by the accumulation of facts and calculating processes" (Jordan, 68). No defender of poetry or criticism, not even Aristotle, can deny Plato's charge that the poets and rhapsodes (who are also critics, like Ion) tell lies. Plotinus tried, but he referred the whole matter to an isolated, transcendent sphere to which Shelley is much less serenely devoted than he is often said to be. What a defense of poetry *can* do, and this is what Shelley's *Defence* does, is to claim that although poetry distorts the truth, science distorts it just as much and in just the same way. Science too, at its most "poetic" and least self-oblivious, nothing affirms and therefore never lieth. It need only divest itself of the omniscience that Peacock accorded to Euclidean geometry and admit that the poetical faculty alone, as Shelley says, "creates new materials for knowledge" (p. 69).

The dynamic thinking of the imagination becomes static when it is repeated by the reason, inevitably so without the intercession of new "poetry." "Ethical science," for example, "arranges the elements which reason has created" (p. 39). The crystallization of classes and systems, suspended in space—as we conceive of them—rather than successive through time, resembles the change from the vital sciences of the nineteenth century to the structural ones of the twentieth as it is described by Foucault. During the course of this period the paradigmatic science for other scientists was first biology, then economics, then linguistics; and within these three sciences over the same period the focus of attention shifted from the processual to the formal: from function to norm in biology, from conflict to rule in economics, and from signification to system in linguistics.[36] Shelley would argue that shifts of this kind are what poetry must guard against or, if need be, reverse. What begins as a vital sense of resemblance, a link forged by sympathy, ends all too soon as an enforcement of uniformity, whether by government, religion,[37] or mere mental habit.

III

The notion that the thinking of one faculty loses vitality when repeated by another suggests an equivalent notion that must pertain to language. If poetic language is "vitally metaphorical" (Jordan, 30), the language of reason must consist of dead metaphors, including equations, laws, and identifications, all bearing traces of their figural origins that are almost too faint to notice.[38] Although considerations of this sort would imply that there is a very close relationship between thought and language, Shelley is most frequently inclined not to accept this implication. In some places he thinks that his contrast between imagination and reason must itself reflect the immemorial contrast between the spirit and the letter. At the same time, however, his coup against rationalism does entail the supposition that imagination and reason are not generically distinct and that the materials with which they function differ only in being alive or dead. In that case the opposition between spirit and letter is by no means absolute.

Without always quite wishing to, Shelley reveals in the argument of the *Defence* that the activity of the imagination is not ineffable but can be understood as a kind of language. "The coloring of imagination" is an expression that Shelley uses in common with Wordsworth and many others. It is a rhetorical as well as a psychological process, *colors* being a traditional term for rhetorical devices. Shelley's poetry had been abused for its surfeit of "colouring epithets,"[39] and if only for this reason it is safe to assume that, although he was no great reader of rhetoric manuals, he was aware of this sense of his term. Wordsworth intends to discriminate at least slightly, in the 1800 "Preface," between the "colouring of imagination" and the "selection" of everyday language that gets colored, but this distinction in itself shows that the metaphorical and the literal share a common medium.[40] Shelley uses the notion of "color" with much the same result. Instead of enforcing the contrast between spirit and letter, he turns out to have questioned it.[41]

The image-making faculty is itself an image, the "Spirit of BEAUTY, that dost consecrate / With thine own hues all thou dost shine upon / Of human thought or form" ("Hymn to Intellectual Beauty").[42] It is at this strange point of overlap between cause and effect that one encounters Shelley's figure of the veil: "Oh, that words . . . / Were stripped of their thin masks and various hue" ("Ode to Liberty," 234–37; *Poetry*, 609). In contrasting the spirit and the form of a work, Shelley likes to think of the latter, its "accidental vesture" (Jordan, 39), as a raiment that includes language and conceals "the beauty of [poets'] conceptions in its naked truth and splendour" (ibid.). And yet, as the 1816 "Hymn" declares, the imagination itself, the creative sun, is what supplies those colors that the poet wants to strip away from his expression—in order to reveal the colorless transparency of his imaginings. Even if one attempts to resolve the paradox by saying that a concrete expression is like a prism, or "dome of many-coloured glass," that refracts "the white radiance" of the imagination (*Adonais, 462–63; Poetry, 443*)—even then, the spirit and the letter are still intermixed in their common light.

On many occasions, as we have seen, Shelley wishes to preserve the notion of language that had prevailed almost universally since its exposition by Locke, namely, that words are arbitrary signs that obscure the pure essence of thoughts. But the position taken up by Shelley in the *Defence* reveals that words and thoughts are very similar to each other. Here in full is Shelley's description of the movement from living to dead metaphor in expressions that derive from "poetry": "[The poets'] language is vitally metaphorical; that is, it marks the before unapprehended relations of things and perpetuates their apprehension, until the words which represent them, become, through time, signs for portions or classes of thoughts instead of pictures of integral thoughts; and then if no new poets should arise to create afresh the associations which have been thus disorganized, language will be dead to all the nobler purposes of human intercourse" (Jordan, 29–30). This passage leaves no place for thought. Language itself supplies what Hume calls ideas, or the combination of impressions. Apart from that innovation, Shelley here follows nearly all the theorists of the origin of language by supposing that in being repeated language grows inflexible because it is less and less immediately connected with archetypal impressions and more and more determined, therefore, by its internal relations as a system. From the scientific point of view this development is a good thing: only in being abstracted from immediate impressions can language serve the purposes of generalization. But for Shelley, as for Blake, generalization is mere lunacy, a pale fire stolen from a forgotten original: "The copiousness of lexicography and the distinctions of grammar are the works of a later age, and are merely the catalogue and form of the creations of poetry" (pp. 30–31).

In implying that language at its origin was and is, in Eliot's phrase, "as immediate as the odor of a rose," Shelley can suggest that it is at once bodily, or concrete, and quintessentially distilled, or abstracted, without being merely a formal sign of either condition. Poetic language, in short, is dynamic and has no arbitrary structure: "The grammatical forms . . . are convertible with respect to the highest poetry without injuring it as poetry" (p. 32). Now, it is in this respect most obviously that poetry "in a general sense" (p. 26: "the expression of the imagination") differs from poetry "in a more restricted sense" (p. 32). The latter from the outset must all too

closely anticipate the expression of the *reason* in that it expresses "arrangements of language" (ibid.) that differ from rational utterances only in being
more delicate. Far from being convertible without injury, then, the verbal
arrangements of poetry in the restricted sense cannot be translated at all
(viz., pp. 33–34)—whereas the highest poetry, Shelley has wanted to say,
has nothing verbal about it. It is at once the inspiration and the eternal
meaning of poetry in the restricted sense and of all the other art forms.
Again a wedge appears to have been driven between spirit and letter.

Well and good, but how can the realm of concepts, even of universals, be
shown to exist at all, short of being the One indivisibly, if it does not itself
participate in some medium that is concrete enough to allow for, nay, to
forge, differentiation? If it contains all colors, even the white radiance itself
must therefore be a system of signs. That this conclusion at least sometimes
governs Shelley's own thought may be shown with reference to his concept
of "allegory." Only one kind of allegory can plausibly be defined as a form
referring to something ineffable, and that, of course, is the story told by
religion: "All original religions are allegorical, or susceptible of allegory,
and, like Janus, have a double face of false and true" (p. 31). Here the
dualism is explicit and neat, but in any less purely theistic allegory, when
interpretation is a matter of finding parallels for certain figures, then plainly
the hidden sense is not ineffable but a para*phrase* that has its own definite
shape and purport. To this effect Shelley quotes with approval from the *Vita
Nuova* in his Advertisement for *Epipsychidion* (1821): "Great were his
shame, who should rhyme anything under a garb of metaphor or rhetorical
colour [*sotto vesta di figura o di colore rettorico*], and then, being asked, should
be incapable of stripping his words of this garb so that they might have a
veritable meaning [*e poscia . . . non sapesse denudare le sue parole da cotale vesta,
in guisa che avessero verace intentimento*]" (*Prose,* 335; Shelley slightly mis-
quotes the Italian, which I have here interspersed with Rossetti's translation
as given by Clark). In general, therefore, allegory does not uphold the
duality of language and pure thought. Rather it refers from one sentence to
another. The difference in degree between the two sentences, between
concealment and exposure, is just the difference—and no more—between
Shelley's "restricted" and "general" senses of poetry.

IV

The Italian of the passage quoted above may have furnished some of the
language of the *Defence*: "vesture," "colour," "naked truth." An anomaly in
all of Shelley's work that has frequently been noticed concerns the question
of what covers what: "The veil of error and the figured curtain of imagination," writes one commentator, "have a mutuality that is ambivalent:
sometimes ironic, sometimes liberating."[43] In part this is simply a question

of relative values: what is mundane and dreary needs dressing up, what is celestial and bright needs to be unveiled. Shelley himself is sure that from this point of view his veil-symbol is not anomalous: "Whether [poetry] spreads its figured curtain, or withdraws life's dark veil from before the scene of things, it equally creates for us a being within our being" (Jordan, 74). As in the case of allegory, the anomaly obtrudes itself only if one attempts to identify nakedness with ineffability or transcendence. Shelley speaks of "the scene of things," and again he says that by lifting "the veil," poetry "makes familiar objects be as if they were not familiar" (p. 39). This is perfectly intelligible; it is Wallace Stevens's making "the visible / A little hard to see," and it anticipates the "defamiliarization" of the early Russian Formalists.[44] Yet in all these instances the similarity between surface and subsurface is greater than the contrast: something specific, concrete, and quotidian is torn aside to reveal something specific, concrete, and unusual. We have to do with either a language-event or an object-event, but never, given the logic of these figures, with a transformation of language into matter or spirit. Either appearances are bottomless or else they are realities; the deep truth is not imageless but an image.

Two passages from the *Defence* are illuminating in this regard, even though each of them does little more in intent, perhaps, than to rehearse a commonplace of empirical psychology in a lyrical vein. The first passage recalls the psychology of Hume: "A word, or a trait in the representation of a scene or a passion, will touch the enchanted chord, and reanimate, in those who have ever experienced these emotions, the sleeping, the cold, the buried image of the past" (Jordan, 73). In Hume, the memory houses lingering and resonating impressions that may be reactivated by some kindred impulse. This is of course the process of association. The memory for Shelley is a "lyre [that] trembles and sounds after the wind has died away" (p. 27). Unless reanimated by a new note of "poetry," the chord in the memory simply dies away until its echo becomes reflexive—and is then claimed, we may add, as an a priori truth by the reason. Now, Shelley's associative "madeleine," his catalytic word, can take effect only if in some sense it resembles what it reanimates. The resemblance cannot be the resemblance of a sign to a corresponding "thought," furthermore, because that which is lodged in the memory, the "chord," already belongs within the system of the sign that is added to it. A new sound gives renewed life to an old sound and not to some forgotten signification either of the old sound or of itself. Thus Shelley's "word, or trait" establishes a connection between signs and not between a sign and a thought.

At this point, when it is no longer possible to avoid terms that will seem anachronistic, it will be reassuring to glance at a theoretical challenge to the empiricist view of language that Shelley himself had read as early as 1813, Horne Tooke's *Diversions of Purley* (1786–98).[45] In a rarely discussed passage in the *Treatise on Morals,* Shelley delivers his opinion of this work: "The discoveries of Horne Tooke in philology do not, as he has asserted, throw light upon metaphysics: they only render the instruments requisite to its perception more exact and accurate. Aristotle and his followers, Locke and most of the modern philosophers gave logic the name of metaphysics" (*Prose,* 185; as we noted earlier, "metaphysics" for Shelley is the science of subjective "facts"—i.e., of thoughts—and logic is the science of words [cf. ibid.]). Concerning Aristotle, Shelley may have in mind the *Categories,* which has often been criticized for having founded its distinctions in language, not reality;[46] concerning Locke, Shelley is in fact echoing Tooke himself, who advises us to reread Locke and "substitute the composition &c. of *terms,* wherever he was supposed a composition &c. of *ideas.*"[47] Tooke adds in this place that Locke actually wished, too late, to recast his *Essay* as a study of the linguistic determination of thought.

Tooke begins his treatise with a surprising observation that would be of interest to Shelley's Demogorgon: "Truth, in my opinion, has been improperly imagined at the bottom of a well: it lies much nearer to the surface" (ibid., I, 10). He takes his stand against the then universally accepted premise, after Aristotle and Locke, that words are "the signs of *ideas*" (I, 22). Tooke's own position, shored up by vast learning in sundry alphabets, closely anticipates not only the view of Saussure but also, even in phrasing, that of Jacques Lacan. Words are signs of *sounds,* says Tooke (viz., Saussure's "acoustic images"), and then he continues: "There may be not only signs of sounds; but again, for the sake of abbreviation [i.e., short-cuts in thinking], signs of those signs, one *under another* in a continued progression" (I, 25; italics mine).[48] It is significant that Shelley apparently accepts this much of Tooke's argument; that is what is implied, in any case, by the word *discoveries* in the *Treatise on Morals.* What Shelley does not then proceed to accept is Tooke's further claim that "Hermes has blinded Philosophy" and that his own researches will discredit "all the different systems of Metaphysical Imposture" (I, 23; II, 510). But if Shelley has accepted the premise, he can reject the conclusion only with the greatest difficulty. There is nothing implicitly materialistic about Tooke's argument, however it may have appeared to Shelley or to Tooke himself. On the contrary, reading Tooke may encourage one to take the *Logos* literally. What Tooke will not accommodate, though, is the possibility of any ideation that is transcendent in the sense of being beyond, or other than, signs.

In the third Book of the *Essay,* Locke introduces the idea of "general signs," or words for classes of thoughts. By Shelley's day this idea comprised the standard explanation, variously attached to theories of progress and decline, of how language forgoes the direct reliance on things that was said to have characterized its earliest stage of development. Both

Wordsworth's "Preface" and Shelley's *Defence* react against the prevalency of general signs by calling for a return to the natural signs of language at its origin. Coleridge in the *Biographia* undermined Wordsworth's "real language of men" by pointing out that the *lingua communis* even of rustics is never prompted directly by nature but is always mediated either by reading, especially of the Bible, or by spoken models like that of the parish priest. Hence, he concludes wittily and truly, the language of nature began in the Schools. Not Coleridge, however, but a kind of undertow from within is what breaks down Shelley's Wordsworthian idea, similarly derived from the Enlightenment literature on the origin of language, that "in the infancy of society language itself is poetry" (Jordan, 30). All such formulas aim at the subordination of language to thought: in the beginning was the sense-impression. Wordsworth's position is at least consistent in that he takes the original language to have been plain-spoken, nonfigurative. For Shelley, on the other hand, if the originary language is "vitally metaphorical," then the first word was already, somehow, a transfer of sense from one word to another.[49] Thus, Shelley's view of language, held in spite of himself at times but at other times deliberately worked out, is ultimately that of Tooke and of Coleridge's refutation of Wordsworth, not that of Locke and Wordsworth. While wishing to preserve the truths of metaphysics, he is obliged to admit that their formulations are dead metaphors.

A second passage in the *Defence* which has the effect of bringing the deep truth to the surface is a commonplace made available to Shelley by the currency of such studies of ancient language and myth as Anathase Kircher's *Polygraphia Nova* (1663), Warburton's *Divine Legation of Moses* (1737–41), and, most recently, Drummond's *Oedipus Judaicus*. Poets both ancient and modern, writes Shelley, "have employed language as the hieroglyphic of their thoughts" (Jordan, 33). Here, in seeking a Romantic analogue, we find Coleridge on the side of natural signs after all; language at its origin is already arbitrary, yes, but used by the poet it *becomes* a repository of natural signs like the hieroglyphic Symbol which, in *The Statesman's Manual,* "always partakes of the reality which it renders intelligible."[50] Coleridge's Symbol and Shelley's hieroglyphic are invoked with the purpose of elevating language to a plane that is above its normal one. Both have the opposite effect, however, which consists in drawing the universe of reference down onto the plane of language. Shelley's hieroglyphic makes a sign of thought rather than the other way around.

Shelley's writings harbor plenty of other challenges to the binary concept of expression. There are the "signs" of Cythna which have already been noticed in this context by Yeats and Earl Wasserman, signs devised for making "a subtler language within language" (*The Revolt of Islam*; VII, 32, *Poetry,* p. 113).[51] And there is also the rarely noticed passage in the "Essay on Life" in which Shelley comes close to imagining the universe itself as a system of signs. Speaking solely of "the misuse of words and signs," he nevertheless offers a description of the world as it is perceived to which exceptions would be hard to find: "By signs, I would be understood in a wide sense, including what is properly meant by the term, and what I peculiarly mean. In this latter sense, almost all familiar objects are signs, standing not for themselves but for others in their capacity of suggesting one thought which shall lead to a train of thoughts" (*Prose,* 173–74). I do not mean to overlook the qualification expressed in "almost all familiar objects"; it is just these from which, in *The Statesman's Manual,* the Symbol redeems us and from which, in the *Defence,* the language of poetry lifts the veil. It should be clear by now, though, that for Shelley more continuously and graphically than for Coleridge, the lifted veil discloses another veil of like texture.

V

Shelley's idea of poetry "in a general sense," then, which is most often thought to derive unrevised from Wordsworth's "breath and finer spirit of all things," is not altogether vague; it can be understood with some precision as a colored region behind the colors of expression. Carefully considered, the difficult passage on the superiority of verbal poetry to the poetry of stone, sound, and so forth will support this view:

> Language, colour, form, and religious and civil habits of action, are all the instruments and materials of poetry; they may be called poetry by that figure of speech which considers the effect as a synonyme of the cause. But poetry in a more restricted sense expresses those arrangements of language, and especially metrical language, which are created by that imperial faculty, whose throne is curtained within the invisible nature of man. And this springs from the nature itself of language, which is a more direct representation of the actions and passions of our internal being, and is susceptible of more various and delicate combinations, than colour, form, or motion, and is more plastic and obedient to the control of that faculty of which it is the creation. For language is arbitrarily produced by the imagination and has relation to thoughts alone; but all other materials, instruments, and conditions of art, have relations among each other, which limit and interpose between conception and expression. The former is a mirror which reflects, the latter is a cloud which enfeebles, the light of which both are mediums of communication. (Jordan, 32–33)

When the mimetic mirror is trained inward, as it is here, and not upon phenomena, as it still is in the *Republic* and to some extent in *Hamlet,* the binary concept of expression is apt to be undermined rather than confirmed. The idea that thoughts could mirror things had been an unobtrusively figurative premise of the realistic tradition in English philosophy before

Locke. But to suggest that language can mirror thought, especially when the clarity of the reflection in that case is contrasted with the fogging of the mirror by everything else, is to suggest in turn that language reflects itself, or else something that closely resembles it.

But still, *all* the media are said here to participate, to a lesser extent, in thought. By a metonymy of cause and effect, says Shelley, they are all "poetry." Presumably, again, Shelley's "figure of speech" can be valid only if there is something poetry-*like* about the imagination, something that is itself a system of signification; similarly all the nonlinguistic media are also systems of signification, like the "things" of the *Treatise on Morals*. Their drawback, in contrast with language, is that even as systems they can only partly reflect the system of mind. Because as materials they can never be wholly transformed into conception, they continue to share the nature of what they represent more than that of what shapes them. Pigments taken from the earth are needed to paint a landscape; clay is used to mold a Venus whose human model has feet of clay herself, and so on. Thus in his "Notes on Sculptures in Rome and Florence" (1819; editor's title), Shelley looks at a statue representing Sleep and regrets that "the hardness of the stone does not permit the arriving at any great expression" (*Prose*, 352).

Poetry in the more restricted sense, on the other hand, touches upon the quasi-material world of dead metaphor called "fact" only insofar as it has ceased to be poetry in the general sense. As a linguistic medium it is in direct and exclusive communion with the power that is enthroned within and curtained from view. Thus it is most concealed just where it is most truly poetry, and for this reason its meaning can never be confidently uncovered by the interpreter. The imagination reveals different aspects of its hidden nature to different eras, but there is another kind of partiality involved as well: one or another worn-out code of perception will distort even that which is revealed. The spirit of revenge, "self-conceit," chivalry, and sensuality are four such codes, or frames of reference, that Shelley mentions. Each fresh insight shrivels and dries up the instant it is exposed, as it were, to the air and must be peeled away in its turn. Shelley hopes that this process will prove to have been cumulative but its admitted endlessness makes one wonder: "Veil after veil may be undrawn, and the inmost naked beauty of the meaning never exposed" (Jordan, 63). Two other sorts of nonprogressive distortion are guaranteed, in any case, by the passage of time. The first results from the failure of the historian to retain the whole truth concerning the facts, or non-poetry, of the past, and the second results, again, from the limitless partiality with which the imagination declares itself: "Time, which destroys the beauty and the use of the story of particular facts, stript of the poetry which should invest them, augments that of Poetry, and for ever develops new and wonderful applications of the eternal truth which it contains" (p. 36).

VI

Evidently for Shelley, as for Longinus, the reader who is engaged in the crucial, although imperfect, transmission of "eternal truth" from generation to generation plays the role of poet. A new facet of this truth must be presented as poetry at every new turn of history, otherwise the vitality of what is known and considered morally, scientifically, or legislatively binding will soon dwindle. Shelley hopes, again, that these changes will be progressive. Despite his clichés about the origin of language, he is no primitivist, as his "Essay on Christianity" makes clear: "Later and more correct observations [than those of the ancient mourners for the Golden Age] have instructed us that uncivilized man is the most pernicious and miserable of beings and that the violence and injustice which are the genuine indications of real inequality obtain among these beings without mixture and without palliation" (*Prose,* 211). To come to Shelley's most famous hyperbole: The progress that culture owes to poetry and that poetry in turn partakes in consists in the forging of ever new and better legislation. Shelley's favorite example of how this progress works is the literature of "chivalry" in the Middle Ages, mainly that of Dante, which advanced the condition both of slaves and of women toward equality (viz., Jordan, 59).

Shelley thus agrees with Peacock concerning the progress of society, differing only as to its causes. Institutionalized laws, whether scientific, moral, or political, cannot change, in his view, because they are inert. They can be altered only from without, by revolution or by some kind of revolutionary poetry. Wishing to discover this process at large in the world, the startling misinformed Shelley wrote late in 1819, in *A Philosophical View of Reform,* that in America "there is a law by which the constitution is reserved for revision every ten years" (*Prose,* 234). Poetry is also a law that repeals laws. So when Shelley writes of reactionaries who "are willing to think things that are rusty and decayed venerable," he is thinking at the same time of a mental state in which language has become an inflated currency, "dead to all the nobler purposes of human intercourse," that is revered more and more as the repository of ceremonial forms and unimportant facts. It is in this spirit that Nelson Goodman asks, "Is a metaphor . . . simply a juvenile fact and a fact simply a senile metaphor?"[52]

Poetry "creates anew the universe, after it has been annihilated in our minds by the recurrence of impressions blunted by reiteration" (Jordan, 75), and thus poetry constantly struggles against the senescence of culture. It is with this purpose in mind that Shelley adopts the Renaissance conceit of the poet as creator. With Sidney in the background and a quotation from Tasso ready to hand (*Non merita nome di creatore, se non Iddio ed il Poeta*), Shelley turns this idea to his own use. We have seen that the poet's "creation" replaces an old set of *eidola* with new ones which in turn must be renewed.

For this reason Shelley's poet-creator is not exactly the secondary god of the Neoplatonists. He is much closer to the God of Descartes, a God who must sustain the universe by recreating it at every minute.[53] Although Shelley appears not to have been familiar with Descartes, he seems to have known him, and perhaps Spinoza, by osmosis. In a place where he cites Machiavelli so vaguely that scholars have not been able to find the reference, he says something decidedly Cartesian: "All language institution and form, require not only to be produced but to be sustained: the office and character of a poet participates [*sic*] in the divine nature as regards providence, no less than as regards creation" (Jordan, 48).

Of necessity poetry resembles revolution, and T. S. Eliot rightly identifies the *Defence* as "perhaps the first appearance of the kinetic or revolutionary theory of poetry."[54] The risorgimento that poetry affords must be iconoclastic and offer violence of some sort to existing orders. The "great secret of morals" may be Love, and love may indeed prove to be the poet's positive contribution to social history, but there is still, first and last, the present fabric of things to be undone, a veil to be *torn* aside. The innovation required of the poet is technical, furthermore, as well as prophetic: "Every great poet must inevitably innovate upon the example of his predecessors in the exact structure of his peculiar versification" (Jordan, 34). The need for variety is so pressing that most regular meters should be avoided, and the rhythm of prose writers who qualify as poets will scarcely amount to a prosody at all: "[Plato] forebore to invent any regular plan of rhythm which should include, under determinate forms, the varied pauses of his style" (p. 35). Thus whereas for Peacock versification, or "harmony," was a reactionary, precivilized kind of violence—"language on the rack of Procrustes"—versification for Shelley is a radical kind of violence carried out against the tyranny of the past. It is an aspect of the poet's adversary attitude toward his own age and toward the poets of the past.

Here recurs another theme of Longinus. Among other inspiring enemies the poet wrestles, as Longinus pointed out and Dryden repeated, with the mighty dead. The posture of the poet in Shelley is still more complex. On the one hand he represents the world, especially its "language, gesture, and . . . imitative arts," which thus "become at once the representation and the medium" (Jordan, 27); while on the other hand that same world, whether as the arena of language or as a language itself ("almost all familiar objects are signs"), is just what the poet must set out to destroy in the course of transforming it. "Sounds as well as thoughts," writes Shelley further on, "have relation both between each other and towards that which they represent" (p. 33). In other words, poetry is the record both of its stimulus and of its response, which latter must be, to some extent at least, a reaction-formation. The recorded stimulus, consisting of all influences including those of the past, comprises the continuity of poetry with the past, while the recorded response is the answer of the individual to those influences. This has always been so, even where the answer is not violent but only a playful emulation: "A child at play by itself will express its delight by its voice and motions; and every inflexion of tone and every gesture will bear exact relation to a corresponding antitype [i.e., prototype, not opposite] in the pleasurable impressions which awakened it; it will be the reflected image of that impression; and as the lyre trembles and sounds after the wind has died away, so the child seeks, by prolonging in its voice and motions the duration of the effect, to prolong also a consciousness of the cause" (p. 27).

Poetry reveals its influences by reacting to them, not by replicating them, but it always does reveal them. It is never isolated and independent. When Shelley writes in the Preface to *Prometheus Unbound* that "one great poet is a masterpiece of nature which another not only ought to study but must study" (*Prose,* 328), he seems to believe that study of this kind is a compulsion depriving duty of its merit. Apparently the great poet, being part of nature, can no more be resisted than the light of day. Quite frequently Shelley brackets nature and art with such equal attention that although they are supposed to be opposites, alternatives, they become in effect interchangeable, just as they were for Longinus. In choosing the best language, for example, one must be "familiar with nature" as well as "with the most celebrated productions of the human mind" (Preface to *Laon and Cythna, Prose,* 317) because, as we have seen, nature is a kind of language and language poetically used has the palpability of nature.

In this way the poet takes an adversary stance toward both nature and art. Even in descriptions that are solely aesthetic Shelley stresses the part played by resistance: "There is a principle within the human being, and perhaps within all sentient beings, which acts otherwise than in the lyre, and produces not melody alone, but harmony, by an internal adjustment of the sounds or motions thus excited to the impressions which excite them" (Jordan, 26–27). There is an element of salutary discord in this harmony; what is at issue for Shelley in such passages, as also for Socrates when he takes up the metaphor of "attunement" in the *Phaedo* (94c–95b), is nothing less than the autonomy of the "soul," or poetic faculty. The "internal adjustment" that makes a more complicated music possible has as its deeper function the manifestation of freedom. Hence true poetry by its very existence symbolizes the moral and political condition to which humanity can aspire. It is really for this reason, then, that the reaction of poetry to any and all impressions is in part adversary, "promethean." Poetry alone, apparently, can contradict the refrain of Shelley's metaphysical fragments, that "mind . . . cannot create, it can only perceive" ("Essay on Life," *Prose,* 174). However, this is a point that Shelley can never resolve, much as he would like to. The same argument may be used to deny the originality of poets that Shelley had often used, in his youth, to deny the divine origin of the universe: There must be "an infinity of creative and created gods, each more eminently requiring an intelligent author of his being than the foregoing" (*Prose,* 131).[55]

It is interesting that Shelley's liveliest expressions of cordiality toward the contributions of both nature and art to the poet appear in the "Preface" to the poem that most vividly dramatizes the tyranny of external and internal forces, *Prometheus Unbound.* Jupiter is a patriarchal tyrant, and only the assertion of the enchained Prometheus that Jupiter exists by his sufferance, that the tyrant is a created embodiment of his own mind, can change the existing order. Thus although Jupiter plays the father, Prometheus the Titan is really the older of the two. This conflict over precedence seems at first to be a stalemate, leaving the two gods as coevals sustaining each other with their mutual hate. Displacing his unusually intense dislike of fathers, Shelley tends in general to concentrate on fraternal rivalries for the palm of originality.[56] Thus it is not the past but the present that makes a poet: "A poet is the combined product of such internal powers as modify the nature of others; and of such external influences as excite and sustain these powers; he is not one, but both. Every man's mind is, in this respect, modified by all the objects of nature and art. . . . Poets, not otherwise than philosophers, painters, sculptors, and musicians, are, in one sense, the creators, and in another, the creations, of their age" (Preface to *Prometheus Unbound, Prose,* 328).[57]

Or, as he had put it in the earlier Preface to *Laon and Cythna,* each poet is, like Prometheus, "in a degree the author of the very influence by which his being is pervaded" (*Prose,* 318). Shelley's treatment of the freedom of the poet is always thus ambivalent. He can write about "Visionary rhyme,—in joy and pain / Struck from the inmost fountains of my brain" (*Letter to Maria Gisborne,* 168–69, *Poetry,* 367), but the figure is not persuasive. What is the source of the fountains? "Internal powers" are given, after all, as much as "external influences." In *Prometheus Unbound,* beyond all rivalries for preeminence there stands Demogorgon in the role of Necessity.

VII

Shelley's mentors at Oxford no doubt overlooked the fact that the word *necessity* in "The Necessity of Atheism" was not only a call to arms but the indication of an unavoidable conclusion in logic. Perhaps they would have found both implications equally pernicious, but had they noticed both, they would also have noticed that they contradict each other. These two senses of *necessity* anticipate Shelley's lifelong dilemma concerning the freedom of the will. An exhortation is made in the interest of some necessary moral good that may be freely pursued or rejected; a declaration of logical or practical necessity, on the other hand, enjoins no mode of action, supposing merely that what cannot be altered (here, the irrefutability of atheism) cannot properly be countered with persecution. Faced with this contradiction, most commentators suppose that Shelley was indeed a Necessitarian in his youth but later embraced the autonomy of the will under the influence of various transcendental ideas, the more willingly so because he must always have realized that a determinist cannot voluntarily support—or reject—social reform. Shelley never achieved this faith, however. At no time did he arrive at a theory of the autonomy of the poet or the integrity of the poem as an intended and achieved design.[58] What Shelley did succeed in doing, as we shall see, was to discriminate between lower and higher forms of determination. Both his poetics and his politics benefited from this distinction, but the alteration it effected upon his earlier view was at most a subtle one.

Shelley affirms the freedom of the will least hesitantly in the voice of personae like Julian in *Julian and Maddalo,* who is "passionately attached to those philosophical notions which assert the power of man over his own mind" ("Preface," *Prose,* 325). In general Shelley remains much closer, however, to such earlier assertions as this one in 1812: "Man cannot make occasions, but he may seize those that offer" ("Proposals for an Association," *Prose,* 60). Statements such as these only put off the problem of the will until a later stage of argument. Is one's grasp of an occasion voluntary? In the *Defence* Shelley will still be found worrying about this problem. Thus he speaks of "the Provençal Trouveurs, or inventors" (Jordan, 57), begging the question whether invention is active or passive. We still have no satisfactory answer to this question, which is raised again, knowingly, by Bruno Snell when he insists that the Greeks had to invent the intellect in order to discover it.[59]

Shelley wavers concerning the poetic will because he cannot decide what kind of connection there is between stimulus and response. Following Hume, he claims to have no reliable knowledge of the relation between cause and effect in general; he can only say with certainty that they are repeatedly contiguous events. It is simply not clear whether this skepticism affords a greater or a lesser degree of freedom to the poet in carrying out what I have called his reaction-formation. The child's reaction to stimuli seemed on consideration to be precisely dictated by them—"every inflexion of tone and every gesture will bear exact relation to a corresponding antitype in the pleasurable impressions that awakened it"—and yet the "chord" of the child's response, although apparently predetermined as to its structure, was still drawn from within and not plucked, as it were, by the impressions themselves. In addition, the staying power of the response plainly exceeded the force of the stimulus.

The two facets of the child's answering chord, the bound and the apparently unbound, are represented in isolation from each other, and thus in more open contradiction, elsewhere in Shelley's late writing. On the one hand there is this remark in a letter to the Gisbornes: "Poets, the best of them, are a very chamaeleonic race: they take the colour not only of what they feed on, but of the very leaves under which they pass" (*Letters*, II, 308).[60] On the other hand, there is the assertion in the *Defence* that "poetry defeats the curse which binds us to be subjected to the accidents of surrounding impressions" (Jordan, 74). From these passages and others like them two conclusions can be drawn. We can conclude that in creative activity there is a measure of independence from impressions, but this cannot be proved and will have to be accepted as an article of faith. Or, more circumspectly, and with more support, I think, from Shelley, we can conclude that there are two sorts of impression, one direct and one indirect, which comprise the whole of poetic inspiration. Indirect impressions, the ideas that appear to well up from within, leave us with at least the illusion of freedom.[61] Predetermination of this kind, if it exists, is so very indirect that it cannot be fathomed and need not affect the poet's sense of his role as an agent of reform.[62] "The word *liberty* as applied to mind," writes Shelley in a note to *Queen Mab*, "is analogous to the word *chance* as applied to matter: they spring from ignorance of the certainty of the conjunction of antecedents and consequents" (*Prose*, 109).

One source of indirect impressions, undermining voluntarism but hardly to be compared with direct stimuli, is the unconscious. Shelley's extraordinary picture of the mind in his *Treatise on Morals* resembles Keats's Chamber of Maiden-Thought, the mental landscape of *Kubla Khan*, and the child psychology of Wordsworth in "Tintern Abbey." It also evokes Shelley's own complex odes to Power of 1816. In short, it is a summa of Romantic conjectures about the dark side of the mind and deserves to be better known. People should not attach certainty to their opinions in metaphysics, says Shelley, because they cannot know their own minds well enough to judge their biases. It were best if they "beheld their own reflections and, in dim perspective, their shadowy hopes and fears—all that they dare not, or that daring and desiring, they could not expose to the open eyes of day. But thought can with difficulty visit the intricate and winding chambers which it inhabits. It is like a river whose rapid and perpetual stream flows outwards—like one in dread who speeds through the recesses of some haunted pile and dares not look behind. The caverns of the mind are obscure and shadowy; or pervaded with a lustre, beautifully bright indeed, but shining not beyond their portals" (*Prose*, 185–86).[63]

From these regions the visitations of inspiration and poetry come. Like the lady in *Alastor*, they may be inward or outward in their origin, but regardless of their source, they are imperatives, compulsions, that drive the poet along his course. In being clearly higher than, or at least other than, the data of sense, these visitants offer an escape from the materialistic determinism that had made all "beautiful idealisms" too obviously chimerical for the young Shelley. They may still be sublimations, but now at least their connection with the instinctual basis of desire is concealed. Here then are two levels of determination, duly distinguished, in the "Essay on Christianity": "Our most imperial and stupendous qualities—those on which the majesty and power of humanity is erected—are, relatively to the inferior portion of its mechanism, indeed active and imperial; but they are the passive slaves of some higher and more omnipresent Power. The Power is God" (*Prose*, 202).

VIII

Having first argued that the inspiration consisting of thoughts and the expression consisting of words or other media do not differ in kind but only in degree, and having then argued, in the last few pages, that the poet's inspiration is not autonomous but consists in two kinds of influence, I shall now attempt to bring these two contentions together. I shall try to show that for Shelley, as also for Longinus and Dryden, Hermes and Urania are the same divinity. In *Paradise Lost,* Milton tactfully provides the reader with more than one way of accounting for his inspiration, saying that Urania either "dictates to me slumbering, or inspires / Easie my unpremeditated Verse" (bk. IX, 23–24). That is, either she puts words in his mouth or else she enables him to invent his own words, albeit unreflectingly. In slightly misquoting this passage, Shelley leaves out the alternative he himself is usually said to espouse, the one that leaves the poet at least a shadow of originary power. We have Milton's "authority," says Shelley, "for the Muse having 'dictated' to him the 'unpremeditated song' " (Jordan, 72). The difference is clear, and it is characteristic of Shelley. We have already noted a good many places in which Shelley seems to say that poetry is inspired by poetry.

Because he has made the distinction between higher and lower determinations, Shelley can emphasize the operations of the will without misgivings while at the same time denying that it has the power of origination. So it is that without severe contradiction he can list certain principles in the *Defence* that are "alone capable of affording the motives according to which the will of a social being is determined to action" (Jordan, 28). In other words these principles shape and determine the mind before the mind can claim to have constituted them for its own purposes. They *are* the inspiration that "acts in a divine and unapprehended manner, beyond and above consciousness" (p. 37), and their anticipation of the mind's control explains why poetry "has no necessary connexion with consciousness or will" (p. 77). These "principles" are "equality, diversity, unity, contrast, mutual dependence" (p. 28). Together they comprise not only the fundamental ties of man in society but also the principles of both syntax and poetic meter. There is a sense, thus, in which mind itself, in its poetic and its moral operations alike, is shaped and informed by language or by a system like a language.

There are two well-known passages in *Prometheus Unbound* that seem to assert the priority of language among the operations of mind. The first, from the Earth's hymn to Man ("one harmonious Soul of many a soul"), makes language the demiurge of thought, if not exactly its forerunner:

> Language is a perpetual Orphic song,
> Which rules with Daedal harmony a throng
> Of thoughts and forms, which else senseless
>   and shapeless were.
>
>   (IV, 415–17)[64]

The analogy between the rule of language over thought and Ocean's rule over the "unpastured Sea hung'ring for Calm"—a "Monster" (III, ii, 48–49)—suggests that language in Shelley's drama is a means both of actualization and of government. The chief emblem of its power is the curse that was once voiced and is now revoked by Prometheus. The second passage that is pertinent in this regard is from Asia's description of Prometheus's gifts to man in compensation for Jupiter's having put an end to the happy ignorance of the Golden Age:

> He gave man speech, and speech created thought,
> Which is the measure of the Universe;
> And Science struck the thrones of Earth and Heaven
> Which Shook but fell not; and the harmonious mind
> Poured itself forth in all-prophetic Song.
>
>   (II, iv, 72–76)

Here, more clearly, language precedes thought—which is to say, it is thought itself. The whole of the *Prometheus* is a pagan reinvention of the divine *Logos* and its fruits.

"All the inventive arts," writes Shelley in his "Discourse on the Manners of the Ancient Greeks," are "no more than various expressions of one internal power . . . either of an individual, or of society" (*Prose,* 217). In society this power is the Spirit of the Age, while in the individual it is creative genius, but the force that infuses both in common in Shelley's later thinking is a kind of demiurge,[65] the Greek *nous.* So too Coleridge, in a manuscript note to *The Statesmen's Manual,* calls his transcendental Reason the *nous,* in contrast to *gnosis,* which Shelley would have identified with the mechanistic "reason"—or, in Coleridge's parlance, the understanding.[66] It is widely assumed, I think rightly, that Shelley's idea of the creative *nous*—and perhaps Coleridge's too—derives from the *Timaeus* (28ab, 36de, and especially 44b), in which language also seems to enable thought: when the soul becomes accustomed to its mortal body, "the several circles return to their natural form and their revolutions are corrected, and they call the same and the other by their right names and make the possessor of them [i.e., the circles] to become a rational being" (44b; trans. Jowett).

Now, to "call the same and the other by their right names" means, I take it, that through the articulation of difference in its various forms (e.g., Shelley's list of "principles") the agencies of the soul can parcel out the world syntagmatically. This then is the primary activity of mind in general. Individuality would simply be the lodging in each person of somewhat different segments of the divine *semiosis*. In Shelley's "Essay on Christianity," this view of individuality corresponds to that of Bacon's cave, which Shelley hoped to expose to the light in refuting Peacock: "Every human mind has what Lord Bacon calls its *idola specus*, peculiar images which reside in the inner cave of thought" (*Prose*, 199). The determination of personality by these several images becomes more clearly a tyranny when Shelley describes the mechanics of stock response: "We combine words, combined a thousand times before. In our minds we assume entire opinions; and in the expression of those opinions, entire phrases, when we would philosophize. Our whole style of expression and sentiment is infected with the tritest plagiarisms. Our words are dead, our thoughts are cold and borrowed" (*Treatise on Morals, Prose*, 184). Shelley would have it that this is just the state of affairs that the creative demiurge will revolutionize, but in his writing, with unusual consistency, the originary language remains simply a more dynamic version of the derivative one.

Being One, the language of the *nous*, like that of "poetry in the general sense," transcends subject–object relations. This is one reason that it allegedly cannot be pigeonholed, unlike the language of individuals, which imposes perspectives of vision merely by virtue of being grammatical: "The words *I, you, they* are not signs of any actual difference subsisting between the assemblage of thoughts thus indicated, but are merely marks employed to denote the different modifications of the one mind" ("On Life," *Prose*, 174). It is with reference to this plane and this plane only, I believe, that Shelley is preoccupied with unity. Our thoughts have a natural bias toward reunion with all the thoughts from which they are distinguished in being ours, but they cannot achieve unification without sacrificing the signature that makes them ours. To acknowledge the will to unity in Shelley, then, is still not to accept Wasserman's presentation of him as a Coleridgean enthusiast in behalf of organic form. When Shelley distinguishes between "a story and a poem" in the *Defence,* this being its most Aristotelian moment, he affirms the universality of the "poem" but *not* its wholeness; to do that, in light of the discussion of grammatical person in "On Life," would be mistakenly to proclaim the identity of mind and Mind. For Shelley, the perception that there is even a connection between the many and the one is itself, if it is vividly achieved, the profoundest act of which the individual imagination is capable.

A "poem," in any case, is "the creation of actions according to the unchangeable forms of human nature, as existing in the mind of the creator, which is itself the image of all other minds" (Jordan, 36). One model of the individual mind that proposes itself in this context is the proto-Jungian one described by Yeats in his essay on Shelley: "Our little memories are but a part of some great memory that renews the world and men's thoughts age after age."[67] An objection to this way of putting it, however, must be that in Shelley it is not as evident as it might be whether each mind is fully contained within the one Mind. Shelley speaks too often of the "visitation" of Power, of Intellectual Beauty, and so on, for the notion of the mind's containment by whatever it is that houses these agencies to seem quite plausible. In imagining that creative power surges up from within us, as he also sometimes does, Shelley evokes the "fountain," but this metaphor is not easy to reconcile with the more common metaphor of the wind—which is needed to fan the fading coal. Wherever these tropes clash with each other, the problem of the will, of poetic autonomy, is still making itself felt: "The mind in creation is a fading coal, which some invisible influence, like an inconstant wind, awakens to transitory brightness: this power arises from within" (Jordan, 71).

Possibly this contradiction can be set aside or made at least to seem less blatant if we introduce yet a third way of describing the mind's bearing toward its inspiration. Godwin's *Mandeville,* wrote Shelley late in 1817, "is a wind which tears up the deepest waters of the ocean of mind" (*Prose,* 311). This is either a wind that make furrows in the ocean or else, like the wind in the *Ode to the West Wind* two years later, it is a responsive wind that blows along the floor of the ocean in sympathy with the wind in the sky. I think that it is the former; Shelley was still in England when he wrote this review and had not yet taken the boat excursion on "Baiae Bay" that was to furnish the submarine imagery of the Ode.[68] Supposing Shelley to be describing the kind of wind that makes ripples, the review of Godwin can then be said to anticipate and reinforce the passage in the *Defence* which is in many ways more interesting, and is certainly more consistent, than the one about the fading coal:

> We are aware of evanescent visitations of thought and feeling . . . always arising unseen and departing unbidden, but elevating and delightful beyond expression: so that even in desire and the regret they leave, there cannot but be pleasure, participating as it does in the nature of the object. It is as it were the interpretation of a diviner nature through our own; but its footsteps are like those of a wind over a sea,

which the coming calm erases, and whose traces remain only, as on the
wrinkled sand which paves it. (Jordan, 72)

Whatever this experience may be like at the moment when it happens, in the
memory it becomes a sense of having been written upon or imprinted by
some force. In light of these observations, possibly the most precise notion
to be arrived at concerning the relation between mind and Mind, especially
if one recalls the dictation of Milton's Muse, is that the Mind makes a verbal
impression on the mind, leaving "eternal truths charactered upon the
imaginations of men" (p. 66).

This notion lends accuracy to still another of those Shelleyan topics that
are generally dismissed as grandiose and vague, namely, the "great cyclic
poem."[69] Thus for example Shelley may mean something very precise when
he describes the great actions of the Roman epoch as "episodes of the cyclic
poem written by time on the memories of men" (Jordan, 52). Now, from
Shelley's correct use of the term *cyclic poets* elsewhere (p. 41) in reference to
Homer and the other authors of the Trojan Cycle, we can assume that he has
a "restricted" as well as a "general" sense of the "cyclic poem" in mind—
and that, like the two senses of *poetry,* these two poems are meant to be
linked as effect and cause. The Greek cyclic poets in effect compiled an
encyclopedic chronicle that was the main source of education and inspiration for those who came after it. Because Shelley evidently knew this, it can
be assumed that in the sentence "Homer and the cyclic poets were followed
at a certain interval by the dramatic and lyrical poets of Athens," the word
followed has the slightly obsolete sense of "imitated" as well as "succeeded."
From this evidnce it can be deduced that Shelley's more figurative references
to the cyclic poem will evoke a pattern, or model, in which specific poems
are already implicit.

As Eric Havelock argues in his *Preface to Plato,* the cyclic poem supplies its
readers with a *lexis* and with a mnemotechnic. Shelley begins his *Treatise on
Morals* in a comparable vein by arguing that the One Mind is an exhaustive
chronicle containing all the ideas that all other minds can ever have: "A
catalogue of all the thoughts of the mind and of all their possible modifications is a cyclopaedic history of the Universe" (*Prose,* 182). The phrase
possible modifications indicates that the history is written before the fact. This
vocabulary characterizes the cyclic poem in the restricted sense. What
shows once again that organic unity is not the property of any given work
of art is that each actual poem will necessarily be a fragment of the poem it
refers itself to. Despite the waggish mood of the Dedication to *Peter Bell the
Third* (1819), Shelley can be seen there to outline a theory of literary history
that corresponds to that of the *Defence*:

Allow me to observe that so much has been written of Peter Bell that
the present history can be considered only, like the *Iliad,* as a continua-

tion of that series of cyclic poems, which have already been candidates for bestowing immortality upon, at the same time that they receive it from, his character and adventures. In this point of view I have violated no rule of syntax in beginning my poem with a conjunction; the full stop which closes the poem continued by me being, like the full stops at the end of the *Iliad* and the *Odyssey,* a full stop of a very qualified import. (*Prose,* 321)

This passage is the best gloss for Shelley's treatment of the Greek bucolic poets in the *Defence.* Their poems are "episodes," he says, resembling in this the actions of the great Romans. They are also preordained, both because they furnish one note in the chord of poetic possibility (the epic and dramatic modes furnish others) and also because they are fully anticipated by the gentler moments of Homer himself—his pastoral similes, his erotic interludes, and so on. All these factors bear directly on what Shelley says about the Greek idylls. Those for whom they were written "may have perceived the beauty of these immortal compositions simply as fragments and isolated portions; those who are more finely organized, or born in a happier age, may recognize them as episodes to that great poem, which all poets, like the co-operating thoughts of one great mind, have built up since the beginning of the world" (Jordan, 51).

In Peacock's "Four Ages," the cyclic poem, with its record of everything knowable, is crudely anticipated in his Iron Age, but it is distinguished in quality as well as being culturally important only in the Golden Age, that is, in the age of Homer: "All men love to look back into the days that are past. In these circumstances traditional national poetry is reconstructed and brought like chaos into order and form" (ibid., p. 7). For Shelley on the other hand, poetry at its most seminal cannot become anachronistic: "All high poetry is infinite; it is as the first acorn, which contained all oaks potentially" (p. 63). This exalted notion refers us to the "extended sense" of the cyclic poem, but it still retains more precision than one would think. Shelley repeatedly calls actual poems "immortal"; they are so insofar as they participate in that "poem" which is not just their soul or spirit but, more precisely, the preexistent mode of their writing, their genre. The *Paradiso* is "a perpetual hymn of everlasting love" (p. 58), a hymn like that of the angels, in other words, that is eternally sung.

Thus it is not really his own poem that a poet writes. The bird in the "Ode to a Skylark" is "Like a poet hidden / In the light of thought, / Singing hymns unbidden" (*Poetry,* 602); the bird is not compared to the poet who sits pen in hand, but to the poet hidden within the poet, dictating unpremeditated song. Shelley's "nightingale" in the *Defence,* "who sits in darkness and sings to cheer its own solitude with sweet sounds," is similarly hidden. If we refer this passage back to its source in Milton, the bird more clearly becomes the voice of a tradition singing through its chosen vessel, the Poet:

> nor sometimes forget
> Those other two equall'd with me in Fate,
> So were I equall'd with them in renown,
> Blind *Thamyris* and blind *Maeonides,*
> And *Tiresias* and *Phineus* Prophets old.
> Then feed on thoughts, that voluntary move
> Harmonious numbers; as the wakeful Bird
> Sings darkling, and in shadiest covert hid
> Tunes her nocturnal Note.
>
> (*Paradise Lost,* III, 32–40)

In all these passages, starting with the one about the Greek bucolic poets, both the singer and the auditors are blind. The predetermined nature of the singer's unpremeditated prophecies is in some measure concealed from him, both to preserve his illusion of freedom and in order to "temper this planetary music for mortal ears" (Jordan, 39). The auditors in their turn cannot see the hidden singer; they neglect him and overlook the value of his hymnody because they are blind to its celestial origin.

At its *most* extended, Shelley's cyclic poem refers not to any poetic tradition but to the Pythagorean planetary music: "Listen to the music, unheard by outward ears, which is as a ceaseless and invisible wind, nourishing its everlasting course with strength and swiftness" (p. 55). It is most significant that in a draft note Shelley criticizes this passage: "But this is not argument—not illustration" (p. 55n.). *Caveat lector:* clearly he feels that other and equally vague-sounding passages actually do function as arguments with legitimate frames of reference, whereas the present passage, he says, really *is* too vague. For the moment he has permitted his concept of poetic truth to float into an ether where it can no longer be identified as a mode of signification in its own right. More adequately imagined, even celestial harmony should be an avatar of actual language: thus the "periods" of all poets—and prose poets—"are harmonious and rhythmical, and contain in themselves the elements of verse; being the echo of the eternal music" (p. 35).

It is difficult to think about Shelley's "cyclic poem" without calling to mind its latter-day equivalent in T. S. Eliot: "The whole of the literature of Europe from Homer . . . has a simultaneous existence and composes a simultaneous order."[70] Also similar is the "aesthetic horizon" elaborated by recent German theorists of literary reception. In each formulation the literary field is a totality prior to the appearance of each new work, a totality which the new work, if it *is* new, then subtly reorders. For H. R. Jauss and his compeers this change is called the *Horizontswandel;* for Eliot "the *whole* existing order must be, if ever so slightly, altered" by "the supervention of novelty" (*Sacred Wood*, p. 50); and for Shelley, finally, what is new effects a change necessarily,[71] although its effect may be canceled if the novelty turns out to be ephemeral. Thus in 1817 Shelley read Apuleius with excitement, but he suspected that "this light will pass away, & when I am at a sufficient distance from this new planet, the constellations of literature will reappear in their natural groupes" (*Letters*, I, 542). Once more, thinking of this kind evidently understands the whole of literature and only that whole to comprise an "order." Each new work is a fragmentary contribution. During the last few decades, a period in which the literary work has been highly valued as an autonomous object, the fact that there is no aesthetic of the whole to be found in Shelley has been noticed more often by those who criticize the *Defence* than by those who like it. M. H. Abrams distastefully observes that individual poems are viewed by Shelley "as though they were fundamentally simultaneous and inter-convertible,"[72] and René Wellek objects that in Shelley's hands "Poetry loses its identity completely."[73]

In the same vein Wellek also remarks, perhaps sympathetically recalling the unfortunate social history of the Russian Formalists, that Shelley's "great cyclic poem" is a "collectivist" idea (*History of Literary Criticism*, II, 128). This observation will serve to clarify the quasi-linguistic attributes of poetic inspiration in Shelley somewhat further. What brings new poems into being is not exactly the sum of existing poems; these are all isolated, in Shelley's metaphor, as constellated stars. What accounts most fully for the new poem is the collectively shared medium that all poems have in common, the existing language itself. Although this notion of a *langue* that dictates the poet's *parole* looks new-fangled, I have been trying to show— and not only in reference to Shelley—that it is not. It is a view that was very precisely worked out in Shelley's time by Horne Tooke, and before him, more diffusely, by Enlightenment theorists of the origin of language. It is from these sources, I think, that Shelley derives a passage in the *Defence* that will certainly seem enigmatic until it is viewed in the manner suggested here: "Every original language near to its source is in itself the chaos of a cyclic poem" (Jordan, 30).

IX

In the foregoing discussion I have maintained that there is a functional equivalence, if not in all cases perfect synonymity, between a number of key terms in Shelley's thought, even though some of these terms belong traditionally to the domain of feeling, spirit, and thought while others belong to that of the signifying media. These terms are: mind, power, imagination, the "great cyclic poem," and language. The three former terms are not opposed to the two latter; rather the whole cluster offsets a group of terms that have likewise traditionally been distributed between the two categories of signified and signifier. These are: mechanism, calculation, reason, lexicography, and grammar. To all these terms there should be added another, Time, which belongs essentially in the domain of imagination but has a dual nature that allows it to mediate more easily than any other term between imagination and reason. Its doubleness comes from Shelley's conviction that the universe had no beginning, that there was no time, in other words, when time was not. Hence the single word, *Time,* indicates eternity in some places and temporality in others. Time is Shelley's ultimate "destroyer and preserver" for this reason. If time destroys the vitality and novelty of language, it is also the "redeemer" that brings new language into being. If its accidental vestures cover up the truth of poetry, it is also that which "writes the great cyclic poem."

Thus time is the medium of all media and imposes its nature on every form of expression. If in its eternal moment (to borrow a theological concept) time is the medium in which the universal harmony is suspended, in its aspect as sequence time obscures the universal by reducing all forms to linearity. Here again is Shelley's paradox of the veils. His most profound contribution to a philosophical basis for poetics, a contribution that can be found also in Longinus and Dryden, is his having questioned the dualism at the heart of most accounts of knowledge and creation: content and form, thought and expression, truth and verification, and so on. The reason for his questioning, which was not congenial to him and in the long run only vexed him, is that Shelley had an acute and in some ways tragic sense of being immersed, saturated, in temporality. Under the unremitting erasure of time, the cognitive process cannot in actuality have two sides because the allegedly stabler side constantly slides, as Horne Tooke says, "under the other." This sense, or sensation, accounts for the *manner* of Shelley's poetry, for the flurries of partly successive, partly aggregative images and for the prismatic, kaleidescopic fragmentation of vision. The spirit of his skepticism, an essentially lyrical impulse that nevertheless qualifies his idealism, is much closer to that of Heraclitus than that of Pyrrho or Hume.

His thinking is unstable because it is rigorous enough to remain in suspense between ideas of order and ideas of diffusion. On the one hand, the unifying tendency of his work sets at defiance the isolation of the individual; it is indeed "collectivist," both spiritually and socially. On the other hand, his awareness that we receive and make use of knowledge piecemeal until we lose ourselves in its veils returns the individual to his isolation, with no objective basis for coherence or for a definite place in any "history" that could be fully or systematically grasped. Here again, in the *Defence,* is time presented in its two aspects: "Time, which destroys the beauty and the use of the story of particular facts, stript of the poetry which should invest them, augments that of Poetry, and for ever develops new and wonderful applications of the eternal truths which it contains" (Jordan, 36).

X

Far more than Longinus or Dryden, Shelley resists the atomistic conclusion that being is merely being in the world. The formula of his resistance is the most central and also the most willful reduction in the *Defence,* the one the implicitly equates love with metaphor.[74] It is a daring and instructive reduction in that obviously it could not have been thought in the hylomorphic terms of most critical theory. As Shelley's most entrenched idol, however, it is also naive because it forgets temporality and implies that in the world of tropes and the world of persons alike a truly simultaneous union is possible.

I shall begin to sketch in the concept of love as metaphor by returning to the passage in the *Defence* declaring that "every original language near to its source is itself the chaos of a great cyclic poem." This moment near the source of language crucially determines the shape and values of social life forever after: "The social sympathies, or those laws from which, as from its elements, society results, begin to develop themselves from the moment that two human beings coexist" (Jordan, 28). This is just the time, of course, when language becomes necessary, and at this same time what Shelley calls "laws" are established once for all, quite irrespective of the coming and going of institutions. Shelley had arrived at this concept, with the help of Godwin and Paine, as early as 1812: "Government cannot make a law; it can only pronounce that which was the law before its organization; viz., the moral result of the imperishable relations of things" ("A Declaration of Rights," *Prose,* 71). Apparently those who made this law were those two coexisting human beings whose exploitation of the first tools and utterance of the first words were, as I have suggested, on much the same order of signification. Peacock would have agreed that these persons were perforce poets. He even calls them, among other things, "legislators" (Jordan, 6).[75] Shelley differs, again, in calling all poets, not just the first poets, "the institutors of laws" (p. 31). He refuses "to resign the civic crown to reasoners and mechanists" (p. 63).

What sort of law does Shelley have in view? Never allowing a place for law in the institutional or political sphere, Shelley confines it solely to the sphere of moral relations. He really has only one law in mind: "Love is celebrated everywhere [in *Laon and Cythna*]," he writes in the preface to that poem, "as the sole law which should govern the moral world" (*Prose,* 320). This is to say, as Shelley said in the *Defence,* that "the great secret of morals is love" (Jordan, 40). By "love," it is clear that Shelley means everything from the various definitions of it in the *Symposium* to the "wedded bliss" of Milton. But it is difficult to see at first how poetry as Shelley understands it can promote, much less constitute, the presence of love in the world. On reflection, however, it will appear that poetry performs these functions both with its themes and with its mode of rhetoric, perhaps more profoundly with the latter.

To turn first to themes, an instance of *non*-poetry for Shelley is the reasoning of Malthus, which Shelley particulalry abhorred despite appreciating the political economist's analytic skill (see *Letters,* II, 43). There is little doubt that what Shelley most disliked about Malthus was not his advocacy of birth control per se, though that in itself was objectionable,[76] but his disapproval of contraception and recommendation of abstinence. Malthus's calculated repudiation of the "human tie" that binds society together was a fit emblem, for Shelley, of the conduct of that faculty which typically murders to dissect. Poetry by contrast celebrates love. If I may cite an example of my own, Virgil turns to a new Muse, Erato, in book VII of the *Aeneid* in order to describe preparations for war and for what might otherwise seem a loveless marriage, and all other epics after Virgil to an increasing degree make erotic relations the microcosm of their account of the whole social fabric. The lyric desires, celebrates, or mourns the bliss of union, whether spiritual or erotic; and the modern drama, as Shelley says (surprisingly echoing Dryden's *Essay of Dramatic Poesy* in this regard), is superior to the ancient drama at least in having made love its main theme.

However, these thematic evidences do not sufficiently explain the radical equivalence of poetry, love, and law that Shelley insists upon. If poets' representations of love were in themselves efficacious, they would be *acknowledged* legislators. Readers who condescend toward the proclamation that poets are "the unacknowledged legislators of the world" (Jordan, 80) think that Shelley is having a final dig at reviewers who abuse and neglect poets like himself. Perhaps he does mean this to some extent but it would make no sense whatever for him to mean it primarily; in that case he might as well confess outright that his *Defence* is a failure and let Peacock carry off the palm. But the *Defence of Poetry* is not, in fact, an expression of longing for some impossible realm of poet-kings. Rather it concerns, in the main, what Shelley takes to be an actual and constantly operative power of poetry that is unacknowledged because it is unnoticed by everyone, including the poets themselves, whose "words . . . express what they understand not" (ibid.). Thus it is not quite fair to say that Shelley's essay reflects "the sentimental or Utopian idealizing of the mere communication of kindness and love."[77] Shelley is getting at a quality that is more integral to the nature of poetry itself.

It is not much kinder to declare ironically, with J. Bronowski, that for Shelley "the imagination is the act of feeling at one with one's neighbor,"[78] but Bronowski's witticism does help to show what Shelley means in calling poetry the law of love. It is true that Shelley conceives love to be the perception of likeness to oneself in others: "There is something within us which, from the instant that we live, more and more thirsts after its likeness" ("On Love," *Prose*, 170). This is the idea that lends drama to Shelley's lyrics, from *Alastor* to *Epipsychidion*; it justifies his recurrent treatment of incest and hermaphroditism, and it also prompts the apology for homosexuality in his "Discourse on the Manners of the Ancient Greeks, Relative to the Subject of Love." On all these occasions, says Shelley in the "Discourse," an "archetype" to be desired exists in "the mind which selects among those who resemble it that which most resembles it" (*Prose*, 220). The soberest formulation of this idea is probably that of Hume's *Treatise of Human Nature*: "The stronger the relation is betwixt ourselves and any object, the more easily does the imagination make the transition, and convey to the related idea the vivacity of conception, with which we always form the idea of our own person."[79] It has been suggested that one reason for Shelley's having given up the atomistic materialism of philosophers like Holbach is that such a view afforded no basis for social cohesion; hence "with the discovery of the immaterial philosophy [of Berkeley, according to this critic] this terrible separateness of persons vanished."[80]

Be this as it may, poetic thinking for Shelley is, as Northrop Frye has explained it, "the dialectic of love: it treats whatever it encounters as another form of itself."[81] Frye adds that this thinking is "never abstract: abstraction is the product of a repetition of experience without fresh thought" (*Study of Romanticism*, p. 122). In other words, abstraction is the dessication of figures that is the special province of reason. Something similar may be said of vagueness, though its source is apt to be unrefined feeling rather than the intellect. Shelley himself is neither abstract nor vague, nor is the poetry, as he describes it, that legislates love. His theory of poetry as love has been most succinctly described by Frye: "Love still has for Shelley a great deal of its earlier speculative associations with attraction, an association still preserved in our word 'like.' 'Like' is the sign of analogy, and analogy is a weakened form of the identity which is the fulfillment of love" (ibid., p. 124).

Love is the perception of similitude in dissimilitude of which the emblem and vehicle is metaphor. Aristotle had likewise said that tragedy concerns the relationship of *philoi* and that metaphor, which is the mark of a good poet, is the perception of similitude in dissimilitude. We must now consider how it is that Aristotle, presumably in an opposite camp, could so much resemble Shelley in this regard. Admittedly the line is fine between a poetic of wholeness and a poetic of the grace beyond the reach of art; the enormous polemical gulf between these two positions is in fact probably a relaxation into pathos of the intellectual strain that is needed in order to maintain the actual and proper distance between them. Both viewpoints are worthless, furthermore, unless they carry with them a very full acknowledgment of the role played by the opposite viewpoint in their own critical procedures. But the difference remains crucial; it is the difference between repression and its relative absence. Shelley's *Defence* is also a psychic "defence," it is true, but it is less defensive by far than the *Poetics*. Whereas Aristotle had said that crimes between *philoi* make the best tragic subjects, Shelley remarked in a letter that incest is "a very poetical circumstance" (*Letters,* II, 154).[82] The difference between these observations is twofold. First, Aristotle does not acknowledge the presence of the incest motif in the crimes he catalogs, and second, he always supposes those crimes, even in their slightly inhibited reflections, to be intrinsically tragic. Shelley on the other hand hesitates to call them crimes, approaching them affirmatively or negatively depending on their literary context, as in *Laon and Cythna* and *The Cenci,* respectively.

The danger of a taboo, then, resides in the likeness on which Aristotle's formalism is based. In Shelley's *Defence* there is no such danger. It is possible for him to describe the connection between the microcosm of poetic figures and the macrocosm of likeness in love by referring to exactly the incestuous situation that Aristotle banishes from view. Recalling the time of Dante, Shelley writes, "The freedom of women produced the poetry of sexual love. . . . The familiar appearance and proceedings of life became wonderful and heavenly; and a paradise was created out of the wrecks of Eden. And as this creation itself is poetry, so its creators were poets; and language was the instrument of their art: 'Galeotto fù il libro, e chi lo scrisse' " (Jordan, 57). The allusion is, of course, to the illicit union of Francesca and her brother-in-law, a renewed fortunate fall—from the Romantic standpoint—reflecting that of the incestuous Adam and Eve. The love of Paolo and Francesca points to a likeness not only between Lancelot and Guinevere but also between readers and those they read about. The go-between is language, and its message concerns the perfect happiness of mankind in the absence of institutional restraint.

Needless to say, this is going too far. Shelley's unwillingness to endure things as they are, the weakness nearly everyone has held against him, really does restrict his view of poetry in the end. Poetry and the criticism of poetry are not only dialectics of love; they are more comprehensively to be described as dialectics of likeness and difference within which it is crucially necessary to register dissimilitude. The only danger is that the poet's or critic's eye for difference will harden into the formulas of unqualified contrast and mutual exclusion. Early in his career as a pamphleteer Shelley took a duly circumspect view of perception: "The laws of nature perpetually act by disorganization and reproduction, each alternately becoming cause and effect" (*Prose,* 68–69). A little more of this balance would have usefully qualified Shelley's hymn to the union of spirits in the *Defence*. Still, Shelley's naiveté must not be overstressed. Unlike Coleridge, whose mind is in most ways subtler than Shelley's but whose aesthetic refers all considerations to a single Kantian machine, Shelley does understand the awareness we must retain, as creators and perceivers, of having been cast adrift amid fragments with no means, given our own fragmentary natures, of putting them together. Although poetry may well be an unheeded exemplar of love as law, or of Jakobson's "principle of equivalence" (Jakobson's star examples of this principle are "Russian wedding songs"), it remains a law that is imperfectly and incompletely proclaimed—at least insofar as it appears in the "accidental vestiture" of consciousness and of the real world in time. "The criteria of order and disorder," Shelley writes, "are as various as those beings from whose opinions and feelings they result" (*A Refutation of Deism, Prose*, 134). Form is certainly both the modality and the end of art, but there is a great deal that militates against its full realization. It was easier for Shelley than for Coleridge (speaking of them both solely as theorists of literature) to recognize that the form in question is what Thomas McFarland, in describing "Shelley's fragmentariness," has called "diasparactive form."[83] McFarland insists that the only kind of totalization for which Shelley ever displayed any penchant was the "pantheistic effusion in which all things are felt to be parts of a wonderful whole" (*Romanticism and the Forms of Ruin*, p. 52). Shelley himself knew quite well that this whole is something that is "assumed rather than perceived or imaged" (ibid., p. 53).

XI

The debate between poetry and science, in which Shelley's is one of the earliest and best documents, is closely related to the debate between criticism as an art and criticism as a science that is in full cry today. In this concluding section I would like to suggest, first, why I think that Shelley's is the best response that can be made to the Peacocks of modern science, and second, why I think that his line of argument is the best one to follow in resisting the claims of criticism to be a science, "exact" or otherwise.

Shelley's is a better defense of poetry than that of Arnold in "Literature and Science" or that of Richards in the *Principles, Science and Poetry*, and elsewhere[84] for essentially the same reason in each case. He refuses to accept the contrast admitted by these writers between statement and pseudostatement, confining himself instead to the subtler contrast between seminal and derivative pseudostatements. To concentrate on the case of Arnold: Of all his masterpieces of polemical prose, I think that "Literature and Science" is the most readable. It is a worldlier document than Shelley's and also a more ecumenically humane one. It strikes a more palpable blow against the menace of philistinism that Shelley's rather crude and unmodulated prose voice could ever have mustered. But as a defense of poetry it fails almost completely. Peacock would not probably have confessed defeat when he finally saw Shelley's *Defence* in 1839, but he must have had to admit that he had had the tables turned on him very neatly. Thomas Huxley on the other hand emerges wholly unscathed by Arnold's ultimately self-consuming ironies.[85]

The reason for this is that Arnold never lays claim to the territory of fact, except at one point early in his lecture. In response to Huxley's charge that by "literature" he means *"belles lettres,"* Arnold replies that "literature is a large word; it may mean everything written with letters or printed in a book. Euclid's *Elements* and Newton's *Principia* are thus literature."[86] This is Shelley's tack, and it is the safest one. It is significant, though, that Arnold omits the names of, say, Darwin and Lyell at this juncture. Both Euclid and Newton retain enough of the *symmetria prisca* (cf. Arnold, 395) to qualify almost as belles-lettrists themselves—and to have been discredited already, in some ways, as practitioners of the kind of science that Huxley wished to promote. Still, Arnold is strongest, again, when he thus broadens his definition of *literature* and assimilates to it each and every tendency to bring isolated facts, whether scientific or philological, "under general rules, to relate them to principles." To this extent Arnold retains the idea of poetry developed by Shelley and first hinted at by Wordsworth as the "breath and finer spirit of all knowledge."

By and large, however, Arnold concedes that there are two separate but equal modes of knowledge, thinking that his ironies by themselves will suffice to make them unequal in the way he desires. Evidently he feels that the only truly disputable territory between them is "the constitution of human nature" (ibid., 387). We have only to recall how readily the "human sciences" stole even this province away from the novelists, poets, and essayists only a few years after the delivery of Arnold's lecture to see how indefensible his last bailiwick was, given his too generous concession of fact to the scientists. If today at last we find literature beginning to steal its old territory back from the "human sciences," which themselves seem daily more futile as science and more interesting as literature, that trend should vindicate Shelley's defense of poetry. The positivism of Richards is shared by few today, and his emotive-psychological defense of poetry, itself a kind of scientific analysis, camps insecurely in a rented field. Arnold continues to fare better with us only because under the spell of his urbane condescension toward science we fail to notice his exaggerated awe in the presence of scientific fact. It could scarcely be otherwise in his age, when, as Whitehead pointed out, science and poetry (and religion) delivered more "jarring interpretations" of the world than ever before or since; no wonder that, in the time of Arnold and the Tennyson of *Locksley Hall* and *In Memoriam,* "each individual was divided against himself."[87] It should be said in justice to Arnold that it was easier for Shelley to avoid the pitfall of scientism because the science of his day still consisted primarily of refinements of Euclid and Newton or in the patently obvious oversimplifications of "the constitution of human nature" by the Utilitarians. And perhaps it is easier for us once again to avoid the worship of science because from the scientists themselves we hear less of "certainty" and more of such values as "tentativeness" and "elegance"—with which, as belletrists, we have long been familiar.

In his lecture Arnold is helpless once he has conceded that he is defending "a knowledge of words" against "a knowledge of things" (Arnold, 387). After this invidious contrast, which in any case the epistemology of Locke had discredited two hundred years earlier, there is little to be done, and Arnold proceeds to make his case even worse. He brings forward some recent claims of science concerning "things" by which he is evidently appalled: The earth is an insignificant planet in the vastness of space, man in turn is not the "cynosure" even of the earth, man's "ancestor was a hairy quadruped," and so on. These are not elegant propositions like those of classical science, nor are they merely dull but harmlessly trivial data like the fact that a taper when it burns is converted to carbonic acid and water. Rather they are "conceptions of the universe fatal to the notions held by our forefathers" (p. 391). In mentioning these new conceptions almost in the same breath with the cosmology of Scholasticism, Arnold may be hinting that they in turn will prove ephemeral, but he makes nothing of this line of counterattack, either because he feels compelled to accept the new cosmology and all its implications or, perhaps, because he does not want to be mistaken for a Creationist. His final complaint can only be that there is nothing in the revelations of science to *comfort* us: "Under the shock of hearing from modern science that 'the world is not subordinated to man's use, and that man is not the cynosure of things terrestrial,' I would, for my own part, desire no better comfort than Homer's line which I quoted just now,

τλητὸν γὰρ Μοῖραι θυμὸν θέσαν ἀνθρώποισιν—

'For an enduring heart have the destinies appointed to the children of men!' " If this is Arnold's crowning illustration of the need for literature, the two sides are badly matched.

The idea that literature, or literary criticism, is worthwhile simply as a comforting reassurance that humanity is worthy of special attention is not a vain or trivial or wholly illusory idea. It would be enough, possibly, if we were not enjoined to expect so much more. It troubles us that there is nothing certifiably *true* about Homer's statement. It is rich in pathos, even a little sentimental—an Arnoldian touchstone, in short. There is no harm in shoring such things against one's ruins, if one is in ruins, but all the surrounding sciences seem to be offering sturdier materials, solid truths not all of which are as depressing as the ones that shocked Arnold. Hence to defend poetry as a form of knowledge there is no choice but to follow Shelley onto the offensive, to point out the limits of objective knowledge and conclude that the best science is literary, not the other way around. Fortified by the belief that there is really no version of the scientific method that does not block out nearly as much legitimate knowledge as it is designed to reveal, one returns to Homer, and to *belles lettres,* as forms of knowledge that are neither true nor false but open, that do not decide but amplify and include.

FIVE

The Instance of Walter Benjamin: Distraction and Perception in Criticism

In the preceding chapters I have shuttled for the most part without comment between the concerns of literature and those of criticism because I think that although these concerns *can* be distinguished, just as the concerns of poetry and science can be distinguished, they overlap to a great extent and do not differ absolutely in any particular.[1] I have taken it for granted that form is to literature what method is to criticism. Of the texts I have considered, all but one anticipate this view. Aristotle alone preserves a complete distinction between poet and critic; criticism as such he takes up as a separate topic starting at chapter 25. The other three allow literature and criticism to merge: Longinus's poetics of response and transmission locates the poet and the critic in similar moments of in-betweenness; Dryden makes a "fable" of his Preface; and any criticism that Shelley could have brought himself to tolerate he would have called "poetry in the general sense."

In the Longinian mode, the critical act, like the poetic act, is not an event, or object, that can be radically isolated and distinguished from others. Rather it is a movement that cannot be recognized for what it is except as one in a series of movements that constitute the open-ended structure of aesthetic experience in general: a structure of continuous mediation. Both literature and criticism, in short, are essentially interpretive. Both to an equal degree are aspects of what Hans-Georg Gadamer understands to be the hermeneutical nature of all historical experience, of experience, that is, in its "historicity." But the recognition by Gadamer (to whom my own views are much indebted) that experience is invariably hermeneutic is qualified by an unwarranted exception. Just as Freud more piously than cannily exempts the work of art from the psychopathology of everyday life, so Gadamer accords the power of origination solely to the work of art among the modes of cognition.

Gadamer draws an analogy between interpretation and stage perform-ance. The work of art, in his view, the work that is performed, remains always itself; it is never that which is constituted in performance or by the response of an audience. And yet, he admits, the work of art in itself is not objectively accessible. It can nowhere be revealed as itself, in its own being, except through the inevitable distortion of it by the "prejudice" and the historical estrangement of the performer and the audience. "All encounter with the language of art," he writes, "is an encounter with a still unfinished process and is in itself part of this process" (*Truth and Method*, p. 88). This statement explains the limits of interpretation very helpfully, leaving only the status of the work of art somewhat obscure. The revision of Gadamer's view that I wish to offer in order to recover a "poetics" that is as unified— i.e., as undifferentiated—as that of Longinus, is simply that the work of art is indeed inaccessible, as Gadamer implies, unless it is reconsidered as an interpretation in itself.

The relation between art and interpreter, Gadamer argues, can be compared with the relationship between a game and its player. The game, in its self-contained, to-and-fro "play," is always itself, constituted as such not by any player but by the centripetal force of its rules, and yet the game is never actualized except in the being-played accorded to it by a player. But this qualification entirely vitiates the assertion it is meant to qualify. How can we identify the "proper spirit" (ibid., p. 96), or essence, of the work of art—qualities which we may provisionally grant it—other than as this very being-played? I do not mean to imply only that a game is gradually but irreversibly reshaped by the history of its being-played (in one form or another, this is the answer to Gadamer that informs German "reception-aesthetics"); I mean also that the game even at its inception cannot appear except as, or apart from, its being-played. This was the gist of my critique of Aristotle: that the poet's invention is itself a concrete *praxis,* a being-played and a playing not a play or a foreplay, before which, or apart from which, the idea of the play "as such," or pure torque, simply cannot appear on any horizon of perception. Gadamer himself writes that "all playing is a being-played" (p. 95), that games play us as much as we play them, but omits to apply this principle to the case of the game's "inventor."

Everywhere guided by his sense of the unity of being and structure (in which sense I think he departs further than he realizes from his mentor Heidegger), Gadamer wishes to preserve the aesthetic of the autonomous artistic whole that was introduced by Aristotle and recast as an apprehension of the perceiving subject by Kant. At the same time, however, Gadamer denies the actualization of the whole except *through* the perceiving subject and furthermore denies the availability of the whole in itself *to* any such subject. But where, then, *is* the whole? Recognizing the need to locate it concretely, E. D. Hirsch calls it an "intentional object," but that object vanishes in its turn as soon as one reflects that no experiential activity is ever fully intended by an agent except in pure, reconstitutive phenomenology.[2] In this regard I have argued hitherto that the work of art is intended in irreconcilable ways by consciousness and by the coercive manifold that comprises the unconscious. If this is so, if the work is intended in these ways at once by and through its author, clearly it can be said that it is intended in these same ways by and through its interpreter, whose secondariness to the author and the work does not then differ in any crucial respect from the secondariness of the author to what one could call (to put the matter ecumenically) his or her "precursor milieu."

Obviously, in order to say this one must question the distance, often the polar opposition, that is traditionally preserved between invention and text, bringing the former close to language and viewing the latter experientially rather than as an autonomous structure. Once this distance has been diminished, as it is, I have argued, in texts as diverse as those of Longinus and Dryden, the work of art can be viewed as an experience in transit for writer and reader alike. The "text" itself is both everywhere and nowhere in this experience; it is the condition, the ground, of the experience, but it is never the experience itself or even, itself, the determining structure of that experience. Furthermore, the distance between text and experience varies in ways that defy generalization. As the ground of the hermeneutic experience the text may play its most extensive role at the time of its appearance or—as sometimes happens—at some later time in which it is more properly at home, and the degree to which the properties of the text fail to predetermine its interpretation and reception is, for many reasons, impossible to measure.

Interpretation is affected, in all cases, for any reader in any generation, by the necessarily wandering course of attention which no critical theory has ever taken fully into account, perhaps because it is assumed that the purpose of theory is precisely to eliminate it. "Prejudice from over-hastiness," writes Gadamer, "is to be understood . . . as the source of all error in the use of reason" (*Truth and Method,* p. 242). But even Gadamer supposes that such prejudice can be overcome. In previous chapters I presented the phenomenon of inadvertence as the nonantithetical tension between conscious and unconscious determination. Here I would repeat especially that the tension is indeed nonantithetical. In other words, one cannot forecast the extent of the gulf that is occasioned by repression. At its most dialectical, repression becomes, in Freud's late formulation, the negation *(Verneinung)* whereby all utterance is a defense by denial. According to this notion, it is not just that we never say what we mean; rather, we always say the opposite of what we mean. What I propose here is a deliberately moderate revision of this idea, one that returns incommensurability to the pattern of error in interpretation. Agreeing with Schleiermacher that every hermeneutic act begins with misunderstanding,[3] and with Harold Bloom that every reading is a misreading, I am concerned only to loosen the structure of error, to deny that it can be quantified, say, as a "margin of error," and thus to resist Schleiermacher's derivation of understanding from misunderstanding and Bloom's structuration of literary history as Verneinung.

I do not intend to veer toward a dogma of the random; there is little doubt that the several modes of error are each in themselves structurally constituted. What remains doubtful is that, given the complexity of each succeeding "precursor milieu," and given above all the irreducible temporality of experience—such that there can be no true identity, simultaneity, or coincidence in language or any other medium—it could be possible to register the manner and degree to which error, however clearly structured in itself, will determine cognition. As Walter Benjamin puts the matter very soberly in one of his Baudelaire studies, "Experience is less the product of facts firmly anchored in memory than a convergence in memory of accumulated and frequently unconscious data."[4] It is a buildup, a sedimentation, rather than a definite force. There is a need, if this is so, for a theory of asystematic understanding, a theory that will account for what is called "distraction" by Benjamin, to whom I shall presently turn as my final exemplary critic. In discussing Benjamin, I shall develop the concept of *distraction,* which he himself does not recognize to be a key issue in his work, into a final caveat against method.

I

Before pursuing Benjamin's thought and its implications, however, I should like to work out a final critique of formalism in terms which Benjamin would not use but which nonetheless clearly reveal the advantages of his outlook. The terms are those of Freud, to whom Benjamin was largely indifferent,[5] and with them I shall attempt a kind of psychoanalysis of the thinking which takes form for its object and method as its means.

My remarks on Aristotle's *Poetics* were meant to show that the special distortion attendant upon formal criticism, or any criticism that purports to retail the full "meaning" of a fully "intentional object," is determined by the aversion of all such criticism to extremes beyond commensuration. I also tried to show, both in that chapter and in some of the examples given in my introduction, that formal criticism typically undermines both its premises and its conclusions, unwittingly staging its own "recognition scene" in the course of narrowing its object. This occurs because the "eye for resemblances" that produces the metaphors and the turnings of plot in Aristotle is always Oedipal in tendency. That is, in excluding the domain of incommensurable difference in both perception and its objects, the eye for resemblances regroups its field of vision as a matrix of kinship. Tragic conflict is filial, with fear and pity expressing the emotionally two-sided relationship of the parent (not necessarily male) to ourselves, while eroticism, still more problematically, is incestuous. In the logic of formalism, attraction and revulsion are yoked together as one in the trope of metaphor, which Aristotle describes as the affinity of an "alien name" with one's proper name. What the formal method assigns to "conscious artistry" is precisely the dynamic of the primal scene in the unconscious. Although these terms may seem lacking in generality, they readily suggest analytic parallels from other standpoints. In political terms, for instance, a parallel argument accounts for the frequently noticed conservative ideology that underlies the formalism of the present century. Here conflict would appear as a tension between classes, and eroticism, the attraction of similitude, would unnaturally reinforce the status quo, reflecting the unnatural solidarity of competitors under Capitalism and thus increasing the likelihood of revolution.

In short, the main achievement of the eye for resemblances is to raise troubling questions about the interdependence of like and dislike. Johnson's famous description of "Metaphysical" images "yoked by violence together" through the "discovery of occult resemblances in things apparently unlike" shows how disturbing this faculty can seem, and in the early days of the New Criticism the notion of *ambiguity* was received in the world with similar unease. But it is characteristic of formalist thought itself not to consider the implications of the obverse patterning that governs its procedure. This oversight, the unnoticed "recognition scene" in the plot of Aristotelian thought, particularly colors the "objectivist" arguments for cognitive certainty, for the discrimination of one object from another based on the perception of anomaly against the backdrop of resemblance. It will be understood that the ensuing argument is not meant to dismiss the objectivists' position out of hand. I am not certain to what degree the view of cognition set forth here is valid; I would only assume that the very plausibility of this view, even if it is accepted in only limited or occasional instances, must undermine the serenity with which the objectivist "recognizes" things in themselves.

"Our expectations strongly structure what we see," writes Israel Scheffler, "but do not wholly eliminate unexpected sights."[6] E. D. Hirsch remarks comparably that, e.g., "the unexpected phoneme can . . . cause us to revise or correct the word we were expecting."[7] These observations are unobjectionable, and the argument they bolster, the argument that we can see incongruous objects from a single perspective, is complemented by the equally appealing argument, most ably propounded by E. H. Gombrich in aesthetic matters, that we are able to infer—or "complete," as it were—a single, unchanging object from any number of partial perspectives.[8] In either case a *synonymy* is alleged,[9] whether of objects or viewpoints. It is important to have done so because if synonymy can be established, the idea that knowledge is a storehouse dwindling as fast as it increases can be refuted, and the progress of knowledge toward general truth can be affirmed. (In literary interpretation the equivalent of this progress would consist in the defiance of the hermeneutic circle by advancing toward a single meaning based on "configuration.") Apparently, then, we can store up perceptions for reuse, according to either the rigorous principle of synonymy or the more flexible—but also more agnostic—principle of "family resemblance."

But there is another, less reassuring explanation of the availability of synonymy to perception, one that also serves to explain why constructive disagreement is possible. This explanation depends only on the acceptance of the idea that unconscious factors play a role in the cognitive process, an idea which has many adherents but which, perhaps not surprisingly, has yet to make the slightest impression on formal hermeneutics or on the so-called scientific (neurological, quantitative, and cybernetic) studies of cognition. A distinction is necessary here: by *unconscious* I do not mean that which is merely unthought-of, or what Freud would call preconscious. That material has always been accounted for in cognitive science. It is what Michael Polanyi calls "tacit knowledge," and what Hirsch accepts as the tacit implications of a "willed type."[10] Thus the word *tree* will entail "roots" and "branches" without the speaker's awareness, but the words *heads* and *tails,* according to this view, would not belong to his or her "meaning." It is said only to be in this limited sense that, in keeping with a slogan of the hermeneutic tradition, an interpreter can know more about a text than its author did. When one introduces the factor of the unconscious, however, the region in which knowledge is repressed and not merely ignored, "heads" and "tails" are very much part of the speaker's meaning, and set the interpreter thinking profitably about totems—despite the significantly vehement dissent of the speaker. This then is the zone that I understand here to be "unconscious."

In any case, what I wish to call attention to here, in pursuit of a psychoanalysis of formalism, is the phrasing that characterizes a particular moment of triumph in the proof of objective knowledge based on the existing possibility of disagreement with others. In general this proof states that it is precisely the ability of another to disagree with my argument that shows that argument to be an independent object, wholly intelligible to the other's categories of perception and yet free from the coercive distortion they supposedly exert. It is possible, in the first place, simply to deny that one *can* fully understand what one does not already believe owing to a shared perspective. Negative capability in these matters varies but perhaps never approaches very close to perfection. It would be difficult to show that conversion in argument does not always consist in the recognition of some unnoticed aspect of one's own opinion. Sometimes we do find ourselves to be converted to an opinion of which we cannot find the slightest prior trace in ourselves, but perhaps it is there nevertheless. This is where the oedipal structure of unconscious identification comes into play: not only will another's view turn out to have been mine on examination, but there is a sense in which the other will turn out to have been me.

Here is the language of E. D. Hirsch at the moment of triumph I mentioned. He quotes the most fascinating part of it from Charles Bally, the student of Saussure's theory of communication, and thus derives the idea of our cognitive freedom from our social capacities as speakers in dialogue: "Far from being an extraordinary or illusory feat," Hirsch writes, "this entertaining of two perspectives at once is the ground of all human intercourse, and a universal fact of speech which the linguists have called the 'doubling of personality.' "[11] The rhetorical strategy of this passage is significant. The "universal fact" is externalized, if not universalized, in being identified with the opinion of another. The danger that is minimized here in the very moment of being illustrated, the danger that the universal will be contaminated by subjectivity, is further reduced by the placement of the universal in the service of "intercourse." But this is an interesting word that the vagaries of modern usage have somewhat corrupted. Here too the danger of what is seen by the eye for resemblances returns in the very place where its elimination had been intended. The universal is said, in any case, not to be personal but rather interpersonal, and as if spontaneously in support of this assertion, Hirsch assigns it to "the linguists," subtly implying his *own* conversion to the bracing scientificity of colleagues who study the "external features" of their topic, language. In short, every rhetorical detail of this passage serves to reinforce the idea that its argument is objectively verifiable and thus keeps us from noticing that whatever we know, after all, about the "doubling of personality" we first learned not from linguistics but from psychology, which holds that doubling is not a triumph of detachment but, on the contrary, an instinctive mimicry.

As Schleiermacher says, "Everyone carries a tiny bit of everyone else within himself, so that divination [of meaning] is stimulated by comparison with oneself."[12] But conversion experiences are not solely a matter of projection, identification, or transference any more than ingrained and stubborn disagreement is solely oedipal. Disputes and their resolution need not be accounted for exclusively in such terms even by psychoanalysis. There is another aspect of Freud's thought that brings us closer, and in a more constructive context, to the *experience* of cognition. The objectivist argument we have been considering is based on "the recognition of anomaly." That whole phrase is interesting: we see the anomaly, notice it, that is, because its unaccountability strikes us as uncanny, at least for the moment, and our mode of seeing it, as the phrase suggests, is not cognitive but re-cognitive. We see the anomaly, in short, or come to agree with the argument of another, not because they are new to us but because we have forgotten that they are not new to us.

Freud's essay on "The Uncanny," which is his *On the Sublime,* is very loosely constructed, as befits the disorienting power of his theme, but one thread, from the first antithetical dictionary definitions to the final series of oddly disjointed afterthoughts, does seem more or less steadily to run through it: the uncanny accompanies our recognition of what was once familar but has been forgotten. The object in question can be almost anything, as long as it was once *heimlich* (familiar) and is now *heimlich* (secret); but in particular, to come to the word Hirsch passes along to the linguists, that object is likely to be a "double." By way of illustration Freud records an experience he had on a train:

> I was sitting alone in my *wagon-lit* compartment when *a more than usually violent jerk of the train* swung back the door of the adjoining washing-cabinet, and an elderly gentleman in a dressing-gown and a travelling cap came in. I assumed that he had been about to leave *the washing-cabinet which divides the two compartments,* and had taken the wrong direction and had come into my compartment by mistake. Jumping up *with the intention of putting him right,* I at once realized to my dismay that the intruder was nothing but *my own reflection in the looking-glass of the open door. I can still recollect that I thoroughly disliked his appearance.*[13]

The scene in which Hirsch locates the intercourse of free intellects could be a recognition scene like this one, which I have italicized in places to bring out the allegory. Bearing in mind that nearly all argument arises between orthodox and rebellious viewpoints, one may note that the dislike one feels for the *semblable,* who mirrors one's own arrogance so disagreeably, may be directed against a discarded self. Conversion, being won over by argument, would then be intelligible as a recognition of authenticity either in one's former rebelliousness or else in one's former identification with authority, as the case may be.[14]

What was not already in the self as a precognition is probably just that which the self will never be able to grasp. It is perceived, insofar as one is cognizant of it at all, not as an anomaly but as a blank. One cannot even put a name to it. This is scarcely an alarming state of affairs because it need not occur very often; nearly every idea we encounter has already been lodged, at one time or another, in our memories. Learning is thus more precisely than we may think the discovery of our own potential. This is not a new idea, although it may be that the Socrates of the *Meno* would disapprove of the use to which his "all inquiry and all learning is but recollection" has here been put.[15] In any case, memory is poor at recall but amazingly efficient at storage, and it is this gulf between performance and potential in the mind which gives us the satisfaction, every day, of "recognizing" anomaly. It is also, however, the gulf in which every theory of constitutive form and every formula for hermeneutic success, for achieved presence to meaning, must come to grief. Longinus called it the sublime, Freud the uncanny, and I hope to be able to demonstrate, in the long run, that it is nothing other than the irreducible margin of error in interpretation.

In critical polemic, people who agree with each other are sometimes said by their opponents to be "incestuous"; perhaps we have now come some way toward seeing why, and also toward seeing why supporters of any widely held opinion are so fond of portraying themselves as rugged individualists and voices crying in the wilderness. This is because, according to the structure of his or her own formalism, the methodological loyalist must choose between combative solitude or unwilling incest—the latter being the only state of agreement that is perceptible to any eye keyed for resemblances. Thus the arch-conformist Robert Southey, at the height of British anti-Jacobinism, could imagine himself to be "speaking out" when he accused Byron and Shelley—each of whom had already been driven into exile by public opinion for entirely unrelated reasons—of having formed "a League of Incest."[16] As we have seen, the chief difference between Southey and Shelley in this respect is that the latter, for whom incest was "a very poetical circumstance," could freely acknowledge the presence of shocking bad form in the constellation of desire, and hence could not be forced into a posture of repression by the necessity of denying it.

There can be no question of domesticating the *Unheimlich,* the sudden sensation of being possessed by another, of possessing another, for in that case it would no longer be uncanny. What is possible and desirable, rather, is to come to terms with the experience in its strangeness, to recognize it as the breach of decorum, necessarily within the fabric of decorum, that Longinus calls sublime. This is not the wild posturing of Horace's mad and shaggy poet turned critic. It is a position that is taken up on the border, *within* the border, indeed, of formalism. It is a crucial contention of Geoffrey Hartman, one that the intricate precision of his own criticism justifies, that "there are many ways to transcend formalism, but the worst is not to study forms."[17] Form is an important object, and method an important concern, of any responsive interpretation; but recognition can only come, and reconciliation with what one recognizes is only possible, when form is no longer an endgame.

II

The preoccupation with the form of the Whole, with totality, is not exclusively to be found in the formalist critical tradition. It is the essential object of traditional metaphysics, and even Heidegger, who sought to supersede metaphysics, could still write of "Dasein's possibility of being-a-whole"—though significantly he denied this possibility "as long as Dasein *is* as an entity."[18] Even the most daunting materialist philosophers of our century, the Lukács of *History and Class Consciousness* and the Adorno of, say, *The Dialectic of Enlightenment,* base some aspects of their work on the desideratum of the whole. The Marxian category of totality, which serves to rationalize the nostalgia for what Marx calls the "primeval" community of land but which most closely resembles agrarian feudalism among the phases of recorded history, involves the interrelated but undialectical categories of the "human" and of completeness. Together they form a tautology: The human is authentic if it is total (for Lukács, this comes about with the synthesis of subject and object at the end of bourgeois "prehistory"), and totality, understood as a victory over self-alienation and reification, is what in turn characterizes the human. In Marx's depiction of the Greeks as the "normal childhood" of the historical present one can already find the theory of alienation, derived in turn from Winckelmann and Schiller, that governs the values of the intellectual tradition referred to here.[19] Gradually, first in Marcuse and later in the so-called greening of America, this sort of talk has come to serve cultural forces that would have appalled the Lukács of the 1920s and actually terrorized the Adorno of the 1960s. Yet it is not merely present already as a latent strain in these remarkable writers; it is in fact the fulcrum, the fixed point of unquestioned value that enabled them to question the fixed ideology of bourgeois culture.

In short, the notion of the authentically human, of the "self," itself constitutes an ideology. Neither the early nor the late Walter Benjamin can be dissociated from it altogether, and it entirely conditions one of his most interesting essays, "The Storyteller." But he could never rest content with this ideology, which he knew for what it was. The ensuing remarks are meant to describe the irresolution in his thought that preserves him, or at least distances him, from the unexamined fetish that reunites most Marxist intellectuals with the mainstream of bourgeois ideology—the fetish of the Whole.

I wish to consider Benjamin as a continuator, then, albeit of course an unwitting one, of the thinking that I have associated with Longinus and have located as well, in part to show the diversity of its presence, in texts by Dryden and Shelley. The leading trait of this thinking, perhaps, is its evasion of the polarities that shape most philosophical thinking from Plato forward. Thus for Longinus the sublime is neither immanent nor transcendent; nor is it a hypostasized entity, such as form, but a movement, instead, between hosts, each of whom is possessed by it rather than of it. Similarly in Dryden no stable contrast is discernible between language and thought ("invention"), translation and original, forebear and successor, creation and inspiration. It is Dryden, too, following the "thrid" of his discourse as docilely as though it were a leading string, who makes a point of being distracted from consecutive reasoning. For both Longinus and Dryden, clearly, openness to the movement of inspiration depends on passivity, on the suspension of the will to create or to formulate. Understandably, the dialectic of freedom and determinacy is kept for the most part out of view in these writers, but it does play its part figuratively. Dryden's "Almighty Poet" becomes Shelley's "great cyclic poem" of which all successive poems are fragments. The heat of inspiration comes, in Shelley, as the tearing of a veil, a rift in the ground of decorum—of what Longinus called "persuasion"—and when inspiration begins to cool in set forms of language that are already en route to their future as dead metaphors, then it is no longer itself.

For Shelley, as for Longinus, the movement of inspiration is not smooth but violent, a "sword of lightning" (Jordan, 47), not only because it is disruptive, a breach of the whole, but also because it is received in a posture of defense and answered in a countermovement, a "responsive chord." What is common to all three writers above all, and what follows from the themes I have just passed in review, is the assumption that the literary experience is fragmentary. Not only does it appear as an interruption of texts themselves, a fragment that leaves its context broken apart as well, but it also implies—or better, imposes—the fragmentation of both the constitutive and the reconstitutive subjects. Rather than signaling the freedom of wholeness, as it does for Kant, the actual aesthetic experience displaces the unities of self and other, reality and representation, by merging these erstwhile entities in uncanny ways. One is led to conclude, then—and this is the formula at which I shall arrive in pursuing the foregoing themes in the work of Benjamin—that the movement of the sublime is the movement of distraction.[20]

III

To begin with the question of dualism, of the "hylomorphic dichotomy" that Longinian thinking unsettles: As Benjamin makes clear in his anecdotal-analytic "The Image of Proust," the border between reality and representation is not easy to determine.[21] That is the theme of Jacques Derrida's "Ein Porträt Benjamins," in which Benjamin is "read" by way of Valerio Adami's portrait of him, itself a reading of a photograph by Gisele Freund. Derrida treats the truncated forehead (*front:* translated *Stirn*) in the drawing as an amalgam of "fronts," at once war-torn, physiognomic, and emblematic of Benjamin's indecisive vanguardism; and he reads the horizontal line bisecting the drawing as though it were at once the border between extremes in Benjamin's work and the Franco–Spanish border on which Benjamin committed suicide in 1940. He is, exclaims Derrida, "ein Mann der Grenze."[22]

Now, because Benjamin is a "man of the border," his thought, like that of Longinus, cannot be expected to be programmatic, a construction made out of fully formed, unvarying ideas. As Peter Demetz remarks in his introduction to *Reflections* (p. xiii), "he works with a few intimate leitmotifs that fascinate him throughout his life, regardless of the particular stage of his ideological transformations." However, despite warnings such as this one, efforts to organize Benjamin's thinking according to paired categories continue to be widespread. Many see him as an intellectual victim of polarities so gaping and so resolutely adhered to that they cannot be reconciled. Thus Jürgen Habermas says of him concerning the issue that has generated the most polemic among students of Benjamin: "An anti-revolutionary conception of history cannot be tacked onto historical materialism as if it were a monk's cowl."[23] Just as frequently those who interpret Benjamin programmatically suppose, unlike Habermas but still with respect to the dichotomy he identifies, that Benjamin effects a triumphant synthesis of materialism and messianism. The text most frequently cited in support of this synthesis is the first of the 1940 "Theses on the Philosophy of History," in which the hunchback of theology, "an expert chess player," huddles inside the automated puppet labeled "historical materialism" and calls, as it were, the shots of history (*Illuminations*, p. 253). But is everything explained by this Thesis, as the programmatic reader wants to argue? Or is Benjamin's figure very pointedly the explanation of nothing at all?

Benjamin's Thesis proposes a strange alliance between handicapped beings, the halt leading the blind. Which came first, the Marxian puppet or the Hegelian hunchback—rival emblems of causation between which there is obviously no alliance possible in any case? And what of the figures themselves? Under the sway of Stalin it must have meant something for Benjamin to compare the official Marxist version of history with a puppet, a mindless congeries of gestures (*gestus* is one of Benjamin's favorite words for the reflexes of ideology in the 1930s) manipulated by—well, by the hunchback, who, far from appearing as the Messiah, most closely resembles the crippled and degenerate spirit of absolutism, the hand pulling the strings of the Hitler–Stalin Pact. It is well known to students of Benjamin that the hunchback is the mischief-maker of folklore which haunted his childhood imagination, anticipating his recognition of the hunchback in Kafka as a figure somewhat ambiguously connected with suffering, variously as agent and as victim—an attenuated Messiah indeed.

The lineaments of Kafka's hunchback can be seen even in the small, puppet-like figure of Odradek, who is "the form," says Benjamin in "Franz Kafka," "which things assume in oblivion" (*Illuminations*, p. 133). In the logic of these figures, then, the "theological" is not only stunted and neglected (that in itself would not be a bad thing for the future of theology, as we shall see), but in fact it ceases to be theological at all and simply becomes a *thing*. Kafka's Odradek, in a passage quoted by Benjamin, is "star-shaped," residually a star. It is perhaps astrological or perhaps Davidic. It is in any case a stellar influence: "a small wooden cross-bar sticks out of the middle"—so that by the most distant metonymy it also becomes a star of Bethlehem—"and another small rod is joined to it at a right angle. With the aid of this latter rod on one side and one of the extensions of the star on the other, the whole thing can stand upright as if on two legs" (ibid.). Odradek is, in short, a puppet, an allegory at once of humanity and of the stellar influence under which humanity seems to move of its own accord.

What has become of the duality that purportedly sustains Benjamin's first Thesis? The puppet as automaton becomes the hunchback, and the hunchback, crouched inside and roughly similar in shape, passes over into the "image" (Benjamin's *Bild,* as in "Zum Bilde Prousts," or *Dialektik im Stillstand*) of the puppet. What remains is not a synthesis of intellectual strains but a broken-down figure of doubt within which the differences between form and content, spirit and substance, essence and appearance— not to mention the differences between superstructure and structure— cannot be demonstrated except insofar as the figure itself, redoubled but not dual, implies a *margin* of difference available to us as an open question. Benjamin's puppet, "in Turkish attire and with a hookah in its mouth," sitting "before a chessboard," is a perfect figure of the attenuated sublime, poised between trance and automation.

IV

Reflection on this figure and on Benjamin's work as a whole suggests that history is neither materially nor transcendentally shaped but has the properties, rather, of what Heidegger calls Being-in-the-world. Hannah Arendt incurred a good deal of understandable displeasure when she compared Benjamin's thinking with Heidegger's in the introduction to *Illuminations* (p. 46). Benjamin himself disliked Heidegger before Heidegger's "common cause with fascism" (Benjamin's phrase for the reactionary politics of Ludwig Klages and Jung) became an issue. We can reasonably date his antipathy from 1927, when *Being and Time* was published perhaps in part— if the suspicion of Lukács is to be trusted—as a refutation of *History and Class Consciousness.*[24] But if Heidegger's purpose, or one of them anyway, was to universalize the class-bound category of production for consumption under the rubric of "equipmentality" (the transient, consumable features of all production), it is difficult to see how that undertaking would differ from Benjamin's fundamental project as we shall consider it.[25] Furthermore, that which makes Benjamin elusive is what makes Heidegger elusive also—nothing less than the considered inability to maintain any clear sense of the duality between essence and appearance upon which the dialectical treatment of any topic must rely. Benjamin is no more capable than Heidegger of answering the question, "What is a Thing?" in a straightforward way. Indeed, his later work incurs its most brilliant and constructive lapses into irresolution when it attempts to domesticate the Marxian category, elaborated by Lukács, of "reification."

For Lukács in 1927, reification was anything that "objectified" both consciousness and objects themselves, whether through specialization, alienation of the worker from the means of production, or the hardening of intellectual arteries caused by the pressure of ideology on bourgeois philosophy. His political motives aside, Lukács was well advised, in a new preface of 1967, to reject this blanket conception of reification. He blames his error on the persistent influence of Hegel, for whom "the term alienation . . . includes every type of objectification [*Vergegenständlichung*],"[26] and he now realizes that if he hews to this line he must repudiate objectivity itself. Thus he must now say, necessarily, that "objectification is a natural means by which man masters the world and as such it can be either a positive or a negative fact" (ibid., p. xxxvi). In 1927 Lukács had considered "fact" itself to be a reified, undialectical concept (ibid., p. 184). Hence whereas the "early middle" Lukács had inadvertently entered into agreement with Heidegger, whose view of alienation as the ground of existence itself led— in being simplified—to the grim homilies of modern Existentialism, the late Lukács gave himself a way out. Just as there are authentic and inauthentic concepts of the individual subject, he argues, so there are objects that are "reified" and objects that we know to have been "objectively" understood. (Just so, Gadamer in a different context enables his entire hermeneutic by distinguishing between true and false prejudices [see *Truth and Method*, p. 266].) Unfortunately, though, however necessary this distinction may be if Lukács is to celebrate unalienated man's potential for world-building, and however plausible the diagnosis of the modern predicament that is empowered by this distinction, it remains a distinction without a difference, except as a vehicle for ad hoc ethical judgments.

In order to make sense of the distinction between clear, objective thinking and reified, ideological thinking, one must persist in the effort to locate its basis in actuality. It is that stubborn quest, with its equally tenacious burden of doubt concerning the place of transcendence, that informs the work (although in dissimilar guises) of both Heidegger and Benjamin. What is "substance," then? And, correlatively, what is "thinking"? Can the hermeneutic circle that governs the relation between category and percept be broken? Can the difference between *idea* and *eidos* be described, with Plato, as a difference in materiality? And above all, how are any of these questions to be understood apart from a theory of representation in language? These are Heidegger's questions, and, early and late, they are Benjamin's as well.

V

Benjamin's opinions on the subject of language, his earliest philosophical concern, are at first blush bizarre to the point of crankiness. He was an Adamist; that is, he believed with Cratylus and his friends—and likewise with Hamann—that the first given names were natural signs of their objects, mimetic, onomatopoetic, or hieroglyphic in varying degrees, and that with the Fall Babel asserted itself instantly in the proliferation of tongues that were merely instrumental. "The word must communicate *something* (other than itself)," he wrote in 1916: "That is really the Fall of language-mind" (*Reflections,* p. 327). Note that what is stressed here is not the relatively commonplace regret for the loss of contact with nature, although that is certainly entailed, but instead the regret that the self-sufficient intransitivity of words themselves has been lost. Only the *Ursprache,* language in its original and quintessential form, could manifest creative self-delight and a oneness with nature so absolute that to "communicate" it would itself suggest the intervention of a gulf of self-consciousness. Both these lost attributes of man's language once identified that language very precisely as an echo of God's Word. But all that is past, absolutely and irrevocably past, and it is the vividness of Benjamin's consequent knowledge that there is nothing prelapsarian about language as we use it that places him, despite the mystical yearning that he shares with Shelley, squarely among the skeptics—also like Shelley—as a theorist of reference. Since the Fall, for Benjamin, language has become the mask of truth, a mask which it is "The Task of the Translator" (1923; *Illuminations*) to strip away.

Nearly every commentator on Benjamin has held that in his later work he had to modify these notions (allowing, for the moment, that he ever entertained them unequivocally), just as he had, in general, to modify his "mysticism." It seems to me, however, that no matter how intensely the early Benjamin may have wished to evoke a theological atmosphere for his views, there is in fact nothing necessarily immaterial about them—just as the disclosure of the hunchback in the late first Thesis does not necessarily mark the resurgence of a transcendental perspective. Consider this passage, purportedly *against* the semiotician who must be the Adamist's natural opponent, from the 1916 "On Language as Such and the Language of Man": "The view that the mental essence of a thing consists precisely in its language—this view, taken as a hypothesis, is the great abyss into which all linguistic theory threatens to fall, and to survive suspended precisely over this abyss is the task" (*Reflections,* p. 315). To be sure, Benjamin wants always, as here, to mark a difference between essence and language. But the difference is of the subtlest kind, and it can be maintained only by the willful defiance of gravity. Even for Adam the ontological truth, though it was not identical to language, could not appear apart from language because it still participated in the mystery of the Logos: "*In naming the mental being of man communicates itself to God*" (ibid., p. 318; italics Benjamin's). And *only* in naming, he might have added. Arguably, for Benjamin language always precedes thought, as it does, I have argued, for Shelley. That would explain, in any case, why Benjamin approvingly quotes André Breton: "After you, dearest language" ("Surrealism," in ibid., p. 179).

Thus the change wrought by the Fall is less pronounced than it first appeared to be. Ontological truth is still virtually immanent in language, only now it is concealed rather than revealed by its medium. Language remains the home of truth, its only available hiding place. Hence in "The Mimetic Faculty" (1933), a late draft of a much earlier essay, Benjamin, already well along in his "materialist" phase, does *not* break appreciably with any earlier doctrine when he says that "the mimetic element in language [i.e., its mode of natural signification, here specifically onomato-poesis] can, like a flame, manifest itself only through a kind of bearer. This bearer is the semiotic element [i.e., its mode of artificial signification]. Thus the coherence of words or sentences is the bearer through which, like a flash, similarity appears" *(Reflections, p. 335)*.

The affinity of this view with the late Heideggerian concept of the *Riss*, the fissure or painful threshold in the ground of existence through which Being appears, should be clear;[27] it should likewise be clear that Benjamin here aligns his view with the theory of the sublime as the disruption of a smooth and familiar surface that is as old as Longinus and has as its contemporary equivalent the surfacing of material from the unconscious. What I want to stress is that in this "bearer" (the *phor* in words like *metaphor*) Benjamin locates his concept of allegory, a concept in itself so ambivalent that from it we can trace all his key dilemmas.[28] In *The Origin of German Tragic Drama* (1925), allegorical phantasmagoria ("emblems" in more conventional scholarship) together with certain reified locutions of mourning for the emptiness of the world (the *Trauer* of *Trauerspiel*), are said to constitute an alienation, a distance, that makes visible a radical truth: the fact that postlapsarian emptiness itself is the ground of redemption. Thus it is the very secondariness of allegory, its hypostasis and conventionality, its failure to communicate or even to convey emotion, that calls attention to the truth content of language as such; whereas symbol, the more attractive figure, is by nature such an efficient "bearer" that it transfers meaning from the mimetic to the merely semiotic level, where it remains condemned "to communicate *something* (other than itself)."

What is crucial is to recognize that, without reduction, "allegory" for Benjamin, as for Paul de Man on somewhat similar grounds, simply *is* "the language of man"—though it is not quite "language as such," which remains the forever inaccessible Ursprache. The contrasting figures of allegory and symbol themselves imply all of Benjamin's other distinctions between the redemptively inauthentic and the authentic: between mere "information" and immanent "meaning," between "beauty" and "truth" (which it is the role of beauty in art to conceal), and finally between the two, mutually supportive modes of interpretation: "commentary," which concerns both the aesthetic form and the facticity of a work, and "criticism," which tears aside the formal and merely communicative veils of the work, "mortifies" its worldly significance ("je mehr sie in der Welt absterben"), as Benjamin says in his 1922 essay on Goethe's *Elective Affinities,* and identifies its semantic essence (*Gesammelte Schriften,* I, i, 125). ("Without commentary," writes Charles Rosen concerning this contrast, "criticism is self-indulgent revery; without criticism, commentary is frivolous information."[29]) There are in fact many more parallel dyads even than these, all of them consequences of the dialectical character of the allegorical sign, which consists, essentially, in the dependence of revelation on concealment. It is the effect of the communication-function, for example, to conceal truth-content, to repress it, in order finally to ensure the revelation of truth-content precisely as that which is *not* transmissible, not for another but for itself. From this point of view Benjamin's continuous recognition that the Proustian *mémoire involuntaire* derives from daydream, rather than from alertness or an effort of will, becomes intelligible. One only wants to ask, in all these cases, whether the two sides of the allegorical sign, the semiotic and the semantic, are as decidedly opposed as they seem to be, even and especially in Benjamin's own thought.

"Nowhere does Moscow look like the city itself; at most it resembles its outskirts" ("Moscow," in *Reflections,* p. 125). A playful engima, this, ostensibly a piece of concrete "information." But in "meaning" it is crucial Benjamin, and deeply anti-Platonic. The city is not the idea or essence or even the "sum" of its parts; it can only resemble certain of its parts among others. Just so, in language, the kernel or "truth" of a message turns out simply to be more language: "a proverb . . . is a ruin which stands on the site of an old story" ("The Storyteller," in *Illuminations,* p. 108). This and many similar passages call to mind the maxim from Goethe's *Maximen und Reflexionen* quoted by Benjamin in his doctoral thesis on Romanticism: "Do not look behind the phenomena; they themselves are the truth" *(Gesammelte Schriften,* I, i, 60). Benjamin freely elaborates on this notion in the essay called "Surrealism":

> We penetrate the mystery only to the degree that we recognize it in the everyday world, by virtue of a dialectical optic that perceives the everyday in the impenetrable, the impenetrable in the everyday. The most passionate investigator of telepathic phenomena, for example, will not teach us half as much about reading (which is an eminently telepathic process), as the profane illumination of reading about reading. . . . The reader, the thinker, the loiterer, the *flâneur,* are types of

illuminati just as much as the opium eater, the dreamer, the ecstatic. *(Reflections,* pp. 189–90)

One should note with momentary surprise the way in which this passage about experience passes smoothly into the remarks about reading. For Benjamin, to be conscious is to read. There is no distinction worth making, that is, between reality and representation since it is quite natural and proper to consider experience to be exclusively one or the other. Experience itself, however, whether it concerns the language of nature or the language of art, has a more legitimately two-fold character, consisting of the *Erlebnis,* in which life is loitered through, and the *Erfahrung,* in which the loiterer notices, on a sandy part of the sidewalk, a pearl.[30] I have permitted myself this last figure in order to put the same kind of question I have been asking heretofore, and which I believe Benjamin himself finally to be asking—the question whether the difference between Erlebnis and Erfahrung is really one of contrast, whether it is not rather a difference of intensity within the same, or nearly the same, medium. "Why should only idealists be permitted to walk a tightrope," asks Benjamin in a passage quoted by Gershom Scholem *(Walter Benjamin,* p. 153), "while materialist tightrope walking is prohibited?" In the remaining pages I shall discuss the advantages that accompany the tightrope walking between dualistic categories that Benjamin permits himself (over the term *materialist,* inevitable to Benjamin after the late 1920s, one need not quibble); but for the moment it must be admitted that the collapse of dualism does entail a sacrifice. On the "border" there can be neither progressive dialectics nor dialectics concerning progress. This built-in limitation in his friend's use of dialectic was what moved Adorno to complain that Benjamin's obscurely organized study of nineteenth-century Paris was "located at the crossroads of magic and positivism."[31] Be this as it may, it is tempting to conclude, especially of one whose father numbered Oriental rugs among his business concerns, that Benjamin characteristically sought the figure in the magic carpet.

But for Benjamin illumination is never, more strictly speaking, the result of a search, of tearing aside veils. It is not a form of *activity.* One need only think of his atypically Freudian acknowledgment that presence of mind depends on forgetting (that is, on repression), or of his more congenial fascination, again, with the *mémoire involuntaire,* which is repressed reassuringly at random in Proust rather than by any one structure of shock absorption. The experience of truth for Benjamin is always a kind of Pauline conversion; it accords, that is, with the likelihood that those who persist in paying attention to the road will never fall off their horse. It is only partly then a Kantian idea, in the "Epistemo-Critical Prologue" to the *Trauerspiel* study, that "Truth is the death of intention": "This, indeed, is just what could be meant by the story of the veiled image of Säis, the unveiling of which was fatal for whoever sought thereby to learn the truth" *(Origin,* p. 36).

Benjamin's analysis of Baudelaire as an allegorist of the Modern begins properly with Baudelaire's dedication "Au lecteur," with its formal allegory (prosopopoeia in this case) of allegory itself:

> C'est l'Ennui!—l'oeil chargé d'un pleur involuntaire,
> Il rêve d'échafauds en fumant son houka.
> Tu le connais, lecteur, ce monstre délicat,
> —Hypocrite lecteur,—mon semblable,—mon frère!

Dreaming of all the forms of *échafaudage* that will seem particularly inter-changeable to a materialist (mounting the scaffold, haranguing a crowd, making a fortune, putting theories and books together), Monsieur Bore-dom is a user of "Hashish in Marseilles." T. S. Eliot, who knew Baudelaire well, who complained about the "dissociation of sensibility" in modern life and letters, and with whom Benjamin has surprising affinities, famously quotes the last line of Baudelaire's poem at the end of the passage in *The Waste Land* that begins with a Dantesque view of city life:

> Unreal city
> Under the brown fog of a winter dawn,
> A crowd flowed over London Bridge, so many,
> I had not thought death had undone so many.

Of similar people—commuters and small house agent's clerks—Benjamin writes: "Baudelaire envisaged readers to whom the reading of lyric poetry would present difficulties. . . . Will power and the ability to concentrate are not their strong points . . . ; they are familiar with the 'spleen' which kills interest and receptiveness" ("On Some Motifs in Baudelaire," in *Illumina-tions,* p. 155).

Unlike Eliot's Tiresias, Baudelaire knew that these readers were types of himself, steeped, to use the phrase Benjamin quotes from the "Salon de 1845," in the "indolence naturelle des inspirés" *(Charles Baudelaire,* p. 67). Baudelaire knew that only the hypocrite could claim otherwise because the dissociation of sensibility, the loss of self-presence and of presence to things that is reflected in what Benjamin calls the allegorical state of language, was quite simply the basis of existence itself. There are many important tensions in this matrix of ideas that merit careful review—beginning with a consider-ation of Benjamin's most complex and ambivalent dialectic, within which, in one form or another, "distraction" is revealed to be inseparable from "the aura."

VI

Some preliminary observations explaining and defending the place I envi-sion for distraction in the theory of interpretation may be useful. In an interesting recent defense of semantic determinacy, Ralph Rader attempts to isolate authorial inattention as an instance of obvious incompetence that can be accounted for and set aside in determining the author's meaning. Thus a vulgarly pert little story that he found "on a shop-counter" depends for its point on a sequence of conception, pregnancy, and abortion that could have taken place only within twenty-four hours. This sort of blunder Rader calls "the intended and unavoidable negative consequence of the artist's positive constructive intention."[32] If, however, he had found the story in an avant-garde fiction quarterly, Rader might not have liked it any better but he would have been alerted to the possibility that the foreshortening of time might not be a mistake. It could represent the finger of God, its own absurdity, the ethically pointed interruption of ordinary life by contagious magic, or any number of other things. Without some sort of presupposition, one can no more ascertain where decorum has been broken than where it has been sustained or reinforced. This necessary uncertainty pertains to the reader's own comprehension as well as to that of the writer. We cannot decide with certainty whether coherence is ever, after all, the true or truly final objective of what we read and think.

At the height of scientific positivism, it was taken for granted that in all minds there exists what I. A. Richards called a "tendency towards increased order," meaning an increasingly complex order, not an increasingly rigid one.[33] In view of the more recent findings of science itself, I doubt whether it is possible today to take such an unflinchingly teleological view of mind, either in the individual or as it is manifest in society. There is certainly some evidence for a tendency toward increased order. Sociobiology, ego psychology, the sociology of the herd instinct, and the various behavioral psychologies would all suggest it—and would suggest also that this tendency is not something to be especially proud of. But there is also evidence of tendencies in the mind toward some zero-condition (Freud's late theory that "the aim of all life is death"), toward entropy, toward increased simplicity (neo-primitivism and the various Negative Ways to beatitude), and toward the kind of disorderly frenzy that is not always cultivated, like the *katharsis* of Aristotle's *Politics,* for the sake of an ensuing calm. With all these conflicting evidences at hand, it seems likeliest that there is no continuously dominant tendency of any kind. The mind appears to be the scene of endless jostling between orderly and disorderly impulses; or rather, if there is a main tendency, a "goal orientation," for example, or even what Gadamer can call "the anticipation of completion that guides all our understanding" (*Truth and Method,* p. 261), it is not furnished by the mind itself, neuroses apart, but by the social context of the individual.

On this view, the rage for order is not "blessed," not intrinsically worthy, but a survival mechanism whose value is a wholly practical matter. Art, which is an elaborated rehearsal and celebration of survival, naturally affirms the "tendency towards increased order" as an unconditional value.

Such is the probable nature of mind, however, that this design of art, the design of achieving design, is certain to be interfered with in incommensurable ways—not only by the unconscious but also by countless environmental factors, by Pierre Macherey's *"unconscious of the work* (not of the author),"[34] by Fredric Jameson's "political unconscious," or negative confluence of silent ideological pressures,[35] and so on. Such revisions of a strictly psychological understanding of mind as these last two are important and deserve elaboration, as long as they do not lend themselves to an antithetical formalism. There is also a grace beyond the reach of unconsciously determined structures; it appears as a happy mutancy, just as the grace beyond the reach of art is a happy mistake.

There is a school of interpretation which supposes the Keatsian ideal of "existing in uncertainty without any irritable reaching after fact" to be a condition of total ignorance. Now, although it is indeed true that one is certain, for the moment, of whatever one says, even of one's ambivalence or one's willingness to reconsider,[36] it would be difficult to show that the certainties even of those who think they are certain accumulate or achieve stability. And yet despite this limitation we all exist in states of greater or lesser knowledgeability. E. D. Hirsch has influentially denied, however, that any meaning can be communicated at all that is not understood with an achieved, invariable certainty. Meaning, in his view, is necessarily determinate, which is to say that it is constituted by a guiding intention. Thus for example he argues that "symptomatic meanings," which are inchoate stirrings of inner discourse beyond the control of the will, "may be of immense interest, but they should not be confused with verbal meanings, because meaning thereby loses its determinacy."[37] Meaning is also to be distinguished from "significance," which is the projection of meaning against its social background, the author's life, our own responses, and so on.[38]

These distinctions derive most directly from Wimsatt and Beardsley's distinction, in "The Affective Fallacy," between "what [the poem] *is* and what it *does*."[39] For Wimsatt and Beardsley, as for Kant, the identity of a poem, as a poem, is constituted by its independence from both author and reader. For Hirsch it is independent of the latter but is bound to the former as an intentional structure. Its intention, its having been willed to exist in one form and not another, *is* its meaning, and "meaning" has no other meaning. This modification of his own position disturbed Monroe Beardsley so much that he insisted in response to Hirsch that meaning without the inference of an intention is still not indeterminate.[40] Both sides have a point. An intentional structure, or *epoche,* in the Husserlian sense invoked by Hirsch that is unintended or not discernibly intended in the everyday sense of the term employed by Wimsatt and Beardsley does exist, certainly, even in automatic writing. But its existence does not prove, other than by the fiat of redefinition, that it has a bearing on meaning. Perhaps all things are intended, then—a point for Hirsch—but regardless of whether they are they have some meaning—a point for Beardsley.

The controversial question at issue, of course, is whether the meaning of a text can be considered open and indeterminate. Interpretation is configuration: contemporary critics agree on this point but cannot agree as to its implications. One group, the group concerned with method, understands configuration to be a narrowing down of meaning so that what began obscurely ends by declaring itself. The other group thinks of configuration as a superfigurative process eddying out from a center that is not authentically central but only heuristic, a point of departure among others. On this latter view, each and every decision to stop interpreting must be arbitrary. One could always go on. Marvell's metaphor, "deserts of vast eternity," could be taken as an emblem of meaning without closure.[41] "Vast" is the bridge between the finitude of deserts and the boundlessness of eternity; by this mediation the former shrinks the latter and the latter stretches the former, but neither can wholly mitigate its difference from the other. Thus, neither Marvell's coy mistress nor the reader can ever be quite certain whether they have world enough and time or not. Left with the impossibility of knowing for certain, one perceives that neither the Christian-moralist nor the Anacreontic "readings" of the poem are adequate except as expressions of the reader's inevitable bias or overcompensation for bias—states of mind which themselves vacillate in intensity.

Precipitated in its indeterminacy by the nature of language, then—by the illogic of metaphor or by some other treachery lurking in the always inaccurate copula "is"—meaning is completed finally by the exhausted patience of the interpreter. Until then, meaning turns and turns; it is not merely twofold or "ambiguous" but gathers new resonance and irony from each return to a former viewpoint. This process is catalyzed not merely by tropes and figures but by every aspect of representation. We can choose quixotic characters in French literature more or less arbitrarily as an example. At first there seem to be two views, supportive or ironic, to be taken of, say, Alceste, Saint-Preux, Julien Sorel, Lucien de Rubempré, or Emma Bovary. They are all either self-centered fools or holy innocents, so defined in either case, usually in disagreement with one another, by their fictional societies and by their readers. Most readers would agree that it is not enough merely to take sides for or against these characters after the manner of the Rousseau who idolized Alceste. But it is not much more adequate to "see both sides." "Implied" as we are in the social milieu of these quixotics even while we are marooned in our own, our most honest and attentive view of them must remain unstable; it will gradually uncover their identities in revealing the ebb and flow of our own discontent with the forms of civilization. Our sympathy for such characters begins as condescension; the resulting irony entails self-recognition, however, and that may be the basis for a subtler sympathy that subsumes irony without malice; but in this more accepting form, our irony may inspire anger at the helplessness our acceptance implies, and that anger may give rise to a fresh wave of sympathy—as Socrates complains in the *Republic*—that takes the form of self-pity. All these—and more—are what I would call interpretive emotions, emotions attendant upon interpretation that cannot exist apart from it. They are "in the reader" from the beginning, yet they can never be separated from the text without ceasing to be interpretive.

Despite the affectivism of these exercises and the view of meaning that it implies, one *could* quite readily accept the logic of Hirsch's declaration that meaning is only what is given by authority. It is not tautological and it is a fair use of the word *meaning,* both etymologically and grammatically. But the consequence of this assertion resembles that of Croce's having put the true work of art in the head of the artist where we can never find it. Hirsch is protective of meaning in just this way and withholds it from us in purporting to guarantee it. Partial, indeterminate, and wrong, meaning can only be where we can find it; to put it another way, meaning is always already what Hirsch calls "significance," a mis-take or special appropriation, not of "meaning" but simply of the text itself.

Mistakes being protean, they help us to interpret as long as we resist the temptation to play Menelaus with them. On just this subject, significantly, one of the least mistake-prone (as opposed to mistaken) of critical theorists, Oscar Wilde, makes a simple mistake in attribution that tells one an enormous amount about the *Odyssey* and about Oscar Wilde. Speaking of a lady, doubtless fictitious, whose life imitated art, he says that "she was a kind of Proteus, and as much a failure in all her transformations as was that wondrous sea-god when Odysseus [*sic*] laid hold of him."[42] Menelaus in book 4, it will be recalled, interrupts his news about Odysseus and about himself to explain obliquely why he has chosen the Elysian fate that Odysseus rejected in tearing himself from the arms of Calypso. Thus in proclaiming his identity Menelaus is wrestling Odysseus, who would never, himself, have wrestled Proteus because he would have recognized Proteus in himself. Odysseus becomes a hero by choosing the protean ways of mortal existence, while Menelaus loses his identity and sinks into oblivion by having tricked Proteus and chosen to pin down that which is eternal and unchanging. Thus Wilde's mistake is a revealing interpretation of Homer, one that portrays in a new light the way in which the *Odyssey* itself is a triumph of the polytropic hero over the single-minded, form-conscious heroes of the war fought in behalf of Menelaus in the *Iliad*.

But this mistake is also a revealing interpretation of Oscar Wilde. At least *he* cannot be accused of having fallen into "careless habits of accuracy"

("Decay of Lying," p. 169); *he* at least withstands the decay of lying. For Wilde as for Benjamin (both are alert counter-Platonists) lying is the truth of masks, and thus it is that in his mistake about Proteus Wilde undermines his pose as an aesthete and reveals, more radically then realism ever can, that in the perpetual error of its appearances art *is* life. He who best wrestles Proteus does not wrestle him at all, never forces him into a shape, because he is, like Odysseus, Proteus himself. One need not stress the subject matter of this mistake, which begins with the comparison of Proteus and a lady, in order to recognize the degree to which, at moments like this, it is precisely the mistake, and not the realism Wilde disliked, that "incriminates" art, as Richard Ellmann puts it, with the atmosphere of experience.[43]

That Wilde's mistake is probably inadvertent or forgetful only increases its significance. Mistakes of his distracted kind are the ones that are most likely to lead somewhere. It is no accident that in choosing instances of the way in which life imitates art Wilde singles out *mist*. Not only "those wonderful brown fogs" that "did not exist until Art had invented them," but the closing remarks of the dialogue bespeak the importance of unclarity—not for its own sake but in context: "At twilight nature becomes a wonderfully suggestive effect, and is not without loveliness, though perhaps its chief use is to illustrate quotations from the poets." Here and only here, when nature has finally been merged with art, Proteus with Odysseus, is there no further need for interpretation: "Come! We have talked enough" ("Decay of Living," p. 196). "Between me and life," Wilde once said, "there is a mist of words always."[44] Although this is said with poignancy and must always prompt a vigorous nod of assent from those who have grown impatient with Wilde, the image of mist is an illuminating one. It identifies the connection between the mystification of "aura"—the rapt concentration of affect shared by object and spectator under certain conditions—and the error, or distraction, that it entails in the work of Benjamin.

VII

Benjamin had many precursors, apart from Freud, in the analysis of modernity as a distracted condition in which consciousness is given over to the warding off of surplus shocks. Two whose influence was perhaps most immediate were the sociologist Georg Simmel, who wrote in "The Metropolis and Mental Life" (1903) that "what appears directly as dissociation is in reality only one of the elementary forms of socialization,"[45] and the Surrealist Louis Aragon, whose 1924 celebration of the Paris Arcades, the phantasmagoric *Le Paysan de Paris,* is introduced by the oddly complacent confession that "the merest summons can distract me from anything, save from my distraction."[46] It seems generally to have been agreed upon by intellectuals in the 1920s that for clarity of mind a certain distance is necessary and can best be assured by the defensive postures of life in the crowd. Thus Simmel goes on to write that every metropolite becomes a "stranger" (the title of another of his essays) and that this reserve "assures the individual of a type and degree of personal freedom to which there is no analogy in other circumstances."[47]

Obviously enough, Simmel's "intellectual distance" is just what the Marxist deplores as the alienation of the bourgeois intellectual, as the aloofness of mind that looks inward and distances itself from social responsibility. However, being aware of this critique, at least in its broadest form, apparently posed no deterrent to Brecht, for one, who deliberately forsook the communal experience of Aristotelian catharsis and embraced his own tellingly named "alienation effect." It was this bold venture, as it were homeopathically dosing the masses with still more of their malaise—alienation—that so much appealed to Benjamin and formed the basis of his own arguments in "The Author as Producer" and "The Work of Art in the Age of Mechanical Reproduction." As Benjamin makes clear in "The Author as Producer," referring to Brecht, the alienation effect aims at an enlightenment that is grounded in distraction: "Here—in the principle of interruption—epic theatre, as you see, takes up a procedure that has become familiar to you in recent years from film and radio, press and photography. I am speaking of the procedure of montage: the superimposed element disrupts the context in which it is inserted" (*Reflections*, p. 234).

The difficulty inherent in ideas such as this should be evident. Aragon's quip reminds us that the moment of being distracted is very different from the *state* of distraction; the former is quite possibly a state of sudden alertness induced by a shock too great to be absorbed by the pre-conscious, whereas the latter is typically a state of revery or dullness in which the subject, overwhelmed by white noise or "fumant son houka," is in no condition to be affected by any *Verfremdung* short of the dynamite in the theater that was later recommended as a last resort by Artaud. In actuality one is apt to conclude—and Benjamin's arguments confirm this, albeit with reluctance—that the "dialectic of enlightenment" is even more dynamic than at first it seems. No reception aesthetic, certainly not Brecht's, has fully accounted for the ways in which rapt, intransitive attention slides into mesmerism unless interrupted, while aesthetic shock leads, conversely, to frustrated indifference unless suspended. What seems certain, though, is that the more complex these issues are, the closer will become the interdependence, if not the experiential similarity, of these seemingly opposite states of consciousness. If distraction is allegorical, whether in discourse or in the realm of fetish-objects, and if illumination is, again, the truth of allegory, it must be asked once more, by analogy with the questions we have put already, whether these two states are really obverse or whether they are not, in fact, kept apart by a narrow, perhaps incalculable difference of degree. The chicken and the egg comprise an inadequate model for dialectics because they have too much in common, as Benjamin perhaps means to imply when he says, in "The Storyteller," that "boredom is the dream bird that hatches the egg of experience" (*Illuminations,* p. 91).

Bad distraction, then, or alienation as dystopia, is a state that cannot be identified unequivocally except by prescriptive sociologies such as Marx's. This is something that Benjamin cannot quite agree to do. For that reason Fredric Jameson finds him lacking in the constructiveness of, say, Marcuse: Benjamin, writes Jameson, "was perhaps more conscious of what prevents us from assimilating our life experience than of the form such perfected life would take."[48] In the attitude that Jameson appears to prefer one generally finds, implied or stated, a longing for an urban, technological equivalent of tribal life. This is a longing shared by Benjamin himself at particular moments, as in the essay called "Naples" (1925): "What distinguishes Naples from other large cities is something it has in common with the African Kraal; each private attitude or act is permeated by streams of communal life. To exist, for the North European the most private of affairs, is here, as in the Kraal, a collective matter" (*Reflections,* p. 171). More characteristic, though, is the uncertainty we must suppose to have overtaken Benjamin on hearing Brecht's opinion of Kafka: Kafka feared, says Brecht, that "people become estranged from themselves by the forms of communal life" ("Conversations with Brecht," in ibid., p. 205). Working on his Kafka essay just at this time (1934), Benjamin would have had to concede that Brecht was right, and that for Kafka the cause of reification is collectivity of absolutely any kind. This sobering thought would afford one important reason why the Kafka essay, alone among the essays of the 1930s, bears little or no trace of Marxist thinking.

The issue of the relation between distraction and its putative opposite, "the aura," is what occasioned the celebrated and well-documented "Adorno–Benjamin Debate" of the 1930s.[49] Contrary to nearly all previous commentators, I must say that I think Benjamin has the best of it, not because his position corresponds better to the actual situation of the arts today, but simply because it avoids the holistic fallacy on which Adorno's aesthetic depends. Adorno brought the charge of "flagrant romanticism" against Benjamin both for his approval of the decline of the aura—viewed in this case as an ideological illusion—and for his optimistic comparison, inspired by Brecht, of the alienated spectator's "expertise" at a play or a movie with the expertise of a sports fan. What Adorno deplores is precisely the element of distraction in jazz-age art appreciation. His opinion rests, whether we agree with it or not, on a distinction that is presented as objective but must remain a matter of taste. Almost alone among antibourgeois critics, Adorno retains the Kantian "purposive manifold" as an aesthetic category governing the complete and self-contained object that calls forth the disinterested and therefore intransitive gaze of the spectator. This equilibrium he is at pains to contrast with the equally wholehearted and total attention that the bourgeois art consumer pays to kitsch. In thus discriminating between good and bad wholes, Adorno eliminates the rationale, as he thinks, for what he sees as a tactical preference on Benjamin's part for montage and fragmentation. Adorno thus offers his own version of the aura, which he calls "freedom," as the only authentic form of production and reception in the arts: "Precisely the uttermost consistency in the pursuit of the technical laws of autonomous art changes this art and instead of rendering it into a taboo or fetish, approximates it to the state of freedom, of something that can be consciously produced or made."[50] Following Kant and Coleridge, then, Adorno affirms the individual, autonomous will, hoping that in its wake, buoyed up by its integrity, the social will can effect comparable achievements. By contrast, Brecht and Benjamin do not expect the masses to will their own enlightenment, either directly or indirectly. They aim, rather, to create conditions for the visitation, as it were, of insight.

Hence, while Adorno reifies distraction as a state of mass torpor and nothing else, Benjamin approaches it dialectically, placing his hope in the abrupt awakening brought about by novel experience and the unprecedented casual participation in artistic production fostered by the mass media. Of course Benjamin did not seem to realize, as Adorno clearsightedly did, that with more money in hand fascism and the democratic bourgeoisie could commandeer technology, the means of "mechanical reproduction," more readily than the forces of progressive subversion could ever hope to do. But Benjamin's key insight, and the path it leaves open to culture as it exists, transcend this error. Throughout his career, from the *Trauerspiel* study to the "Arcades Project" of the 1930s, he recognized, with Brecht, that distraction—the equivalent of which in language is allegory—is nothing other than the principle of differentiation that enables thought; he also recognized that distraction is what liberates reception (experience) from the grip of totality which is, without exception, despite Adorno's struggle to discriminate, the grip of ideology *tout court*. For Benjamin, distraction is the ground of authentic perception.

I have implied hitherto that distraction and the aesthetic aura are squarely opposed in Benjamin's work, but my preceding argument would indicate that this is probably not the case. Benjamin would perhaps prefer to present the aura and the wearing away of authenticity by reproduction as alternatives. But our suspicion that the aura, toward which Benjamin is notoriously ambivalent, is itself the truth of things (like the "melancholy, incomparable beauty" of faces in early photographs, or "the aura of these mountains, of that branch" ["The Work of Art," in *Illuminations*, pp. 226,

223])—that suspicion should prompt us to wonder whether the aura is not inseparable from the moment of distraction in which it is reproduced.

VIII

From hour to hour, distraction, which Freud called the failure of "inhibiting attention,"[51] is simply the interference of life with concentration, ranging from all the unconscious factors we have mentioned to actual interruptions in the environment—visitors from Porlock. Distraction consists in *all* the possible factors that can interfere with form and formalization. But it is this same state and no other, this failure of formal attention, which is our latter-day equivalent, duly pared down to our almost fully naturalized circumstances, of the sublime, of "grace," of the uncanny, and of the aura which remains, for Benjamin, in the vicinity of illumination. The literary equivalent of St. Paul's tumble off his horse, distraction is the Longinian experience described by the poets as the sudden awareness of being interrupted by a voice not their own:

> Biting my truant pen, beating myself for spite:
> "Fool," said my Muse to me, "look in thy heart, and write."

> But as I raved and grew more fierce and wild
>   At every word,
> Methought I heard one calling, *Child!*
>   And I replied, *My Lord.*

> To me alone there came a thought of grief:
> A timely utterance gave that thought relief,
>   And I again am strong.

>   Sudden, they shadow fell on me;
> I shrieked, and clasped my hands in exstacy!

> And they were behind us, reflected in the pool.
> Then a cloud passed, and the pool was empty.
> Go, said the bird. . . .

> This is death, death, death, she noted in the margin of her mind; when the illusion fails. Unable to lift her hand, she stood facing the audience.
>   And then the shower fell, sudden, profuse.
> . . .
>   "That's done it," sighed Miss La Trobe, wiping away the drops on her cheeks. Nature once more had taken her part.[52]

Language as it must be spoken or written precipitates mistakes necessarily. Insofar as these mistakes can be seen through, they do not constitute an aspect of our uncertainty in the long run. But the greater and more permanent confusion that is not subject to direct analysis exists in language that is just coming into being, that rises into expression from all the varieties of reverie. This sort of confusion results in mistakes that are not corrigible or even perceptible according to some definite norm but are not negligibly trivial either; in themselves indeterminate, they spread their influence in untraceable ways from concept to concept. If all definite knowledge is form, the fixing of pattern in the mind, then it must be said to have imprinted itself by passing through a grid, or template, the interstices of which are made up of differentiations of every description: thoughtful observation, received ideas, ideologically and unconsciously motivated prejudices, areas of ignorance, and lapses of attention both slight and severe. In the canon of critical theory there are methods of reading—and writing— that suppress all these factors except the first and concentrate on achieved form, and there are also methods that take all these factors except the first and last into account and concentrate on antithetical form. But there is no method that *can* accommodate the immethodical wandering of the mind, and because distraction of this kind as much as any other cause quite obviously sets mistakes in motion, one can see that method is thus far lacking in comprehension. What is needed is not a method but a theory that accounts for marginal error—not even a new theory, but an openness within existing theories.

The play of mind in "The Work of Art in the Age of Mechanical Reproduction" gestures toward this kind of openness. Benjamin's essay is remarkable for its ambivalence toward the values it juxtaposes, even though its declared duty is to celebrate the supersedence of the aura of unique masterpieces by the more pragmatic effects of mass production and mass reception. Brecht had already complained, in "The Threepenny Trial," of "the old kinds of untechnical, antitechnical 'glowing' art, with its religious links."[53] Distraction, the state of mind in which architecture has always been received and the cinema is now received, should be welcome to a Brechtian as an obvious contributor to the dissolution of "aura"—of "the long-since counterfeit wealth of creative personality"—and, it may be added, of the allegedly perdurable existence of the art object in and for itself that is proclaimed by formalism (see *Illuminations,* pp. 239–41). But the author of "Unpacking My Library" cannot rest content with the revolution he announces. He does not fully control the tone of his attitude toward mass taste, and he cannot resist concluding that distraction has its merely philistine side: "Reception in a state of distraction . . . is increasing notice-ably in all fields of art and is symptomatic of profound changes in appercep-tion" (ibid., p. 240). Nothing good is ever a symptom; Benjamin's ambiva-lence of taste is revealed in his having made distraction a more vulgar phenomenon (a matter of simple indifference) than it necessarily is.

Distraction according to the sense in which I intend it is never a state of complete disregard or mindless imperception; those conditions, of course, a constructive literary theory can safely disregard. What must be taken into account, rather, because it is as much the author's as the reader's share, is little more than a wavering of concentration, a falling away from the Kantian "rapt, intransitive attention."[54] It is a mist, like that of words for Oscar Wilde, that mediates without blocking perception. Benjamin opposes it to "concentration," or "being absorbed by the work of art" ("Work of Art," p. 298) and makes it sound exclusively like woolgathering, but in my view distraction is simply the hum of temporal existence itself, which is always with one except when it precipitates those moments of clearing to which Longinus was the first to address himself as a critic. One is always failing to concentrate, says Benjamin elsewhere in the same essay, as a camera will show when it "introduces us to unconscious optics as does psychoanalysis to unconscious impulses" (ibid., p. 237). There should be no question of wanting to get rid of distraction even if one could, for it is at once the necessary encroachment of reality on interpretation and the necessary ground on which a clearing may suddenly appear.

All the theorists of the reader reading have helped to remove the work of art from its glass case and brought it closer to us, but as yet they have not made "us" recognizably like ourselves. Many readers have been offered as models, but as yet no distracted reader. Affective theorists have been duly skeptical about the limits of objective knowledge and have therefore imagined readers who are "aspect seers,"[55] but in general these readers see their aspects much too clearly. The "sincerity," or self-knowledge, recommended to readers by Richards is already complete in them.[56] Richards's reader can be liberated from the ten malfunctions of reading, Freud's from neurosis, Kenneth Burke's from ignorance of his mode of agency in a scene, Hans Robert Jauss's from rigid expectation-horizons, Jonathan Culler's from "literary [in]competence," and so on. None of these authors supposes that his reader exists, any more than Wallace Steven's "Large Red Man Reading" exists, but each nevertheless proposes his reader as a guiding light. In other words, all tacitly or openly acknowledge that distraction prevents their readers from appearing on earth, yet none makes the crucial decision that appears to be incumbent on them in that case, which is to incorporate distraction into a theory of reading. All deny the possibility of "disinterested" reading, but none fully identifies the factors that constitute the reader's interest. Defects in configurativity are not vacuous or merely idle: they are complexly motivated and excitable conditions which are as likely to inspire interpretation as the state of Keatsian "indolence" or Coleridgean "dejection" is likely to inspire poetry.

All the fictive readers in critical theory are remarkably good at formalization. They notice right away that sonnets have fourteen lines and a certain rhyme scheme. They are demons for the return of images and the dialectic of themes. They never come by all this information haphazardly. It is very probable, though, that one's first impulse toward formalization, one's first intuition of "unity" in the text, comes in ways that cannot be accounted for. Dreaming, musing, one reads "A slumber did my spirit steal" and corrects oneself instantly, but one's first feeling for the emptiness and vertigo of Wordsworth's lyric may come from that mistake. Or, in reading "fields of *sheep*" in the Great Ode, the reader will first come to notice that "bounding lambs" grow up just as children do, and thus he will take fuller cognizance, in this poem, of the pastoral element that Wordsworth was at such pains to emphasize as a crucial part of childhood in the eighth book of the *Prelude*. It is amazing how many blunders of this obvious uncomplicated variety have to do with the evidently contagious themes of reverie, sleep, or distraction itself.

It is more realistic to have gone wrong in these ways—it brings one closer to the modality of literature as well as life—than to have committed only those blunders which are permitted to ideal readers and which turn out to have contributed to an economy of configuration. The "stock response" of Richards and the corrigible "intrinsic genre" of Hirsch are necessary first orientations for the successful reader. Stanley Fish's competent reader could not learn the unifying lesson of his own fallen ignorance without first falling regularly and systematically into the trap of premature semantic closure.[57] Blunders of this kind are not defects in reading but structural principles (like hamartia in Aristotle) that are given a place in theory to explain how the configurative narrowing down of successful reading can be said to have occurred. At least for most of us, though, the reading process is very dissimilar to this sort of configuration, and dissimilar likewise to the description of reading by St. Augustine that is quoted with approval by Hirsch: "The more it progresses forward, so much more the expectation being shortened the memory is enlarged."[58] Only a seer of the Eternal Moment could seriously maintain that the whole of the psalm he repeats to himself stays in his consciousness and increasingly aids the progress of his configuration. Even memorized texts do not remain in consciousness for more than a few lines at a time; they are very little more continuously available to contemplation than merely familiar texts are. Mnemonic devices contain information that we do not remember until we come upon it in reciting the devices. For all texts, I think, we must suppose that during the reading process our tendency to *replace* old data with new, creating a very loose mooring for the purposes of configuration, fully offsets the brief stability of the data that are replaced.

Once more, though, I would want to question the value of successful configuration even if it were possible. Consensus being achieved, all that would remain would be to trace the implications of the "willed type." Kenneth Burke sounds a little like Benjamin, undecided and perhaps somewhat nostalgic, but he understands perhaps even more clearly than Benjamin what role is played by distraction in the literary mind when he says, "if one returns to . . . a work again and again, it is because, in the chaos of modern life, he has been able to forget it."[59] "Has been able": few critics committed to fixed points of view could manage to convey that sense of relief so soon after their avowal of distaste for the conditions that have made forgetfulness possible. Burke's agile sentence perfectly exemplifies what criticism could be like under those conditions.

IX

Very well, one is distracted, and so is one's author. How does that affect what one says about literature? Essentially, what must come into question is the ideal of critical impersonality. Because "the personality of the critic"[60] is never wholly suppressed by the official language of institutions, the critic can only choose, in that case, to reveal his or her personality willingly or to reveal it inadvertently in the ways that my "psychoanalysis of formalism" was meant to indicate. The former choice is "rhetorical" in the pejorative sense commonly deployed against it because it anticipates inevitabilities by staging them. The first person singular either proclaims its arrogance to be its own, not that of its approved method or institution, or else it confesses shortcomings to which method could never admit. Certainly these can be vices of style, the former vainglorious and the latter merely coy, but they at least make their margin of error a personal matter.

Of the three possible attitudes toward voice, the pretense that one does not have one, the effort to speak in someone else's, and the willingness to use one's own, the last is obviously the least offensive and would flourish, I think, if the several methods of criticism did not unfortunately come ready-equipped with their several styles, ranging from ornate to plain. Aristotle's bad style, so unlike the eloquence attributed to him by Cicero and so often apologized for by his modern admirers, is after all a perfect reflection of the distance he cultivates. And the rhapsodic mannerism that creeps into the style of Longinus or Charles Lamb or the late Barthes is a reflection of everything that is good and bad in their *participation mystique.* Style is a matter of "taste," as that quality was understood by Gracián; it tries to catch the flavor, as literally as possible, of a certain kind of civilization. One is uncontrollably irritated by alien styles: indeed it is impossible not to care what civilization should taste like, but it is nonetheless churlish to adjudicate the wars of doctrine with charges and countercharges of provincialism. The wag who remarks that a particular critic's tone reminds him of a bad translation of a minor French poet must be willing to hear that his own style is that of a very minor English poet in the original language.

Certainly there is no occasion to glory in the presence of personality in criticism. Interpretation, as Gadamer subtly establishes, is not self-expression merely. But if personality and self-expression are bound to appear in criticism, they may as well be admitted. Criticism is literature; there is surely no harm in repeating once more that the *Lives of the Poets* affords more literary pleasure than *Irene*. But criticism is only one kind of literature. It can never cease to be a "secondary revision" and it will go on taking its cue, as much as possible, from what it revises. My own taste runs to a personable but philologically keen, densely allusive criticism that takes *more* and more diverse cues from its text than is customary. The criticism of Geoffrey Hartman, which is of this kind, exemplifies what I have called the staging of distraction. The roundabout course of his allusiveness represents the course of interpretive discovery. His criticism is the most *realistic* record we have of what literate reading is like. In this vein, one can say of Benjamin's criticism, as Robert Alter remarks, what Benjamin says of Kafka's parables: it is "a body of Aggadah in search of a Halakhah, lore in quest of law, yet so painfully estranged from what it seeks that the pursuit can only end in a pounce of destruction, the fictional rending the doctrinal."[66] The critic, then, as *Hamlet: ou le distrait?* Possibly there is something in this of what Arnold called the "personal estimate" and Richards, "irrelevant association"; it is the result, in any case, of refusing to pretend not to have been surprised by what one reads.

It is true that few critics are personable enough to risk placing themselves in the foreground of their work. However, it cannot be a principled objection to oppose the promotion of personality in criticism, because the principle in question, if elevated to law, would become absurd. It would silence Johnson, Arnold, Eliot, and the authentic late Romantic Harold Bloom most obviously, but it would at least subdue most other notable critics. To enforce the impersonally custodial role of criticism on principle would be to exemplify the mode of error that I have tried to describe in this book, the derivation of method from instinctual discrimination.

It remains to ask what a criticism that is not positive should be expected to accomplish and what standards it should have for itself. (What is said here will not apply to criticism that is meant for a primer or an introduction. This exemption may seem to rule out a great deal of criticism, but it does *not* disregard the "general reader," in whose name difficult writers are customarily abused, but who has no need, should such a reader exist at all, of sympathetic condescension.) Especially because in every other department of thought and art at present the avant garde has retrenched, it is incumbent on the critic to unsettle received ideas of the sort that Shelley associated with the decline of poetry. Not just anyone's ideas, however, and especially not those of the opponent whom the controversialist delights in calling "naive." The received ideas the responsible critic should attempt to unsettle are his or her own. One's self-consciousness as a reader should be channeled into the analysis of one's own habitual distractions. It is here that we can return to Gadamer, having once admitted—as he would not—that to be aware of one's own distractions is to open oneself to them and cannot entail ridding oneself of them. What Gadamer points out is that the vantage point of the interpreter can never be a "fixed ground," a methodological perspective that transcends the temporality of interpretation: "The horizon of the present is being continually formed, in that we have continually to test our prejudices" *(Truth and Method,* p. 273).

Here is the locus classicus in praise of this kind of thinking from Arnold's "The Function of Criticism." Having quoted Edmund Burke's admission that it would be mere obstinacy to go on resisting if revolution should prove desirable to most others, Arnold continues:

> That return of Burke on himself has always seemed to me one of the finest things in English literature, or indeed in any literature. That is what I call living by ideas: when one side of a question has long had your earnest support, when all your feelings are engaged, when you hear all round you no language but one, when your party talks this language like a steam-engine and can imagine no other,—still, to be able to think, still to be irresistibly carried, if so it be, by the current of thought to the opposite side of the question, and, like Balaam, to be unable to speak anything *but what the Lord has put in your mouth,* I know nothing more striking, and I must add that I know nothing more un-English. [62]

The sentence I quoted earlier from Kenneth Burke is a modern instance of the sort of criticism that is "carried . . . by the current of thought to the opposite side of the question," even from one phrase to the next. Even a circumspect definition can have this property; in Santayana's brilliant "Beauty is pleasure regarded as a quality of the thing," the first part of the predication fitly celebrates beauty and the qualifier faintly censures it for masquerading as what it is not. Somehow one can find compressed in Santayana's axiom the entire literature of amorous delusion. But the text I want to single out finally as a model of what criticism tempered by a fine distraction can do is from T. S. Eliot's later criticism, at the end of the 1944 lecture to the Virgil Society entitled "What Is a Classic?" Eliot spends nearly the whole essay arguing for centrality, almost neutrality, in a classic and insists that its urbanity should be characterized by the absence of idiosyncracy and surprise. Classic prose, he says, develops toward a "common style," [63] and the Latin language can produce a classic because it is "more homogeneous than English." All this is very stuffy; no Spinoza yoked with the smell of cooking here. The emphasis on homogeneity is not unrelated, furthermore, to the uglier emphases of the late cultural essays that I mentioned in the introduction. Even the surprising passage I am about to quote retains some of the smugness of those essays, but it is still an exemplary act of criticism, both in voice and in its stunning imaginative range. Eliot is carried beyond his topic, *The Aeneid,* by the realization that the centrism of the "classic" is not quite an end in itself, however urbane, but exists instead as the necessary origin of something that passes beyond its limits—just as form, as we have seen, is the necessary ground of the sublime:

> In our several literatures, we have much wealth of which to boast, to which Latin has nothing to compare; but each literature has its great-ness, not in isolation, but because of its place in a larger pattern, a pattern set in Rome. I have spoken of the new seriousness—*gravity,* I might say—the new insight into history, illustrated by the dedication of Aeneas to Rome, to a future far beyond his living achievement. *His* reward was hardly more than a narrow beachhead and a political marriage in weary middle age: his youth interred, its shadow moving with the shades the other side of Cumae. And so, I said, one envisages the destiny of ancient Rome. So we may think of Roman literature: at first sight, a literature of limited scope, with a poor muster of great names, yet universal as no other literature can be; a literature uncon-sciously sacrificing, in compliance to its destiny in Europe, the opu-lence and variety of later tongues, to produce, for us, the classic. . . . [Virgil was] the great ghost who guided Dante's pilgrimage: who, as it was his function to lead Dante towards a vision he could never himself enjoy, led Europe towards the Christian culture which he could never know; and who, speaking his final words in the new Italian speech, said in farewell
>
> > *il temporal foco e l'eterno*
> > *veduto hai, figlio, e sei venuto in parte*
> > *dov' io per me più oltre non discerno.*
>
> Son, the temporal fire and the eternal, hast thou seen, and art come to a place where I, of myself, discern no further. ("What is a Classic?" pp. 73–74)

X

The theme of this passage, by which, once more, I am perhaps perversely reminded of Benjamin,[64] returns me to the embattled question of "history," the ground of method and knowledge which promoters of the current backlash against formalism and "deconstruction" alike are most unwilling to lose. The "historicity" of Heidegger, the "temporality" of de Man, the *différance* of Derrida—all these theoretical engagements with time, we are told, are not really historical and harbor a mythic hypostasization of actual social (or literary) change as a return of the same, an always already, or what Benjamin called *das Immergleiche*. Benjamin himself tried steadily to prevent any application of his analytic terms to contexts that were not historically specific. He insisted, for example, that alienation, commodity fetishism, and hence, of course, distraction itself constitute a peculiarly modern and negative kind of allegory, in the exploration of which Baudelaire, as the first Modern, was a pioneer. But I wonder whether this is his most reflective view of the matter. The Eliot of *The Waste Land,* a bourgeois universalist, and Baudelaire too, for that matter, attend to the historical conditions of their diagnosis only as a reflection of the invidious contrast between past and present that both of them deploy ironically. After all, could both find their own *contemptus mundi* already expressed in Dante; but then, just as obviously, whether he would or not, Benjamin in turn could find his own sense of man's estranged condition already present in the seventeenth-century Baroque. And, for that matter, he finds worth quoting Brecht's remark that Virgil and Dante in the *Inferno* are "nonchalant, . . . both promeneurs" ("Conversations with Brecht," in *Reflections,* p. 212).

It will be said—and said purportedly in the spirit of Benjamin—that none of the concepts I have considered, especially concepts such as allegory, distraction, and the aura, has any significant content unless it is differentiated historically. And that is what Benjamin frequently means to do. He discovers himself to have written, for example, under the influence of hashish, that "From century to century things grow more estranged." Many of his commentators have assumed that this sense of narrative in history prevails everywhere in his work and that it signals his reliability as a witness of material change. Without committing himself to this view, René Wellek summarizes this intention on Benjamin's part when he writes, concerning allegory: "What in the book on German tragedy was viewed with sympathy has now become [in the late work] a symptom of capitalist reification."[65] Sometimes Benjamin's miniature social histories of the arts are remarkably ingenious, like the argument of "A Small History of Photography," in which the aura was authentic for the first ten years of the medium, then degenerated into trumpery without disappearing as aura (*here* is Adorno's notion of masscult mesmerism), after which—to complete the dialectic neatly—the photography of Eugène Atget "initiates the emancipation of the object from aura" *(One-Way Street,* p. 250). This development has a pleasing intricacy, comparable to Adorno's wonderful gyre-like schemes for the history of music, but as a chronicle it is wholly ephemeral apart from the interest of the corpus of subjective judgments it affords.

It must be concluded, if not from the failure of arguments such as these then from the success of yet others, that Benjamin himself finally has no stable philosophy of history. The image of the hunchback in the puppet

with which we began suggests as much. It was composed under the shadow
of events that shattered all illusions of progress and engendered countless
formulas of Spenglerian decline. Five years later Adorno and Max
Horkheimer would publish their brilliant tragic narrative, *The Dialectic of
Englightenment*. Benjamin himself sometimes inclines toward a Spenglerism
which, on reconsideration, is all that "From century to century things grow
more estranged" can be said to signify.[66] More reliably, however, Benjamin
understands history itself as a state of distraction from which it is no use
trying to free oneself.[67] History, like Benjamin's prose as Geoffrey Hartman
describes it, is "curiously unprogressive or exitless."[68] From this perspective, one can only cling to the "weak messianic power" (Benjamin, "Theses") with which each generation is in turn invested. (This perceived state of
things is not to be confused with the acceptance of das Immergleiche, for
that too, of course, is a philosophy of history, the hypostasis of change as
myth.) History for Benjamin in 1940 is a growing heap of ruins, from the
retrospect of which even the finest cultural achievements prove to have been
the superstructures of barbarism. Finally, moreover, there is no true pattern
in any of Benjamin's historical arguments. After all, again, his critique of
modern "spleen" had already served as a critique of the Counter-Reforma-
tion melancholy that gave rise to Baroque art. As much could be done,
probably, for the happy Greeks.

Is distraction, then, historically conditioned? Certainly not so much as
Benjamin prefers to suppose.[69] It changes guises, of course, as completely as
"the manners" change even according to those who once believed, with
Thomas Rymer, that "human nature" is always the same. Our problem is
more complex than this comparison may suggest, though, in that everything in our analysis has tended to challenge the distinction between the
superficial and the underlying. Is it the case that the radical reconstitution of
the human that is wrought by history makes the irreducibility of hermeneutic inattention a feature of only one age, our own—a feature that can be
diagnosed, variously, as a symptom and consequence of alienation, urban-
ization, reification, or even (ironically) the decline of mnemotechnics which
accompanied the rise of social concern in academic curricula? No doubt a
history of forgetfulness is required in order to determine whether the topic
itself is, or is not, historical in the radical sense. Nevertheless, what I have
supposed in deciding to place my views on an ahistorical basis is that there
has never been a time without distraction because the medium of distraction
is time itself.

The anodyne that Homer's Helen keeps about her person shows how
long ago forgetfulness became a necessity, a defense mechanism, as well as a
nuisance. Such is the relentlessness of repression by time, as the Greeks
perceived despite their excellent memories, that mistakes attend even a state
of omniscience: "Alas," says the Tiresias of Sophocles,

> how terrible is wisdom when
> it brings no profit to the man that's wise!
> This I knew well, but had forgotten it,
> else I would not have come here.

The oldest notions of distraction are in fact associated with preternatural wisdom, even with holiness. The doctrine of anamnesis in Plato descends via Pythagoras from the Eastern sages, and what would ultimately become the category of alienation in Marx is associated, by a Marxist writer, with the mystical ecstasis, or objectification of the subject, practiced by monks in the Middle Ages.[70] And that which remains confused for us on earth is not harmoniously resolved for the angels, as it is in the "Prolog" to Goethe's *Faust,* but becomes for them, rather, as Benjamin's ninth "Thesis" declares, a still more radical disorder:

> Where we perceive a chain of events, [the angel of history] sees one single catastrophe which keeps piling wreckage on wreckage and hurls it in front of his feet. The angel would like to stay, awaken the dead, and make whole what has been smashed. But a storm is blowing from Paradise; it has got caught in his wings with such violence that the angel can no longer close them. This storm irresistibly propels him into the future to which his back is turned, while the pile of debris before him grows skyward. This storm is what we call progress. *(Illuminations,* pp. 257–58)

This passage will yield, as part of its burden, its farewell to the hope of redemption in time, a last description of the temporality of interpretation, with its necessary chasm between perception and the whole that lies in fragments before it.

Benjamin is, in my view, the most reliable of all the materialist thinkers for the reason, paradoxically, that he retains, albeit solely in the no-time of metaphysics, the religious idea of a Fall, of an absolute alienation into self-consciousness for which, if there can have been a social cause, it must have consisted in a division of labor so rudimentary that it can never be undone. We do not have to substitute a wingèd Hermes for the angel to feel at home with Benjamin's parable. Benjamin may dream of a return to oneness in a realm out of time, prefigured by the intensified *Jetztzeiten,* or "now-times" within time, of the "Theses," but his dream is not eschatological; it is not a theory or a method. As one for whom history and allegory are the same, he rejects the covert nostalgia of synthetic dialectics in favor of the open turning of thought in which meaning, ever present, is always other. With this attitude and by these means, at a time when the habit of certainty is what most threatens the future, criticism and the world can most constructively reflect each other.

NOTES

INTRODUCTION

1 See Feyerabend, *Against Method: Outline of an Anarchistic Theory of Knowledge* (Atlantic Highlands, N.J.: Humanities Press, 1975).

2 Gadamer, *Truth and Method* (New York: Crossroad Publishing, 1982).

3 De Man, *Blindness and Insight: Essays in the Rhetoric of Contemporary Criticism* (New York: Oxford Univ. Press, 1971), p. ix.

4 See Hirsch, *The Aims of Interpretation* (Chicago: Univ. of Chicago Press, 1976), p. 32.

5 See Heidegger, *Being and Time,* trans. John Macquarrie and Edward Robinson (New York: Harper & Row, 1962), pp. 194–95.

6 Lentricchia, *After the New Criticism* (Chicago: Univ. of Chicago Press, 1980), p. 284.

7 Lukács, *The Meaning of Contemporary Realism,* trans. John Mander and Necke Mander (London: Merlin Press, 1972), p. 21.

8 Lukács, *History and Class Consciousness,* trans. Rodney Livingstone (Cambridge, Mass.: MIT Press, 1971), p. 194.

9 Frye, *Anatomy of Criticism: Four Essays* (New York: Atheneum, 1967), p. 62.

10 Jauss, "Literary History as a Challenge to Literary Theory," in *New Directions in Literary History,* ed. Ralph Cohen (Baltimore: Johns Hopkins Univ. Press, 1974), p. 26.

11 Kuhn, *The Structure of Scientific Revolutions* (Chicago: Univ. of Chicago Press, 1970), p. 192.

12 See Frank, "Spatial Form in Literature," *Sewanee Review* 53 (1945), 221–40, 433–56, 643–53.

13 See Mitchell, "Spatial Form in Literature: Toward a General Theory," *Critical Inquiry* 6 (1980), esp. p. 544.

14 Barbaro, "Materialism and Art," in *Marxism and Art: Writings in Aesthetics and Criticism,* ed. Berel Lang and Forrest Williams (New York: Longman, 1972), p. 163.

15 Hirsch, *Validity in Interpretation* (New Haven: Yale Univ. Press, 1967), p. 73.

16 R. G. Peterson, "Critical Calculations: Measure and Symmetry in Literature," *PMLA* 91 (1976), p. 563.

17 Giambattista Vico, *The New Science,* trans. Thomas Bergin and M. Fisch (Garden City, N.Y.: Doubleday, 1961), p. 88.

CHAPTER 1

1 He is not infrequently called a "structuralist," as recently in a letter to *TLS* written by a specialist on the Russian Formalists, F. W. Galan (*TLS* 4087 [31 July 1981], p. 877).

2 Others who have questioned Aristotle's authority are John Crowe Ransom in *The World's Body* (New York: Charles Scribner's Sons, 1938), esp. pp. 183 ff., and Reuben Brower, who is uncomplimentary to Aristotle as a practical critic in "The Heresy of Plot," in *Aristotle's "Poetics" and English Literature,* ed. Elder Olson (Chicago: Univ. of Chicago Press, 1965), esp. pp. 161–67.

3 But see Elder Olson, who claims that it is not an inductive argument, in "The Poetic Method of Aristotle," in *Aristotle's "Poetics,"* ed. Olson, p. 178. His viewpoint (previously published 1951) is in turn criticized by J. M. Gray, "Aristotle's *Poetics* and Elder Olson," *CL* 15 (1963), p. 171. See also Humphrey House, *Aristotle's Poetics* (London: Rupert Hart-Davis, 1956), p. 34.

4 Werner Jaeger speaks eloquently of Aristotle's reverence beneath the stars in "On Philosophy" (*Aristotle: Fundamentals of the History of His Development* [Oxford: Clarendon Press, 1960] p. 159), but I do not think that he could show this attitude to be a typical one. Here and throughout I speak for the most part of "Aristotle" as the *persona* of the *Poetics,* generalizing about the author in the same way one might generalize about "Homer." Very little in what follows need reflect on Aristotle's personality, which is said to have been happy and admirable in every respect. In the few places in which I violate my rule I offer, of course, the merest speculations.

5 I. A. Richards, *Practical Criticism: A Study of Literary Judgment* (New York: Harcourt, Brace, & World, 1966), p. 273.

6 Hulme, *Speculations,* ed. Herbert Read (London: Routledge & Kegan Paul, 1954), p. 86. For an account of the Canadian experience, see Alun R. Jones, *The Life and Opinions of T. E. Hulme* (Boston: Beacon Press, 1960), pp. 23–24.

7 Unless another is specified, my translation will be that of Samuel H. Butcher in his *Aristotle's Theory of Poetry and Fine Art,* ed. John Gassner (New York: Dover Publications, 1951), cited not by page number but by chapter. The Greek texts I have followed are those of Butcher and of D. W. Lucas, *Aristotle: Poetics* (Oxford: Clarendon Press, 1968).

8 Ingram Bywater, *Aristotle on the Art of Poetry,* pref. Gilbert Murray (Oxford: Clarendon Press, 1920), p. 29.

9 *The Basic Works of Aristotle,* ed. Richard P. McKeon (New York: Random House, 1941), p. 1129. The relevance of this passage to the *Poetics* will be found discussed in William K. Wimsatt and Cleanth Brooks, *Literary Criticism: A Short History,* 2 vols. (Chicago: Univ. of Chicago Press, 1978), I, 32.

10 Jones, *On Aristotle and Greek Tragedy* (London: Chatto & Windus, 1962), p. 16.

11 *Basic Works,* ed. McKeon, p. 1129.

12 See D. Lucas, *Aristotle: Poetics,* p. 167, who disputes Aristotle on this issue.

13 *Basic Works,* ed. McKeon, p. 874.

14 For a modern interpretation of the connection between sentence and whole, see Erich Kahler, "The Forms of Form," *Centennial Review of the Arts and Sciences* 7 (1963), p. 139.

15 *Basic Works,* ed. McKeon, p. 9. This sentence seems to me to be as uncompromising, and as generally ignored by its author, as the disjunction between signs and nature that occurs in the *Cratylus,* on the consequences of which for later theories of reference, see Gerard Genette, "Avatars du Cratylisme," *Poétique* 11 (1972), 367–94; 13 (1973), 111–33; 15 (1973), 265–91. On the inevitability of

mimetic impurity in language, see Stephen Pepper's far from wholly skeptical notion of "root metaphors" in *World Hypotheses: A Study in Evidence* (Berkeley: Univ. of California Press, 1961), esp. pp. 84–113.

16 Taylor, *Aristotle* (New York: Dover Publications, 1955), p. 20.

17 Readers inclined to commit the fallacy of misplaced concreteness are often enjoined to remember this passage, together with the one from the *Nic. Ethics* ("It is the mark of an educated man to look for precision in each class of things just so far as the nature of the subject admits") which has been a watchword for the study of critical theory in general ever since it appeared as a motto to M. H. Abrams's *The Mirror and the Lamp* (New York: Norton, 1958), p. 3. I would say, though, that in the *Poetics* it is Aristotle, not his reader, who expects a kind of precision from the work of art that it cannot offer.

18 Else, *Aristotle's Poetics: The Argument* (Cambridge, Mass.: Harvard Univ. Press, 1957), pp. 208 ff. But see, e.g., against this view, G. M . Kirkwood, "*Aristotle's Poetics: The Argument,* by Gerald F. Else," *Classical Journal* 55–56 (1959–61), p. 39.

19 *Aristotle's Theory,* p. 290. Butcher's discussion of time in Aristotle is on the whole, however, helpful and evocative.

20 Kitto, "Catharsis," in *The Classical Tradition,* ed. Luitpold Wallach (Ithaca: Cornell Univ. Press, 1966), esp. pp. 140–47.

21 See D. Lucas, *Aristotle: Poetics,* p. 134.

22 See Else, *Aristotle: Poetics* (Ann Arbor: Univ. of Michigan Press, 1978), p. 94, and also his *Argument,* p. 229.

23 The passage is difficult but most translators agree roughly. Else has "more decisive" for "more" and Bywater has "more a matter for."

24 John Jones, *On Aristotle,* p. 51, suggests that this notion must have been unusual and unpopular. Sir David Ross writes: "[Aristotle] would . . . have thought it no great loss if the actors did their work behind a screen" (*Aristotle* [London: Methuen, 1966], p. 277).

25 This view has been put forward in various contexts, notably by John W. Draper, " 'Aristotelian Mimesis' in Eighteenth Century England," *PMLA* 36 (1921), p. 372, and Leonard Moss, "Plato and the *Poetics,*" *PQ* 50 (1971), 533–42. The reader is also referred, however, to the monumental defense of the term's essential coherence in classical thought by Richard P. McKeon, "Literary Criticism and the Concept of Imitation in Antiquity," in *Critics and Criticism: Ancient and Modern,* ed. R. S. Crane (Chicago: Univ. of Chicago Press, 1954), esp. p. 167.

26 This phrasing is from the translation of R. Hackforth in *Plato: The Collected Dialogues,* ed. Edith Hamilton and Huntington Cairns (Princeton: Bollingen, 1969), p. 521.

27 See his *The Languages of Art* (Indianapolis: Hackett, 1976), especially pp. 3–43.

28 For an incisive if highly personal treatment of *dianoia* in relation to the other parts of tragedy and of literature in general, one that inclines at times to pit the term against *muthos* in a dualistic contrast, see Northrop Frye, *The Anatomy of Criticism: Four Essays* (New York: Atheneum, 1967), esp. pp. 77–79. See also McKeon, "Literary Criticism," in *Critics and Criticism,* ed. Crane, p. 165.

29 Gilbert Murray implies that we are inclined to oversophisticate the distinction

between "plot" and "myth," claiming that plot *is* mythic, archetypal, in the *Poetics*. See his introduction to Bywater, *Aristotle on the Art of Poetry,* pp. 12–14.

30 On this point see Roman Ingarden, "A Marginal Commentary on Aristotle's Poetics," JAAC 20, ii (1961), p. 166.

31 The translator is L. J. Potts, *Aristotle on the Art of Fiction* (Cambridge: Cambridge Univ. Press, 1953), who follows the argument of the early commentary by Thomas Twining (1812). This argument is repudiated by Elder Olson, introduction, *Aristotle's "Poetics" and English Literature,* ed. Olson, p. xiii. In this collection of essays, however, Olson generously prints what I take to be a powerful refutation of his substantialism by Kenneth Burke, "The Problem of the Intrinsic," esp. pp. 123, 125–26.

32 Murray Krieger has interpreted the whole history of criticism as a repeated crossing over wherby "imitation" reveals itself to be "expression" and vice versa. See his *Theory of Criticism: A Tradition and Its System* (Baltimore: Johns Hopkins Univ. Press, 1976), pp. 67–97.

33 To cite the famous (and strictly textual) example of Borges: the *Don Quixote* of Pierre Menard is not that of Cervantes.

34 This problem is carefully discussed by Frederick Pottle, "Catharsis," *YR* 40 (1950–51), p. 629. The problem remains particularly controversial in discussions of the aesthetics of photography, e.g., Walker Evans's photographs of rural poverty.

35 For a lively and still relevant survey of attitudes toward the "emotional effect of tragedy," see F. L. Lucas, *Tragedy in Relation to Aristotle's Poetics* (New York: Harcourt, Brace, 1928), p. 39. For a skeptical view of catharsis to which mine is indebted, see two articles by Kenneth Burke, "On Catharsis, or Resolution, with a Postscript," *Kenyon Review* 21 (1959), 337–75, and "Catharsis—Second View," *CRAS* 5 (1961), 107–32. See also René Girard, "Dionysos and the Violent Genesis of the Sacred," *Boundary 2* 5 (1977), p. 487.

36 Burke, "Catharsis—Second View," p. 118.

37 See Else, *Argument,* p. 449. With some of his implications I cannot agree.

38 W. W. Fortenbaugh, *Aristotle on Emotion* (London: Duckworth, 1975), p. 19.

39 "Preface" to *The Plays of William Shakespeare, Samuel Johnson: Selected Poetry and Prose,* ed. Frank Brady and W. K. Wimsatt (Berkeley: Univ. of California Press, 1977), p. 303.

40 Harsh, "Ἁμαρτία Again," *Transactions and Proceedings of The American Philological Association* 76 (1945), 47–58.

41 Jones, *On Aristotle,* p. 38.

42 Concerning the conditions of epic performance, see Eric Havelock, *Preface to Plato* (Cambridge, Mass.: Harvard Univ. Press, 1963), esp. pp. 20–31.

43 Even those who do not bracket "as they are," as Else does, still remark that the idea of an intermediate character does not suit Aristotle's design in chapter 2. See D. Lucas, *Aristotle: Poetics,* p. 64.

44 Gould, "Gerald F. Else, *Aristotle's Poetics: The Argument,*" *Gnomon* 34 (1962), p. 645.

45 Wimsatt, "Aristotle and Oedipus or Else," in *Hateful Contraries: Studies in Literature and Criticism* (Lexington: Univ. of Kentucky Press, 1966), p. 83.

46 Lucas, *Aristotle: Poetics,* p. 120. Aristotle nowhere implies that nature is perfect:

"Art partly completes what nature cannot bring to a finish and partly imitates her" (*Physics* 2, 8; *Basic Works,* ed. McKeon, p. 250). To say that nature is imperfect, however, does not imply that the works of nature are misconceived or bungled. One could argue, in fact, that the purpose of the *Physics* is to show that nature is nearly as rational as art is. But see, against this position, Richard P. McKeon, "Rhetoric and Poetics in the Philosophy of Aristotle," in *Aristotle's "Poetics" and English Literature,* ed. Olson, p. 215.

47 Else, *Aristotle,* p. 61.

48 The Greek for Butcher's "happy strain of madness" is *manikos.* D. Lucas, *Aristotle: Poetics,* p. 178, writes: "There was no room in [Aristotle's] philosophy for powers which expressed themselves through the mouths of poets." See also ibid., p. 71.

49 Apropos of the parallel that is drawn here between Eurykleia and Jocasta, there may be a lost version of the *Odyssey* in which Penelope herself recognizes the scar. See D. L. Page, *The Homeric Odyssey* (Oxford: Clarendon Press, 1955), p. 122.

50 So Robert Fitzgerald calls him in book 24. See his translation (*Homer: The Odyssey* [Garden City, N.Y.: Anchor, 1963], p. 454). On the subject of Odysseus's name in general, see the superb essay by George Dimock, Jr., "The Name of Odysseus," *HR* 9 (1956), 52–70.

51 All these matters are treated in the vast literature on "organic form," of which the most important texts are: James Benziger, "Organic Unity: Leibniz to Coleridge," *PMLA* 66 (1951), 24–48; Norman H. Holland, "Why Organic Unity?" *CE* 30 (1968–69), 19–30; G. N. G. Orsini, "The Organic Concepts in Aesthetics," *CL* 21 (1969), 1–30; and W. K. Wimsatt, "Organic Form: Some Questions About a Metaphor," in *Day of the Leopards: Essays in Defense of Poems* (New Haven: Yale Univ. Press, 1976), pp. 205–23.

52 See Lane Cooper, *Aristotelian Papers* (Ithaca: Cornell Univ. Press, 1939), pp. 101–21, who gives some excellent examples of the "cosmic" in medieval literature (*Pearl,* "The Tale of Sir Thopas" [i.e., topaz]), erring only in supposing that Aristotle anticipates his insight. See also Angus Fletcher, *Allegory: The Theory of a Symbolic Mode* (Ithaca: Cornell Univ. Press, 1964), pp. 108 ff.

53 See Geoffrey H. Hartman, "The Voice of the Shuttle: Language from the Point of View of Literature," in *Beyond Formalism: Literary Essays 1958–70* (New Haven: Yale Univ. Press, 1971), pp. 298–310.

54 See Else, *Argument,* p. 446, for observations on this topic. The suppression of character in the *Poetics* is what the youthful John Henry Newman mainly complains about in *Poetry, with Reference to Aristotle's Poetics,* ed. A. S. Cook (Boston: Ginn, 1891), p. 2.

55 As I begin these remarks on the *Oedipus,* I should refer the reader to an article that warns against interpretations like mine: Sander Goodhart, "Ληστὰς˸ Εφαηε: Oedipus and Laius' Many Murderers," *Diacritics* 8 (1978), 55–71. Goodhart writes (p. 64) that most *Oedipus* criticism "reveals at its origin an idolatry of the Oedipal perspective and at its conclusion a certain self-destructive violence. . . ." See Kenneth Burke, "On Catharsis," p. 338, however, for an explanation of why these disagreeable predilections may be unavoidable. Quotations of *Oedipus the King* will be taken from the translation, with commentary, of

Thomas Gould, *"Oedipus the King" by Sophocles* (Englewood Cliffs, N.J.: Prentice-Hall, 1970).

56 Jones, *On Aristotle,* p. 213, stresses the "quasi-mathematical symmetries of the play."

57 This connection has been noted (from a very different standpoint) by Katherine E. Gilbert, "Aesthetic Imitation and Imitators in Aristotle," *Philosophical Review* 45 (1936), p. 564.

58 See Gould, *Oedipus the King,* p. 151. See also, concerning this and related issues discussed here, my essay, *"Oedipus the King,"* in *Homer to Brecht: The European Epic and Dramatic Traditions,* ed. Michael Seidel and Edward Mendelson (New Haven: Yale Univ. Press, 1977), pp. 171–90.

59 As Bernard Knox remarks, we find *bursting* wherever we look for catharsis in the *Oedipus* (*Oedipus at Thebes* [New Haven: Yale Univ. Press, 1957], p. 146). See also p. 19: "[Oedipus's] understanding of what has happened to him must be a complete rational structure before he can give way to the tide of emotion which will carry him to self-mutilation." Concerning my assertion about Aristotle's shortcomings as a reader, there exists the view that he confined himself deliberately in the *Poetics* to purely compositional matters. See, e.g., McKeon, "Literary Criticism," in *Critics and Criticism,* ed. Crane, p. 166. I do not agree with this view, but I find it to be more defensible than the one which affirms the adequacy of Aristotle's readings.

60 I would hazard the opinion that Hegel's idea of drama is more comprehensive, though less thorough, than Aristotle's (even though I have just complained of Aristotle's inadequate handling of particulars). On reflection, I believe, this will not seem strange. Hegel's thematic criticism is not a "sententious" thematics of the sort we have mentioned but a concept that is dyed, if I may, into the fabric of his exemplary play, the *Antigone.* Whereas Aristotle's in some ways detailed reading of the *Oedipus* leaves a great deal out in the long run, much more of the *Antigone* can be envisioned from Hegel's generalizations. If we were permitted two sentences to characterize these authors—first, that for Aristotle theater imitates action, and second, that for Hegel theater imitates conflict—would we not then rest more satisfied with Hegel?

• CHAPTER 2

1 For these arguments, see William K. Wimsatt and Cleanth Brooks, *Literary Criticism: A Short History,* 2 vols. (Chicago: Univ. of Chicago Press, 1978), I, 97–111.

2 Olson, "The Argument of Longinus' *On the Sublime,*" in *Critics and Criticism: Ancient and Modern,* ed. R. S. Crane (Chicago: Univ. of Chicago Press, 1954), p. 259.

3 See "ibid.," p. 233. Should there be any doubt of Aristotle's influence on Olson's allegedly "pluralistic" interpretation, Olson's assertion that the sublime "is a kind of mean" between vices of style ("ibid.," p. 242) will indicate what I mean.

4 For the differences between these views as assessed by the participants, see R. S. Crane, "The Critical Monism of Cleanth Brooks," in *Critics and Criticism,* ed. Crane, pp. 83–107; Wimsatt, "The Chicago Critics: The Fallacy of Neoclassic

Species," in *The Verbal Icon: Studies in the Meaning of Poetry* (Lexington: Univ. of Kentucky Press, 1967), pp. 41–65; Elder Olson, "The Dialectical Foundations of Critical Pluralism," *TQ* 9 (1966), 202–30. Under the tutelage of Richard McKeon, the Chicagoans tended to read Aristotle as though the distinction between language and concept, or referent, were the keystone of his sytem. See especially McKeon, "Aristotle's Conception of Language and the Arts of Language," *Critics and Criticism,* pp. 173–231.

5 *Literary Criticism,* I, 101.

6 Thomas Weiskel points to "the confusion of nature and art, author and work, which will become the trademark of the Longinian or affective sublime" *(The Romantic Sublime: Studies in the Structure and Psychology of Transcendence* [Baltimore: Johns Hopkins Univ. Press, 1976], p. 12).

7 *"Longinus" on Sublimity,* trans. D. A. Russell (Oxford: Clarendon Press, 1965), to be cited by section number and marginal number, 1.3. For translations I have also consulted *Longinus on the Sublime,* trans. A. O. Prickard (Oxford: Clarendon Press, 1906), and *On the Sublime,* trans. W. Rhys Roberts (Cambridge: Cambridge Univ. Press, 1899). I have used the Greek edition and commentary of D. A. Russell, *"Longinus" on the Sublime* (Oxford: Clarendon Press, 1964). Although the identity of the author is unknown, I follow the nearly universal convention of calling him "Longinus." It is interesting to note that a leading Longinus scholar, G. M. A. Grube, has returned to the belief, or at least leans toward it, that our author was indeed the third-century Cassius Longinus celebrated by Boileau and Gibbon *(The Greek and Roman Critics* [London: Methuen, 1965], p. 341).

8 The most extreme instance of debunking based on this error is Walter Allen, Jr., "The Terentianus of the *Peri Hupsous,"* *American Journal of Philology* 62 (1941), 51–64.

9 Neil Hertz describes the "oedipal moment" itself, insofar as Oedipus's recognition can be identified with resolution, as the "sublime of conflict and structure" ("The Notion of Blockage in the Literature of the Sublime," in *Psychoanalysis and the Question of the Text,* ed. Geoffrey H. Hartman [Baltimore: Johns Hopkins Univ. Press, 1978], p. 76).

10 The fact that Longinus almost certainly found this remark in Quintilian (*Institutio Oratoria,* 8, 3, 37) makes his assignment of it to the Peripatetics yet more significant.

11 So Roberts. Russell settles for "external trappings" even though the word is *prostragodoumenon.*

12 Grube has also argued (*Greek and Roman Critics,* p. 344) that Longinus must have in mind the emotions of characters, not audiences. Aristotle himself says, however (*Rhetoric* 1408a), that pity, grief, and fear are "low emotions" in oratory. On this point see also Allen Tate, "Longinus and the 'New Criticism,' " in *The Man of Letters in the Modern World* (New York: Meridian, 1955), p. 188.

13 I mean only the structural values of the *Poetics.* In the *Nicomachean Ethics* (1124a) there is a portrait of the "magnanimous man" which closely anticipates the sublime individual in Longinus.

14 I do not think that Longinus's distinctions are completely empty. I would agree, for instance, with Russell's excellent summary (*"Longinus" on the Sublime,* p.

126) of the difference between figures *(schemata)* and *tropoi,* which is, to put it negatively, that if a figure fails the result is a solecism whereas if a trope fails the result is a barbarism. Deconstruction is not the only current school of thought, in any case, which professes a disregard for generic and other such distinctions. See the persuasive article by John Bayley, "Against a New Formalism," *CritQ* 10 (1968), 60–71.

15 See, e.g., Russell, *"Longinus" on the Sublime,* p. 91, and G.M.A. Grube, "Notes on the *Peri Hupsous,*" *American Journal of Philology* 78 (1957), pp. 365–66.

16 Olson's "Argument" notwithstanding, I would agree with Neil Hertz that one cannot keep a fixed pattern or structure of the text clearly in mind ("Lecture de Longin," *Poétique* 4 [1973], p. 292).

17 Readers familiar with Jacques Lacan's "Seminar on 'The Purloined Letter' " (*YFS* 48 [1972], 38–72) will recognize in this chain of dissimulation and enthrallment, which is so much more complex than the Horation *Si vis me flere,* the ring of pursuit as Lacan understands it in Poe's story—and in the psychoanalytic transference.

18 On this point see Tate, "Longinus and the 'New Criticism,' " p. 183.

19 Hertz's reading of Longinus's response to Sappho differs from mine in stressing compositional qualities; I do not agree with his assertion that "La doctrine de l'unité organique a rarement été présentée avec autant de ferveur" ("Lecture de Longin," p. 295).

20 *Romantic Sublime,* p. 17. Weiskel feels on the whole, however, with Hertz, that Longinus is committed to "organic continuity" (ibid., p. 21). Wimsatt is nearly alone among the commentators in having remarked that Longinus's figures "tend to have to do with abnormalities of syntax and peculiarities of structure" (*Literary Criticism,* I, 103).

21 Allen Tate is the most extreme proponent of the notion that the sublime is a quality of words ("Longinus and the 'New Criticism,' " p. 177). See also Elizabeth Nitchie, "Longinus and the Theory of Poetic Imitation in the Seventeenth and Eighteenth Centuries," *SP* 23 (1935), p. 586. Boileau in the "Préface" to his 1674 translation of Longinus insisted persuasively that the sublime is *not* wholly a question of style (*The Continental Model: Selected French Critical Essays of the Seventeenth Century,* ed. Scott Elledge and Donald Schier [Ithaca: Cornell Univ. Press, 1970], p. 272).

22 Iser, *The Implied Reader* (Baltimore: Johns Hopkins Univ. Press, 1974), p. 280.

23 See Hertz, "Lecture de Longin," p. 292.

24 See Geoffrey Hartman on the impossible ideal of "purity" in language in *Criticism in the Wilderness: The Study of Literature Today* (New Haven: Yale Univ. Press, 1980), esp. pp. 115–57.

25 As Weiskel says (*Romantic Sublime,* p. 5), the sublime "is always cloaked in metaphors of aggression."

26 D. A. Russell is especially concerned to deny the similarities between Burke and Longinus. See, e.g., the introduction to his translation, *"Longinus" on Sublimity,* p. xvi.

27 Hertz ("Lecture de Longin," p. 299) discusses the oedipal situation that appears in this and many more of Longinus's quotations, including the passage on Phaethon's flight cited above.

28 Freud, "The 'Uncanny,' " in *On Creativity and the Unconscious,* ed. Benjamin

Nelson (New York: Harper Torchbooks, 1958), p. 156n. I return to this issue in chapter 5 (p. 175).

29 Allen, "Terentianus of the *Peri Hupsous*," pp. 52–53.

30 Burke, *A Philosophical Enquiry into the Origin of our Ideas of the Sublime and the Beautiful*, ed. James T. Boulton (London: Routledge & Kegan Paul, 1958), p. 66.

31 Burke, *Reflections on the Revolution in France* (London: J. M. Dent, 1960), p. 82.

32 Kant, *Critique of Judgment*, trans. J. H. Bernard (New York: Hafner, 1972), p. 83.

33 Perhaps the only commentator who approaches this distinction carefully is George Saintsbury in his eccentric but interesting essay on Longinus in *A History of Criticism and Literary Taste*, 3 vols. (Edinburgh: William Blackwood and Sons, 1900), I, 162.

34 Russell cautions us that grammatically the silence of Ajax is only an analogy and not an example (*"Longinus" on Sublimity*, p. 9n.), but I am not sure it matters which way we take it.

35 On the elaborateness of the frame composition in Homer, which encodes information in specular pairs of the kind I have stressed in this passage, see Cedric Whitman, *Homer and the Heroic Tradition* (Cambridge, Mass.: Harvard Univ. Press, 1958), esp. p. 294–84.

36 A. C. Bradley describes nocturnal silence as "a peace . . . that may make the face of death sublime" ("The Sublime," in *Oxford Lectures on Poetry* [London: Macmillan & Co., 1955], p. 49).

37 Eliot, "Tradition and the Individual Talent," in *The Sacred Wood* (London: Methuen, 1964), p. 52.

38 Not all hearers do so, clearly, but the response which does not in itself become an "influence" becomes, however idiosyncratic and interesting, a terminal mutation. Every significant reader is in some sense also a writer. See the text of Longinus at 7.4.

39 Harold Bloom's theory of influence presides over these next few pages in roughly the form of development, lacking the tropes and defenses, that appeared in *The Anxiety of Influence* (London: Oxford Univ. Press, 1975). Also in this context Weiskel writes admirably as follows (*Romantic Sublime*, p. 32): "To consider the problem of originality is to find the two kinds of sublimation, poet's and reader's, compounded or superimposed."

40 I refer especially to the second of three newspaper essays that are usually entitled "On Genial Criticism": see "On the Principles of Sound Criticism: Essay Second," in *Miscellanies Aesthetic and Literary*, ed. T. Ashe (London: George Bell, 1885), pp. 10–14.

41 There are several versions of this anecdote. All of them are conveniently reviewed by C. D. Thorpe, "Coleridge on the Sublime," in *Wordsworth and Coleridge*, ed. E. L. Griggs (Princeton: Princeton Univ. Press, 1939), pp. 193–94. See also Bradley, "The Sublime," p. 37.

42 Quintilian's well-known anticipation of this passage (*Institutio Oratoria*, 8, 2, 21) is a sarcastic joke at the expense of those who pride themselves on deciphering obscure passages. The relevance of this joke for anyone listening, say, to the priestess at Delphi, should be clear.

43 As Grube writes (*Greek and Roman Critics*, p. 347), "Clearly Longinus uses mimesis in the broadest, not the restricted rhetorical sense."

44 See Prickard, *Longinus on the Sublime*, p. xvi.

45 On the complexities of this passage, see Russell, *"Longinus" on the Sublime*, p. 106. Some scholars have suggested emending *psugmata* (gaps) to *psegmata* (dust, chippings).

46 Hertz argues ("Notion of Blockage," p. 70) that a theoretical concern with "blockage" arises only after the decline of Longinus's influence. I think that this concern is already present in Longinus and can be found in certain phrasings of Addison (especially *Spectator* 412) more apparently than in any author in the decades just preceding Kant.

47 Wimsatt (*Literary Criticism*, I, 109) goes so far as to equate *sunthesis* with rhythm.

48 Yeats, "The Symbolism of Poetry," in *Essays and Introductions* (New York: MacMillan, 1961), p. 159.

49 As I understand it, the meaning of Kierkegaard's allegory, *Repetition: An Essay in Experimental Psychology,* is that repetition, for the reasons here outlined, is a means of finding grace. It is, in any case, as Valéry explained, an enemy of our rational wish to process art as information (see "The Idea of Art," in *Aesthetics,* ed. Harold Osborne [Oxford: Oxford Univ. Press, 1978], p. 28).

50 Kant, *Critique of Judgment,* pp. 86–106. The mathematical sublime is what Thomas Weiskel calls the "hermeneutical sublime," anticipating what I have said earlier in the present essay about the sublime in interpretation (see *Romantic Sublime,* esp. p. 28).

51 Hertz, "Notion of Blockage," p. 74. See also p. 76 and Hertz, "Lecture de Longin," p. 304. It seems to me that in order to project an adequate dynamic into the *structure* of the Kantian sublime, Weiskel has had to draw *imagination* and *reason* dangerously close to their English meanings, so that *imagination* swells into the glorious faculty of Wordsworth, significantly an "unfathered vapour from the abyss," and *reason* shrinks from the radiant proportions Kant awards it to the old patriarchal bogey that the Romantics attributed to the Augustans.

52 Freud, *Beyond the Pleasure Principle,* trans. James Strachey (New York: Norton, 1961), pp. 8–13, 30.

53 Freud, "Notes upon a Case of Obsessional Neurosis" ("The Rat Man"), in *Three Case Histories,* ed. Philip Rieff (New York: Collier Books, 1976), p. 88.

54 It has been speculated that there is a lost section on metaphor; that may be, but I would prefer, of course, to think not. See T. R. Henn, *Longinus and English Criticism* (Cambridge: Cambridge Univ. Press, 1934), p. 65.

55 Jakobson would see metaphor as a basis for repetition in that the "poetic function" is an imposition of equivalence on signs ("Linguistics and Poetics," in *The Structuralists from Marx to Lévi-Strauss,* ed. Richard DeGeorge and Fernande DeGeorge [Garden City, N.Y.: Doubleday Anchor, 1972], p. 95).

56 The definitive discussion of the absence of simultaneity from the functioning of tropes is that of Paul de Man, "The Rhetoric of Temporality," in *Interpretation,* ed. Charles Singleton (Baltimore: Johns Hopkins Univ. Press, 1964), pp. 173–209.

57 What all the faults have in common, says Grube, is "swellings" ("Notes on the *Peri Hupsous,*" p. 364).

58 The use of the topoi of malformation in satire has been treated theoretically by Michael Seidel, *Satiric Inheritance, Rabelais to Sterne* (Princeton: Princeton Univ. Press, 1979), esp. pp. 3–59.

59 I would not have guessed it, frankly, but see the conjecture of Russell, *"Longinus" on the Sublime*, p. 148.

60 For a modern discussion of the politics of sublimity, see Iris Murdoch, "The Sublime and the Beautiful Revisited," *YR* 49 (1959–60), 247–71. For the fullest discussion of Longinus's closing remarks, see Charles P. Segal, *"Hupsos* and the Problem of Cultural Decline," *Harvard Studies in Classical Philology* 64 (1959), 121 ff.

61 Errors of this sort are well discussed by Martin Price, "Form and Discontent," *NLH* 4 (1972–73), 383.

62 See Jonathan Culler, "Beyond Interpretation: The Prospects of Contemporary Criticism," *CL* 28 (1976), 244–56.

63 See Skhlovsky, "Art and Technique," in *Russian Formalist Criticism: Four Essays,* ed. Lee T. Lemon and Marion J. Reis (Lincoln: Univ. of Nebraska Press, 1965), pp. 3–57, and Burckhardt, *Shakespearean Meanings* (Princeton: Princeton Univ. Press, 1968), 285–313. Weiskel (*Romantic Sublime,* p. 19) speaks well in this context of Wordsworth's "great program of defamiliarization."

64 Monk, " 'A Grace Beyond the Reach of Art,' " *JHI* 5 (1944), 131–50.

65 Or somewhat more than a century. Although Burke ignored Longinus and Hugh Blair abused him, his influence is still reflected, according to Monk, as late as 1787 (*The Sublime: A Study of Critical Theories in XVIII-Century England* [Ann Arbor: Univ. of Michigan Press, 1960], p. 25).

66 Monk, "A Grace Beyond the Reach of Art," pp. 132, 150.

67 Saintsbury, *History of Criticism,* I, 154.

68 *Demetrius on Style,* ed. W. Rhys Roberts (Cambridge: Cambridge Univ. Press, 1902), p. 131.

69 Blackmur, "Language as Gesture," in *Language as Gesture: Essays in Poetry* (Westport, Ct.: Greenwood Press, 1974), p. 24.

70 I do not know of a fully developed argument that anticipates what I have been suggesting about the two "forms" and their relations; M. H. Abrams has written interestingly, however, in discussing John Keble, of a "conflict of motives" between composition and repression (*Mirror and the Lamp* [New York: Norton, 1958], p. 146).

71 *Oedipus at Colonus,* trans. Robert Fitzgerald, *Sophocles I,* ed. David Grene (Chicago: Univ. of Chicago Press, 1970), p. 150.

CHAPTER 3

1 Nearly all critics adopt the shirt-sleeve manner from time to time in order to indulge their audience or themselves, but the only modern critics since the decline of belletrism who consistently write with negligent ease (though others write very well in more formal, more severely plain, or more playful styles) are two of the best, William Empson and Kenneth Burke. I suspect that an analysis of their work, especially the "dramatistic" writing of Burke, would take a course very similar to the one that follows here.

2 John Dryden, *Of Dramatic Poesy and Other Critical Essays,* ed. George Watson, 2 vols. (London: Dent, 1962), II, 284. I shall cite this text parenthetically wherever possible.

3 The development of Dryden's thought is not unbroken. In the early 1670s he grew much stricter in defense of the rules of drama and grammar. In the later 1670s he again became conservative for a while in order to compete with Rymer's *Tragedies of the Last Age* (1677), but I think that his editor, George Watson, somewhat exaggerates his retrenchment (see I, 195). It is certainly misleading to insist that the influence of Rymer brought that of Longinus to a halt, when in fact Longinus is freely quoted even in the published text ("Preface to *Troilus and Cressida*," I, 242) that defers most to Rymer's standards. On the influence of Longinus see Alfred Rosenberg, *Longinus in England bis zum Ende des 18. Jahrhunderts* (Berlin: Mayer & Müller, 1917), pp. 19–29; Frank L. Huntley, "Dryden's Discovery of Boileau," *MP* 45 (1947–48), 112–17; and my note in *ELN* 19 (1981), 22–24, "Dryden's Earliest Allusion to Longinus." It will be perceived that I am leaning toward one of the traditional extremes in the dialectic of Dryden commentary, the extreme that is opposed to the objectivist stance definitively taken by Hoyt Trowbridge in "The Place of the Rules in Dryden's Criticism," in *Essential Articles for the Study of John Dryden,* ed. H. T. Swedenberg (Hamden, Ct.: Archon Books, 1966).

4 *The Poet's Calling in the English Ode* (New Haven: Yale Univ. Press, 1980), pp. 12–14.

5 "An Apology for Poetry," in *Criticism: The Major Texts,* ed. W. J. Bate, p. 83 (quoted parenthetically henceforth). Margaret W. Ferguson remarks well that Sidney's exordium "pre-presents" the text ("Sidney's *A Defence of Poetry:* A Retrial," *Boundary 2* 7 [1979], p. 76).

6 In the early 1670s Dryden was to pass through a period of controversy during which he defended the poets of "this age" against the Elizabethans. See the "Preface to *An Evening's Love*" (1671; I, 144), the "Epilogue to the Second Part of *The Conquest of Granada*" (1672; I, 167), and especially the "Defence of the Epilogue," subtitled "An Essay on the Dramatic Poetry of the Last Age" (1672; I, 169). Even in these texts, however, Dryden never really denies the larger capacities of his predecessors.

7 Hobbes, "Answer to Davenant's Preface to *Gondibert*," in *Critical Essays of the Seventeenth Century,* 3 vols., ed. Joel E. Spingarn (Bloomington: Indiana Univ. Press, 1968), II, 55.

8 Earl Miner quotes this passage in a similar context and points out that Dryden's *Essay* proceeds through its arguments from the past to the present ("Mr. Dryden and Mr. Rymer," *PQ* 54, i–ii [1975], p. 144).

9 Mary Thale notes the patriotic poignancy of the role played by the Thames and cites Spenser, but not the refrain of the *Prothalamion* ("The Framework of An Essay of Dramatic Poesy," PLL 8 [1972], pp. 365–66).

10 K. G. Hamilton analyzes passages from both essays and concludes that in the "Preface" there is a "simpler, less closely integrated sentence structure" ("Dryden and Seventeenth-Century Prose Style," in *John Dryden,* ed. Earl Miner [Athens: Ohio Univ. Press, 1972], p. 316).

11 One author, Phillip Harth, has attempted to dissociate Dryden from Montaigne intellectually. See *Contexts of Dryden's Thought* (Chicago: Univ. of Chicago Press, 1968), pp. 3–4.

12 Donald M. Frame, trans., *The Complete Essays of Montaigne* (Stanford: Stanford

Univ. Press, 1965), I: 51. This number denotes the book and essay numbers; henceforth I shall use the same mode of reference parenthetically in the text.

13 Early in the *Essay,* Eugenius censures the ancient playwrights for "building houses without a model" (I, 34). See also the "Preface to *Secret Love*" (I, 105).

14 W. P. Ker remarked that we cannot speak of the "Preface" "except in some such terms as those which Dryden himself employs in it when he has to write about Chaucer" (*The Essays of John Dryden,* ed. Ker, 2 vols. [Oxford: Oxford Univ. Press, 1900], I, 1xxi).

15 Dryden's earlier use of this figure, in the verse "Prologue to *Secret Love*" (I, 108), is far more architectonic.

16 Howard, "Preface to *The Great Favourite,*" in *Critical Essays,* ed. Spingarn, II, 106.

17 This word appears, significantly, in the attack on English plays by Samuel Sorbière, *Voyage to England,* which is said to have prompted Dryden's *Essay* (quoted by George Williamson, "The Occasion of *An Essay of Dramatic Poesy,*" in *Essential Articles,* ed. Swedenberg, p. 66).

18 Details are given by Watson, *Of Dramatic Poesy,* II, 277n., 281n.

19 I am following common opinion here, which dates back to Johnson. I am not sure, however, that Dryden always means "supernatural intervention" when he writes "machine." Speaking of quibbles in this same essay, he says: "Virgil never made use of such machines when he was moving you to commiserate the death of Dido" (II, 279).

20 Dryden welcomed the Restoration, writes David Nichol Smith, "as the return of the nation to a life of greater ease and richer colour" (*John Dryden* [Hamden, Ct.: Archon, 1966], p. 6).

21 See Mikhael Bakhtin, *Rabelais and His World,* trans. Helene Iswolsky (Cambridge, Mass.: MIT Press, 1965), esp. pp. 5–58, 196–302.

22 The shrewdest analysis of this ambiguity of attitude remains that of Dr. Johnson, "Life of Dryden," in *The Works of Samuel Johnson, Ll.D.,* 9 vols. (Oxford: Talboys & Wheeler, 1825), VII, 294–95. Johnson is evidently fascinated by the "Preface" and quotes it far more often than any other Dryden document at his disposal.

23 Huntley, "Dryden, Rochester, and the Eighth Satire of Juvenal," in *Essential Articles,* ed. Swedenberg.

24 But see the attempt by Vivian de Sola Pinto to exonerate Rochester from any wrongdoing ("Rochester and Dryden," *Renaissance and Modern Studies* 5 [1961], p. 36).

25 See Huntley, "Dryden, Rochester," p. 97.

26 I do not know why Huntley does not mention this passage when he lists all Dryden's other citations of Rochester in "Dryden, Rochester," p. 104.

27 See ibid., p. 99.

28 *Essays of John Dryden,* ed. Ker, II, 178–79.

29 There is much dispute about this, but for an opinion comparable to mine, see Achsah Guiborry, "Dryden's Views of History," *PQ* 52 (1973), p. 199.

30 *The Poems of John Dryden,* ed. James Kinsley, 4 vols. (Oxford: Clarendon Press, 1958), IV, 1531.

31 Rymer, "The Tragedies of the Last Age," in *Critical Essays,* ed. Spingarn, II, 184.

32 John Dryden, *Fables, Ancient and Modern, etc.,* 2 vols. (Edinburgh: Robert & Andrew Foulis, 1752), I, xiv–xv.

33 Many commentators downplay the influence of Hobbes that I shall be insisting upon. See esp. John M. Aden, "Dryden and the Imagination: The First Phase," *PMLA* 74 (1959), p. 28. But see Alan Roper, "Characteristics of Dryden's Prose," *ELH* 41 (1974), p. 688, who notes the importance of the parenthesis on Hobbes in the course of his analysis of Dryden's prose. Also relevant is the generalization of Donald F. Bond: "English neo-classicism developed in an atmosphere . . . far different from the predominantly Cartesian climate of French neo-classicism" ("The Neo-Classical Psychology of the Imagination," *ELH* 40 [1973], p. 264). For a good analysis of the associative nature of Dryden's prose, see Gary Stringer, "Ease and Control in Dryden's Prose Style," *SHR* 8 (1974), pp. 306–07.

34 Hobbes, *Leviathan,* ed. C. B. MacPherson (Harmondsworth: Penguin, 1980), p. 95 (I, iii).

35 The most acute contemporary criticism of Coleridge's attempt will be found in Hazlitt, who defends the historical role of Hobbes and gives a lucid account of his associationism ("Coleridge's Literary Life," in *The Complete Works of William Hazlitt,* ed. P. P. Howe, 21 vols. [London: Dent, 1933], XVI, p. 122).

36 Dryden, *Fables,* I, vii.

37 For the comparable exploitation of translation in the Pléiade, see A. F. B. Clark, *Boileau and the French Classical Critics in England* (Paris: Librairie Ancienne Éduard Champion, 1925), p. 109.

38 Eliot, *John Dryden* (New York: Haskell House, 1966), p. 63. See also p. 22.

39 Ong, "Psyche and the Geometers: Aspects of Associationist Critical Theory," *MP* 49 (1951–52), p. 20.

40 Tuveson, *The Imagination as a Means of Grace* (Berkeley: Univ. of California Press, 1960), pp. 7–8.

41 I think in particular of the very helpful but still narrow essay by John C. Sherwood, "Dryden and the Rules: The Preface to the *Fables,*" *JEGP* 52 (1953), 13–26.

42 James Sutherland remarks well that Dryden "was almost alone in the period in seeking to defend tragi-comedy on psychological grounds" (*English Literature in the Late Seventeenth Century* [New York: Oxford Univ. Press, 1969], p. 403).

43 For a convenient summary of the quarrel between "anomalists" and "analogists," see J. F. D'Alton, *Roman Literary Theory and Criticism* (New York: Russell & Russell, 1962), pp. 40–41.

44 See Dean T. Mace, "Dryden's Dialogue on Drama," *JWCI* 25 (1962), p. 89.

45 Dryden is so frequently said to be a proponent of "invention" that I feel I must invoke an authority, Robert D. Hume, who says that "Dryden severely downgrades fable and invention" (*Dryden's Criticism* [Ithaca: Cornell Univ. Press, 1970], p. 60). Later Hume healthily qualifies his own effort to rehabilitate Rymer and to compare Dryden with him by remarking that Dryden's "lesser interest in fable leaves him less bothered by Shakespeare's considerable irregularities" (p. 131). Another critic who notes that Dryden varies on "invention" is John C. Sherwood, "Precept and Practice in Dryden's Criticism," *JEGP* 68 (1969), p. 433.

46 See the character Johnson on "fellows that scorn to imitate Nature, but are given altogether to elevate and surprize" (George Villiers, Duke of Buckingham and others, *The Rehearsal with a Key* [London: T. Waller, 1768], p. 6). The character of Bayes owes something to the beclouded Socrates of Aristophanes. For a sophisticated modern argument to the effect that the *Essay* is antirepresentational, see Dean T. Mace, "Dryden's Dialogue on Drama," pp. 88 ff.

47 See the prefaces of Thomas Shadwell reprinted in Spingarn, *Critical Essays*, II, 147–62.

48 On this point, see William K. Wimsatt and Cleanth Brooks, *Literary Criticism: A Short History*, 2 vols. (Chicago: Univ. of Chicago Press, 1978), I, 202.

49 As this usage of *very* was growing obsolete in 1700 (see *OED* def. Aa), I suspect that Dryden is remembering Chaucer's "verray, parfit, gentil knight."

50 See Sherwood, "Dryden and the Rules," p. 21.

51 See Irène Simon, "Dryden's Prose Style," *Revue des Langues Vivantes* 31–32 (1965–66), 506–30.

52 Clive James, "Waugh's Last Stand," *NYRB* 27 (Dec. 4, 1980), p. 4.

53 Earl Miner, "Dryden and the Issue of Human Progress," *PQ* 40 (1961), p. 123.

54 Hobbes, *Leviathan*, p. 88.

55 David Nichol Smith thinks that this train of thought is original in Dryden (*John Dryden*, p. 84) but the general conception is taken from Longinus.

56 *Poems of John Dryden*, ed. Kinsley, I, 460.

57 W. J. Bate recognizes that Hobbes's empiricism would increase the likelihood of his taking language to be more significant than other factors (*From Classic to Romantic* [New York: Harper Torchbooks, 1961], pp. 16–17).

58 "For myself," writes Montaigne, "I like only pleasant and easy books" (*Complete Essays*, I, 39).

59 See Collier, *A Short View of the Immorality and Profaneness of the English Stage*, in *Critical Essays*, ed. Spingarn, III, pp. 258 ff.

60 Lentricchia, *After the New Criticism*, (Chicago: Univ. of Chicago Press, 1980) p. 169.

61 Benjamin, "Unpacking My Library," in *Illuminations*, ed. Hannah Arendt (New York: Schocken Books, 1969), p. 67.

62 Jacques Derrida quotes the pertinent passages from *Inhibitions, Symptoms, and Anxiety* in "Freud and the Scene of Writing," in *Writing and Difference*, trans. Alan Bass (Chicago: Univ. of Chicago Press, 1978), p. 229.

63 In the opinion of C. S. Lewis, Dryden is "a boor, gross, vulgar, provincial, misunderstanding mind" ("Shelley, Dryden, and Mr. Eliot," in *Rehabilitations and Other Essays* [London: Oxford Univ. Press, 1939], p. 13).

64 So Barthes enjoys Sade because his "pornographic messages are embodied in sentences so pure they might be used as grammatical models" (*The Pleasure of the Text*, trans. Richard Miller [New York: Hill & Wang, 1975], p. 6).

65 I refer here to Dryden's "verbal criticism" of Howard in his "Defence of an Essay," I, 110, of William Walsh in his "Letter to William Walsh," II, 173, and of Settle in his "Preface to Notes and Observations on *The Empress of Morocco*," in *The Works of John Dryden*, ed. Sir Walter Scott, rev. George Saintsbury, 18 vols. (London: William Paterson, 1892), XV.

66 John Hughes carries this notion forward in his "Upon Reading Mr Dryden's

Fables" (1704): "Thus Ennius was by Virgil changed of old: / He found him rubbish, and he left him gold" (*Dryden: The Critical Heritage,* ed. James Kinsley and Helen Kinsley [London: Routledge & Kegan Paul, 1971], p. 250).

67 I should think that the existence of this passage might qualify the opinion of Robert Hume, that for Dryden the infancy of society was "deplorable, not admirable" (*Dryden's Criticism,* p. 160).

68 Sprat, *History of the Royal Society,* in *Critical Essays,* ed. Spingarn, II, 112–13, 117, 118.

69 *The Arte of English Poesie* (1589), in *English Literary Criticism: The Renaissance,* ed. O. B. Hardison (Englewood Cliffs, N.J.: Prentice-Hall, 1963), p. 156.

70 The contrast of Aeneas and Achilles is in Blackmore's "Preface to *King Arthur*" (1699; see Robert Hume, *Dryden's Criticism,* p. 17). M. H. Abrams believes that Dryden's interest in literature as self-expression is more pronounced than comparable interests in any eighteenth-century critic (*Mirror and Lamp,* p. 232).

71 See "On Modern Comedy," in *Works,* ed. Howe, IV, 10–14.

72 As Alan Roper remarks ("Characteristics of Dryden's Prose," p. 689), "What Dryden says . . . of his work on the *Fables* is equally appropriate to the conduct of the preface."

73 Ehrenpreis, "Continuity and Coruscation: Dryden's Poetic Instincts," in *John Dryden II* (Los Angeles: William Andrews Clark Memorial Library, 1978), esp. pp. 17, 21, 23.

74 See Edward Pechter, *Dryden's Classical Theory of Literature* (Cambridge: Cambridge Univ. Press, 1975), esp. p. 20. Rymer on the other hand remarks: "If people are prepossest, if they will judge of *Rollo* by *Othello,* and one *crooked line* by another, we can never have a certainty" (quoted by Emerson R. Marks, *Relativist and Absolutist: The Early Neoclassical Debate in England* [New Brunswick: Rutgers Univ. Press, 1955], p. 31).

75 *The Essays of John Dryden,* ed. Ker, II, 199.

76 See Sherwood, "Dryden and the Rules," pp. 17–18. He cites only the very perfunctory comparison of Carolus Ruaeus in the notes of that scholar on the Delphine Virgil.

77 Quoted by Eliot in *The Use of Poetry and the Use of Criticism* (1932; London: Faber & Faber, 2d ed. 1964), p. 55.

78 See Lévi-Strauss, *Structural Anthropology,* trans. Claire Jacobson and Brooke Grundfest Schoepf (Garden City, N.Y.: Anchor Books, 1967), pp. 202–06.

79 Robert Hume writes that Dryden had "a literary outlook that is far more rhetorical than generic" (*Dryden's Criticism,* p. 59). See also Thomas A. Hanzo, *Latitude and Restoration Criticism* (Copenhagen: Rosenkilde & Bagger, 1961), p. 110.

80 We are inclined to suppose, with Pope's Donne in mind, that the modernization or *refaccimento* (as Johnson calls it) of old authors was a literary fashion; Johnson believes, however, that Dryden's was the first instance of it in English ("Life of Dryden," p. 338). This shows yet more clearly that Dryden felt an unusually strong need to stress the improvement of the language.

81 "An Essay on Virgil's *Georgics,*" in *Eighteenth-Century Critical Essays,* ed. Scott Elledge, 2 vols. (Ithaca: Cornell Univ. Press, 1961), I, 2.

82 It seems to me that Eliot is justified in criticizing Pater for his ironic assertion that

the prosaic Dryden " 'loved to emphasize the distinction between poetry and prose' " (*Homage to John Dryden* [London: Hogarth Press, 1924], p. 17). Dryden loved to do no such thing. For Pater on Dryden, see his "Style," in *Selected Writings of Walter Pater,* ed. Harold Bloom (New York: Signet, 1974), p. 104. Stylistic studies of Dryden's period often stress the close affinities of its verse and prose. See George Williamson, "The Rhetorical Pattern of Neo-Classical Wit," *MP* 33 (1935–36), p. 64. In Dryden's practice, though, as Williamson admits (p. 65), the two harmonies are opposed with respect to the presence or absence of symmetry. See also Williamson, *The Senecan Amble* (Chicago: Univ. of Chicago Press, 1951), p. 325.

CHAPTER 4

1 "Preface to *Laon and Cythna,*" in *Shelley's Prose: Or the Trumpet of a Prophecy,* ed. David Lee Clark (Albuquerque: Univ. of New Mexico Press, 1954), p. 318. All subsequent references to Shelley's prose, apart from the *Defence of Poetry,* will be cited parenthetically from this edition as *"Prose."* Coleridge definitely knew Longinus, but his judgment of him too is doubtful. In two different notes to *The Friend,* Coleridge characterizes Jeremy Taylor as sublime "in Longinus' sense of the word" (see *The Friend,* ed. Barbara E. Rooke, 4: I, p. 347n., and 4: II, p. 176n., in *The Collected Works of Samuel Taylor Coleridge,* ed. Kathleen Coburn [Princeton: Princeton Univ. Press, 1978]). At the same period, in an 1810 essay called "Parties," Coleridge paraphases Longinus 1.4 as "the compacted might of genius" (*Essays on His Times,* ed. David Erdman, 3: II, p. 102, in *The Collected Works*).

2 The scanty catalog of Shelley's references to Kant is given by Earl J. Schulze in *Shelley's Theory of Poetry: A Reappraisal* (The Hague: Mouton, 1966), pp. 62n.–63n. In *Peter Bell the Third* (part six), Shelley says that he had unsuccessfully tried to read "Kant's book" but was disgusted with "the *furor verborum* of the German psychologics" (*The Poems of Shelley,* ed. Thomas Hutchinson [London: Oxford Univ. Press, 1965], p. 357. All subsequent references to Shelley's poetry will be cited parenthetically from this edition as *"Poems."*). C. E. Pulos thinks that for his time Shelley's skepticism was unique in being "free from the influence of German thought" (*The Deep Truth: A Study of Shelley's Scepticism* [Lincoln: Univ. of Nebraska Press, 1954], p. 8). See also Joseph Barrell, *Shelley and the Thought of His Time* (1947; rpt., Hamden, Ct.: Archon, 1967), p. 197.

3 *A Defense of Poetry. The Four Ages of Poetry,* ed. John E. Jordan (Indianapolis: Bobbs-Merrill Co., 1965), p. 43. All subsequent references to these two texts will be cited parenthetically from this edition as "Jordan."

4 John S. Flagg insists that Shelley must be Aristotelian at bottom because of his "very considerable powers of analytic thought in the area of aesthetics" ("Shelley and Aristotle: Elements of the *Poetics* in Shelley's Theory of Poetry," *SiR* 9 [1970], p. 44).

5 This position is taken most notably by M. H. Abrams, *The Mirror and the Lamp,* pp. 126–29; Brooks and Wimsatt, *Literary Criticism,* II, 417–23; and René Wellek, *A History of Modern Criticism 1750–1950,* 4 vols. (New Haven: Yale Univ. Press,

1955), II, 125. The most significant counterstatement rescuing Shelley for formalism (a tactic with which I disagree) is that of Earl Wasserman: "Possibly no other critical theorist has made holistic form so central to his definition of poetry" ("Shelley's Last Poetics," in *From Sensibility to Romanticism,* ed. Frederick W. Hilles and Harold Bloom [London: Oxford Univ. Press, 1965], p. 495). An early editor of the *Defence,* A. S. Cook, can already be found asserting that "harmony," "rhythm," and "order" are key words in the essay (*Shelley. A Defence of Poetry,* ed. Cook [Boston: Ginn, 1891], p. xiii).

6 For an account of the *Defence* that stresses Shelley's interest in boundlessness, see Lloyd Abbey, "Shelley's Repudiation of Conscious Artistry," *ESC* 1 (1975), 62–73.

7 See "A Refutation of Deism," in *Prose,* p. 133.

8 Concerning the interconnectedness of this body of images, see Daniel Hughes, "Kindling and Dwindling: The Poetic Process in Shelley," *K-SJ* 13 (1964), p. 26. Carl Grabo remarks that "Newton, [E.] Darwin, and Davy . . . conceived of matter as no more than one of the manifestations of force" (*The Magic Plant: The Growth of Shelley's Thought* [Chapel Hill: Univ. of North Carolina Press, 1936], p. 432).

9 Shelley often recurs to this notion. The nearest instance in time to the composition of the *Defence* is *Epipsychidion,* 167–72.

10 These essays are: Eliot, *Homage to John Dryden,* and Lewis, "Shelley, Dryden, and Mr. Eliot," in *Rehabilitations* (London: Oxford Univ. Press, 1939).

11 *The Letters of Percy Bysshe Shelley,* 2 vols., ed. Frederick L. Jones (Oxford: Clarendon Press, 1964), II, 152. All subsequent references to Shelley's letters will be cited parenthetically from this edition as *"Letters."*

12 In this regard Ralph Houston has remarked interestingly concerning Shelley's own poetic practice that the "habit of involuntary associative thinking leads Shelley into a form of 'Impressionism' " ("Shelley and the Principle of Associations," *EIC* 3 [1953], p. 57).

13 "Pope, it seems to me, has been selected as the pivot of a dispute in taste, on which, until I understand it, I must declare myself neuter" (*Letters,* II, 290). Later Shelley did muster an opinion on the subject. See *Letters,* II, 322.

14 Abrams, *Mirror and the Lamp,* p. 129.

15 Yeats, "The Philosophy of Shelley's Poetry," in *Ideas of Good and Evil* (New York: MacMillan, 1903), p. 93. To this testimony may be added that of Benedetto Croce, *Aesthetic,* trans. Douglas Ainslie (New York: Farrar, Straus & Giroux, 1972), pp. 352–53. Harold Bloom has called the *Defence* "the most profound discourse on poetry in the language" (*Blake's Apocalypse: A Study in Poetic Argument* [Garden City: Doubleday, 1963], p. 334). G. Wilson Knight has called it "the most important prose document in the language" (*Christ and Nietzsche* [London: Staples, 1948], p. 29). Graham Hough, finally, has more cautiously called it "the best statement in English of the early Romantic theory of poetry" (*The Romantic Poets* [1953; London: Hutchinson, 1979], p. 151).

16 Margaret Ferguson calls this "the *tu quoque* argument" of defenses of poetry ("Border Territories of Defence: Freud and Defences of Poetry," in *The Literary Freud: Mechanisms of Defence and the Poetic Will,* ed. Joseph H. Smith [New Haven: Yale Univ. Press, 1980], p. 151).

17 H. F. B. Brett-Smith, ed., *Peacock's Four Ages of Poetry: Shelley's Defence of Poetry: Browning's Essay on Shelley* (Boston: Houghton Mifflin, 1921), p. x.

18 Concerning this topic, see Joseph E. Baker, *Shelley's Platonic Answer to a Platonic Attack on Poetry* (Iowa City: Univ. of Iowa Press, 1965).

19 For a survey of the important role played by scientists in Shelley's formative years, see Desmond King-Hele, *Shelley: His Thought and Work* (1961; 2d ed. London: MacMillan, 1971), pp. 4–5.

20 Of the many modern studies of this topic, the only one that considers its importance for Shelley is Richard Cronin, *Shelley's Poetic Thoughts* (London: MacMillan, 1981), pp. 3, 251n.

21 I do not mean to suggest that Shelley is original in expressing the general Romantic view of the calculating faculties. Two important statements preceding his (apart from the broadsides of Blake) are that of Coleridge in *The Statesman's Manual* (*Lay Sermons,* ed. R. J. White [London: Routledge & Kegan Paul, 1972], esp. pp. 18–19) and that of Wordsworth, who complains in *The Convention of Cintra* that "Experimental Philosophy" is advancing while the "splendour of Imagination has been fading" (*The Prose Works of William Wordsworth,* 3 vols., ed. W. J. B. Owen and J. W. Smyser [Oxford: Clarendon Press, 1974], I, 324–25). What is unique in Shelley is his eclipse of reason, not his belittlement of it.

22 But cf. Flagg ("Shelley and Aristotle," p. 48), who believes that this is "an Aristotelian way of beginning."

23 On this topic, see Michael McCanles, "The Literal and the Metaphorical: Dialectic or Interchange," *PMLA* 91 (1976), 279–90.

24 To this effect McCanles ("The Literal and the Metaphorical," p. 289n.) quotes A. D. Nuttall, *The Concept of Allegory* (London: Routledge & Kegan Paul, 1967), p. 21.

25 It seems to me that Harry White errs, in an otherwise very useful discussion, in supposing that Shelley never gets past the Baconian contrast of word and thing ("Shelley's Defence of Science," *SiR* 16 [1977], p. 322). Everyone who knew Locke had got past that point.

26 Hume, *A Treatise of Human Nature,* ed. L. A. Selby-Bigge (Oxford: Clarendon Press, 1964), p. 164.

27 Drummond, quoted by G. S. Brett, "Shelley's Relation to Berkeley and Drummond," in *Studies in English by Members of University College, Toronto,* ed. Malcolm W. Wallace (Toronto: Univ. of Toronto Press, 1931), p. 199.

28 John W. Wright, *Shelley's Myth of Metaphor* (Athens: Univ. of Georgia Press, 1970), p. 25.

29 See also "To Constantia" (*Poetry,* p. 541), in which the moon "makes things 'wan with her borrowed light.' " The sun turns sinister, or at least unreliable, in those poems, such as *Epipsychidion* and *The Triumph of Life,* which were written later than the *Defence.*

30 On the significance of esoteric religious lore in Shelley, especially Zoroastrianism, see Stuart Curran, *Shelley's Annus Mirabilis: The Maturing of an Epic Vision* (San Marino, Calif.: Huntington Library, 1975), esp. pp. 32–94.

31 See the 1800 "Preface to the *Lyrical Ballads,*" in *Prose Works,* I, 141. Jordan, ed., *Defence of Poetry,* p. 70n., points out this connection with Wordsworth. Wordsworth also said that poetry is "the first and last of all knowledge," but in

context I would judge that the meaning of his "last" is moral, not epistemological.

32 See Desmond King-Hele, "The Influence of Erasmus Darwin on Shelley,"
   KSMB 13 (1962), p. 31.

33 Bush, *Mythology and the Romantic Tradition in English Poetry* (New York: Norton,
   1963), p. 151.

34 For a diagram of this zodiac, see Curran, *Shelley's Annus Mirabilis,* p. 89. See also
   Ross G. Woodman, "Shelley's Changing Attitude to Plato," *JHI* 21 (1960), p.
   497. A. M. D. Hughes writes of Shelley's "intuitive grasp of the law of
   transformation" (*The Nascent Mind of Shelley* [1947; rpt. Oxford: Clarendon
   Press, 1971], p. 231).

35 Putnam, "Literature, Science, and Reflection," *NLH* 7 (1976), p. 490.

36 See Foucault, *The Order of Things: An Archaeology of the Human Sciences* (New
   York: Random House, 1973), pp. 355–61.

37 Cf. Harold Bloom, who writes: "The *Defence* knows all about the hardening of
   poetry into religion" (*Shelley's Mythmaking* [New Haven: Yale Univ. Press,
   1959], p. 123). David Daiches has also written of the decline from vital to dead
   metaphors in Shelley's essay, in *Critical Approaches to Literature* (New York:
   Prentice-Hall, 1956), p. 114.

38 As Earl Schulze says (*Shelley's Theory of Poetry,* p. 108), "The words of the poet
   . . . become useful conventions to the community."

39 *Literary Gazette,* 9 Sept. 1820, reprinted in *Shelley: The Critical Heritage,* ed.
   James E. Barcus (London: Routledge & Kegan Paul, 1975), p. 230.

40 De Quincey reports Wordsworth to have said that "it is in the highest degree
   unphilosophic to call language or diction 'the *dress* of thoughts' . . . [He] would
   call it the 'incarnation of thoughts' " ("Style," in *Historical and Critical Essays by
   Thomas De Quincey,* 2 vols. [Boston: Ticknor, Reed, & Fields, 1853], II, 186).

41 This affinity between entities that are normally contrasted is felt as confusion by
   the Crocean A. E. Powell. She says that Shelley "confused Art with what was
   not yet Art" (*The Romantic Theory of Poetry* [London: Edward Arnold, 1926], p.
   219).

42 *Poetry,* 530.

43 Jerome J. McGann, "Shelley's Veils: A Thousand Images of Loveliness," in
   Romantic and Victorian: Studies in Memory of William H. Marshall, ed. W. Paul
   Elledge and Richard Hoffman (Rutherford, N.J.: Fairleigh Dickinson Univ.
   Press, 1971), p. 199. See also Schulze, *Shelley's Theory of Poetry,* p. 26; Wasser-
   man, "Shelley's Last Poetics," p. 500; and Paul de Man, "Shelley Disfigured," in
   Harold Bloom et al., *Deconstruction and Criticism* (New York: Seabury Press,
   1979), p. 63.

44 This similarity is noted by Wellek, *History of Modern Criticism,* II, 126.

45 He ordered the book in a letter to a bookseller on 27 December 1818 (*Letters,* I,
   345).

46 E.g., by Emile Benveniste, in "Categories of Thought and Language," in
   Problems in General Linguisitics, trans. Mary E. Meek (Coral Gables: Univ. of
   Miami Press, 1971), pp. 55–64. For a critique of this article, see Jacques Derrida,
   "The Supplement of Copula: Philosophy *Before* Linguistics," in *Textual Strate-
   gies: Perspectives in Post-Structuralist Criticism,* ed. Josué V. Harari (Ithaca: Cornell
   Univ. Press, 1979), pp. 82–120.

47 John Horne Tooke, *Epea Pteroenta, or the Diversions of Purley,* rev. ed. Richard Taylor, 2 vols. (London: Thomas Tegg, 1829), I, 37.

48 "We are forced, then," writes Lacan in his best-known essay, "to accept the notion of an incessant sliding of the signified under the signifier" ("The Insistence of the Letter in the Unconscious," in *The Structuralists: Marx to Lévi-Strauss,* ed. Richard DeGeorge and Fernande DeGeorge (Garden City: Anchor, 1972), p. 297.

49 This is really the point, as Derrida makes clear, of Anatole France's joke against metaphysics in *The Garden of Epicurus.* (The joke is on France himself because he seems not to realize that the primitive formulation is still a version of other words.) If we trace back a pronouncement like "The spirit possesses God in proportion as it participates in the absolute," says France's spokesman in the dialogue, we get "The breath is seated in the shining one in the bushel of the part it takes in what is altogether loosed," which sounds like "some fragment of a Vedic hymn, and smacks of ancient Oriental mythology" (quoted by Derrida, "White Mythology," *NLH* 5 [1974], pp. 10–11).

50 Coleridge, *Lay Sermons,* ed. White, p. 30. Shelley read *The Statesman's Manual* in 1816–17.

51 This passage has been noticed by Yeats, "The Philosophy of Shelley's Poetry," p. 111, and of course by Wasserman in his book, *The Subtler Language.* The idea that for Shelley words refer to words was just the objection of F. R. Leavis; it was met most successfully by Frederick Pottle in "The Case of Shelley," in *Shelley,* ed. R. B. Woodings (London: MacMillan, 1969), p. 48. The self-conscious hermeticism of Shelley's chains of figures is well described by Donald Reiman in "The Purpose and Method of Shelley's Poetry," in *Shelley's Poetry and Prose,* ed. Reiman and Sharon B. Powers (New York: Norton, 1977), p. 537.

52 Goodman, *The Languages of Art* (Indianapolis: Hackett, 1976), p. 68.

53 See, e.g., in Descartes: "From the fact that we now are, it does not follow that we shall be a moment afterwards, if some cause—the same that first produced us—does not continue so to produce us; that is to say, to conserve us" ("Principles of Philosophy," in *The Philosophical Works of Descartes,* trans. E. S. Haldane and G. R. T. Ross, 2 vols. [Cambridge: Cambridge Univ. Press, 1973], I, 227).

54 Eliot, "Shelley and Keats," in *The Use of Poetry and the Use of Criticism* (London: Faber & Faber, 1964), p. 94.

55 Wasserman remarks that in Shelley's "vocabulary 'create' means 'organize,' and not anything *ex nihilo*" ("Shelley's Last Poetics," p. 509n.). This is a fine distinction; I think the word has both meanings.

56 In his most recent essay on Shelley, Harold Bloom writes: "An unacknowledged legislator is simply an unacknowledged influence [Wordsworth, in Shelley's case]" (*Poetry and Repression: Revisionism from Blake to Stevens* [New Haven: Yale Univ. Press, 1976], p. 111). Shelley was not the person, in his youth, to endure the patronizing attitude of a Southey tamely, and by 1819 Wordworth had already become a Jupiter. Thus even the rivalry of Shelley's contemporaries is less fraternal than patriarchal. Shelley could never candidly wish for the death of Sir Timothy, except by betting with Byron on their race to inherit, but there was nothing to keep him from hoping for the death of George III, repeatedly and with startling fervor. He wrote a fragment of fiction called *The Assassins* that was

apparently meant to rehabilitate that word, apparently in the knowledge that it originally designated a person who eats hashish in preparation for a tyrannocide or other political murder. Of the assassins of Caesar Shelley elsewhere wrote that "it was in serious and solemn and reluctant mood that these holy patriots [their father being their *country*, then] murdered their father and their friend" (*Prose*, 204).

57 In his *Enquirer* Godwin wrote in a vein that is relevant here and also recalls Longinus: "The study of other men's writings is strikingly analogous to the invention and arrangement of our own" (quoted by Timothy Webb, *The Violet in the Crucible: Shelley and Translation* [Oxford: Clarendon Press, 1976], p. 21n.).

58 See by contrast, again, the interpretation of Wasserman, "Shelley's Last Poetics," esp. p. 491.

59 Snell, *The Discovery of Mind* (New York: Harper Torchbooks, 1960), p. viii.

60 See also Shelley's letter to Byron saying that the language of *Don Juan* is "a sort of c[h]ameleon under the changing sky of the spirit that kindles it" (*Letters*, II, 358).

61 In this case, as Carl Grabo says, "The problem of the individual in relation to the all-embracing mind is but removed to another . . . plane of argument" (*Magic Plant*, p. 433).

62 C. E. Pulos writes: "The reformer's zeal is not weakened but strengthened if the reformer feels it to be the expression of divine or cosmic power" (*Deep Truth*, p. 62).

63 "Shelley admitted," observes Horace G. Posey, Jr., "that it was impossible to discover the ultimate source of thought" ("Shelley and Modern Aesthetics," *BuR* 19 [1971], p. 101).

64 Gerald Bruns writes pertinently concerning this passage that "language . . . is not a complex of words and structures . . . but an activity *(energeia)* or formative process that mediates between the constructive mind and 'senseless and shape-less' material" ("Poetry as Reality: The Orpheus Myth and its Modern Counter-parts," *ELH* 37 [1970], p. 268). I shall want to insist that it is both.

65 This is widely agreed upon, e.g., by Wasserman, "Shelley's Last Poetics," p. 488.

66 See Coleridge, *Lay Sermons*, ed. White, p. 60.

67 Yeats, "Philosophy of Shelley's Poetry," p. 113.

68 Here is Shelley's record of this expedition (*Letters*, II, 61): "The sea was so translucent that you could see the hollow caverns clothed with the glaucous sea-moss, & leaves & branches of those delicate weeds that pave the unequal bottom of the water."

69 But see Earl Schulze (*Shelley's Theory of Poetry*), who is most helpful with this topic, although he goes astray in not remarking the relevance of the actual "Cyclic Poets," so named (see p. 154). See also Ross G. Woodman ("Shelley's Changing Attitude to Plato," p. 497), who suggests that the Hindu and Orphic mythologies provide "an archetypal pattern in terms of which all classical literature could be understood as a single cyclic poem." Frank Lentricchia remarks shrewdly in passing that "Shelley's Neoplatonic One, Frye's literary universe, and the forces of *langue* in structuralism . . . all serve as determinative agents in relation to a subject" (*After the New Criticism* [Chicago: Univ. of Chicago Press, 1980), p. 12).

70 Eliot, "Tradition and the Individual Talent," in *The Sacred Wood: Essays on Poetry and Criticism* (London: Methuen, 1964), p. 49.

71 Stuart Curran writes very perceptively on this point: "The poet destroys his own vision, the solace of a mere aesthetic serenity, and beyond that, the resolved circle of the world's literature" (*Shelley's Annus Mirabilis*, p. 170).

72 Abrams, *Mirror and the Lamp*, p. 128.

73 Wellek, *History of Modern Criticism*, II, 125.

74 I am again anticipated to some extent in what follows by the thoughtful commentary of Schulze, who discusses Shelley's "analogizing of metaphor with the central forms of community life" (*Shelley's Theory of Poetry*, p. 111).

75 Peacock in turn gets this term from Johnson's phrase, "the legislator of mankind," in *Rasselas* (ch. 10). See Kenneth Neill Cameron, "A New Source for Shelley's 'A Defence of Poetry,' " *SP* 38 (1941), 629–44.

76 The Malthusians, writes Shelley elsewhere (*Prose*, 68), "would tell me not to make people happy, for fear of overstocking the world."

77 Wellek, *History of Modern Criticism*, II, 126.

78 Bronowski, *The Poet's Defence* (Cambridge: Cambridge Univ. Press, 1939), p. 76.

79 Hume, *Treatise of Human Nature*, p. 318.

80 Brett, "Shelley's Relation to Berkeley and Drummond," p. 176. Harold Bloom identifies a third phase of Shelley's thinking, that of *Adonais* and *The Triumph of Life*, when Shelley "had ceased to celebrate the possibilities of imaginative relationship" ("The Unpastured Sea: An Introduction to Shelley," in *Romanticism and Consciousness*, ed. Bloom [New York: Norton, 1970], p. 376).

81 Frye, *A Study of English Romanticism* (New York: Random House, 1968), p. 122.

82 The author of an article in Ollier's *Miscellany* that Shelley had seen declared that "the central principle of practical life, no less than of all life, is love" (quoted by G. F. McFarland, "Shelley and Julius Hare: A Review and a Response," *BJRL* 57 [1975], p. 406). Peter Butter has also called attention to the incest theme in connection with Shelley's idea of love as likeness (*Shelley's Idols of the Cave* [Edinburgh: Edinburgh Univ. Press, 1954], p. 13).

83 Thomas McFarland, *Romanticism and the Forms of Ruin: Wordsworth, Coleridge, and Modalities of Fragmentation* (Princeton: Princeton Univ. Press, 1981), p. 25.

84 For another view of this latter contrast, see Jan Cohn, "The Theory of Poetic Value in I. A. Richards's *Principles of Literary Criticism* and Shelley's *Defence of Poetry*," *K-SJ* 21 (1972), 95–111. Graham Hough has said that "Shelley's argument is more reasoned and his position stronger than Arnold's or Walter Pater's" (*Romantic Poets*, p. 155). I must say, though, that I think Pater's position very different from Arnold's and far less vulnerable.

85 I suspect that Arnold attacks Huxley in proxy for Charles William Eliot in Arnold's Harvard audience, a proponent of "science" who feuded with his cousin and Arnold's friend Charles Eliot Norton about the curriculum and was to be the inventor of "distribution requirements."

86 Arnold, "Literature and Science," in *Poetry and Criticism of Matthew Arnold*, ed. A. Dwight Culler (Boston: Riverside Editions, 1961), p. 385.

87 Alfred North Whitehead, *Science and the Modern World* (New York: Mentor, 1962), pp. 74, 78.

CHAPTER 5

1 I have not dealt at length with this controversial issue because it is the central topic of a recent book by Geoffrey Hartman, *Criticism in the Wilderness: The Study of Literature Today* (New Haven: Yale Univ. Press, 1980), esp. pp. 189–213.

2 See Hirsch, *Validity in Interpretation* (New Haven: Yale University Press, 1967), p. 38.

3 See Friedrich Schleiermacher, *Schleiermachers Werke,* 4 vols. (Leipzig: Fritz Eckart, 1911), IV, 145.

4 Benjamin, "On Some Motifs in Baudelaire," in *Illuminations,* ed. Hannah Arendt, trans. Harry Zohn (New York: Schocken, 1969), p. 157. In addition to this text, I will quote passages from others by Benjamin as follows, all to be cited parenthetically in the text: *Charles Baudelaire: A Lyric Poet in the Era of High Capitalism,* trans. Harry Zohn (London: New Left Books, 1973); *Gesammelte Schriften* (Frankfurt: Suhrkamp, 1974), 9 vols.; *One-Way Street,* ed. Susan Sontag, trans. Edmund Jephcott (London: New Left Books, 1979); *The Origin of German Tragic Drama,* ed. George Steiner, trans. John Osborne (London: New Left Books, 1977); *Reflections,* ed. Peter Demetz, trans. Edmund Jephcott (New York: Harvest/Harcourt Brace Jovanovitch, 1978).

5 According to Gershom Scholem, Benjamin attended Paul Häberlin's seminar on Freud at Berne in 1918 and reached "a negative judgment" (*Walter Benjamin: The Story of a Friendship,* trans. Harry Zohn [Philadelphia: Jewish Publication Society of America, 1981], p. 57).

6 Scheffler, *Science and Subjectivity* (Indianapolis: Bobbs-Merrill, 1967), p. 44.

7 Hirsch, *Aims of Interpretation,* p. 32.

8 See Gombrich, *Art and Illusion: A Study in the Psychology of Pictorial Representation* (Princeton: Princeton Univ. Press, 1960), esp. pp. 63–90, 146–78.

9 So Hirsch describes it in *Aims of Interpretation,* esp. pp. 50–51.

10 See Polanyi, *Personal Knowledge: Towards a Post-Critical Philosophy* (Chicago: Univ. of Chicago Press, 1958), esp. pp. 95–100, and Hirsch, *Validity in Interpretation,* p. 54.

11 Hirsch, *Aims of Interpretation,* p. 49.

12 Schleiermacher, *Schleiermachers Werke,* IV, 154: "Jeder von jedem ein Minimum wird sonach aufgeregt durch Vergleichung mit sich selbst."

13 Freud, "The 'Uncanny,' " in *On Creativity and the Unconscious,* ed. Benjamin Nelson (New York: Harper Torchbooks, 1958), p. 156n. It has been suggested that in 1919, the year this essay was written, Freud would not accept his young colleague and potential rival, Victor Tausk, for analysis because Tausk "would be likely to imagine that ideas he had picked up in his hours with Freud were his own"—and yet it was Freud who said that Tausk made "an 'uncanny' impression on him" (quoted in Neil Hertz, "Freud and the Sandman," in *Textual Strategies: Perspectives in Post-Structuralist Criticism* ed. Josué V. Harari [Ithaca: Cornell Univ. Press, 1979], p. 315).

14 On this point see Theodor Adorno's observations on the narcissistic identification of the demagogue with his audience in "Freudian Theory and the Pattern of Fascist Propaganda," in *The Essential Frankfurt School Reader,* ed. Andrew Arato and Eike Gebhart (New York: Urizen Books, 1978), esp. pp. 122–28.

15 Plato, *Meno,* trans. Benjamin Jowett (Indianapolis: Bobbs-Merrill, 1949), p. 37.

16 See, inter alia, *Byron's Letters and Journals,* ed. Leslie Marchand, 11 vols. (Cambridge, Mass.: Harvard Univ. Press, 1976), VI, 76.

17 Hartman, *Beyond Formalism: Literary Essays 1958–1970* (New Haven: Yale Univ. Press, 1971), p. 56.

18 Heidegger, *Being and Time,* trans. John Macquarrie and Edward Robinson (New York: Harper & Row, 1962), p. 288.

19 Marx, *The Grundrisse,* ed. David McLellan (New York: Harper & Row, 1971), p. 45.

20 The sublime in Longinus is too easily associated solely with the "abundant volcanic metaphors" of the sort that Benjamin himself shows to belong to the rhetoric of fascism; see his "Theories of German Fascism: On the collection of Essays *War and Warrior,* Edited by Ernst Jünger" [1930], *New German Critique* 17 (1979), 120–28. But there are plenty of metaphors of violent disruption in Benjamin's own work, and in any case, as I tried to show, it is a mistake to associate the volcanic in Longinus with autocratic power.

21 On this issue, see Carol Jacobs, "Walter Benjamin: Image of Proust," in *Dissimulating Harmony* (Baltimore: Johns Hopkins Univ. Press, 1980), pp. 89–110.

22 Derrida, "Ein Porträt Benjamins," translated in *"Links hatte noch alles sich zu enträtseln . . ." Walter Benjamin im Kontext,* ed. Burckhardt Lindner (Frankfurt: Syndikat, 1978), p. 173.

23 Habermas, "Consciousness-Raising or Redemptive Criticism—the Contemporaneity of Walter Benjamin," *NGC* 17 (1979), p. 51.

24 Lukács, *History and Class Consciousness,* trans. Rodney Livingston (Cambridge, Mass.: MIT Press, 1971), p. xxii.

25 See *Being and Time,* p. 97, and the further development of this idea in Heidegger, "The Origin of the Work of Art," in *Poetry, Language, Thought,* trans. Albert Hofstadter (New York: Harper & Row, 1971), p. 48.

26 Lukács, *History and Class Consciousness,* p. xxiii.

27 Heidegger, "Language," *Poetry, Language, Thought,* p. 204.

28 For an especially imaginative discussion of allegory in Benjamin that stresses the possibility of its return to a symbolic mode, see Charles Bernheimer, *Flaubert and Kafka: Studies in Psychopoetic Structure* (New Haven: Yale Univ. Press, 1982), pp. 189–98.

29 Rosen, "The Ruins of Walter Benjamin," *NYRB* 24, xvii (1977), p. 33.

30 For a convenient summary of this distinction, see Martin Jay, *The Dialectical Imagination: A History of the Frankfurt School and the Institute of Social Research, 1923–1950* (Boston: Little, Brown, 1973), pp. 208–10.

31 Adorno, "Letters to Walter Benjamin," *New Left Review* 81 (1973), 71.

32 Rader, "Fact, Theory, and Literary Explanation," *Critical Inquiry* 1 (1974), 253.

33 Richards, *Practical Criticism: A Study of Literary Judgment* (New York: Harcourt, Brace, & World, 1966), p. 268.

34 See Macherey, *A Theory of Literary Production,* trans. Geoffrey Wall (London: Routledge & Kegan Paul, 1978), pp. 92, 130–32, 194–96. See also the commentary on Macherey by Terry Eagleton, *Criticism and Ideology: A Study of Marxist Literary Theory* (Atlantic Highlands, N.J.: Humanities Press, 1976), pp. 89–95.

35 See Jameson, *The Political Unconscious: Narrative as a Socially Symbolic Act* (Ithaca: Cornell Univ. Press, 1981), esp. pp. 98–102.

36 This important point has recently been argued by Stanley Fish in *Is There a Text in This Class? The Authority of Interpretive Communities* (Cambridge, Mass.: Harvard Univ. Press, 1980), pp. 359–62.

37 Hirsch, *Validity in Interpretation*, p. 53.

38 For Hirsch's most succinct summary of this distinction, see ibid., p. 57.

39 Wimsatt, *Verbal Icon*, p. 21.

40 Beardsley, "Textual Meaning and Authorial Meaning," *Genre* I, 3 (1968), p. 172.

41 For this example and most of its implications I am indebted to the conversation of Harris Friedberg.

42 Wilde, "The Decay of Lying," in *Literary Criticism of Oscar Wilde,* ed. Stanley Weintraub (Lincoln: Univ. of Nebraska Press, 1968), p. 185.

43 See Ellmann's introduction to *The Artist as Critic: Critical Writings of Oscar Wilde,* ed. Ellmann (New York: Random House, 1969), p. xxiv.

44 Hesketh Pearson, *Oscar Wilde: His Life and Wit* (New York: Harper & Brothers, 1946), p. 129.

45 Simmel, *On Individuality and Social Forms,* ed. Donald N. Levine (Chicago: Univ. of Chicago Press, 1971), p. 332.

46 Aragon, *Nightwalker [Le Paysan de Paris]*, trans. Frederick Brown (Englewood Cliffs, N.J.: Prentice-Hall, 1970), p. 2.

47 Simmel, *Individuality and Social Forms,* p. 332. Scholem says that Benjamin took a seminar on Simmel in Berlin in 1920 and that he read Aragon in 1927 (*Walter Benjamin,* pp. 92, 135).

48 Jameson, *Marxism and Form* (Princeton: Princeton Univ. Press, 1974), p. 62.

49 The best survey of the issues in this debate is that of Susan Buck-Morss, *The Origin of Negative Dialectics* (New York: Free Press, 1977), pp. 136–84.

50 Adorno, "Letters to Walter Benjamin," p. 65.

51 Freud, "The Psychopathology of Everyday Life," the Standard Edition of the *Collected Works,* ed. Strachey, VI, 61.

52 These passages are from Sonnet 1 of Sidney's *Astrophel and Stella,* Herbert's "The Collar," Wordsworth's "Intimations Ode," Shelley's "Hymn to Intellectual Beauty," Eliot's "Burnt Norton," and Woolf's *Between the Acts,* respectively.

53 *Brecht on Theatre,* ed. John Willet (New York: Hill & Wang, 1964), p. 98.

54 The phrase is that of Eliseo Vivas; most students of criticism have become acquainted with it through the distinguished work Vivas's student, Murray Krieger (see, e.g., most recently, *Theory of Criticism: A Tradition and Its System* [Baltimore: Johns Hopkins Univ. Press, 1976], p. 11n.). See Vivas, "The Artistic Transaction," in *The Artistic Transaction and Other Essays* (Columbus: Ohio State Univ. Press, 1963), pp. 3–77.

55 See John Reichert, *Making Sense of Literature* (Chicago: Univ. of Chicago Press, 1977), pp. 1–27.

56 Richards, *Practical Criticism,* pp. 263–64.

57 This is the underlying principle in the education of Fish's reader. It is worked out most fully in *Self-Consuming Artifacts: The Experience of Seventeenth-Century Literature* (Berkeley: Univ. of California Press, 1972), pp. 383–427.

58 Augustine, *Confessions,* XI, 28, quoted by Hirsch, *Validity in Interpretation,* p. 79.

59 Burke, *Counter-Statement* (New York: Harcourt, Brace, 1931), p. 45.

60 This phrase is at the heart of Harold Bloom's essay, "Agon: Revisionism and Critical Personality," *Raritan* I, i (1981), 18–47.

61 Alter, "On Walter Benjamin," *Commentary* 48 (Sept. 1969), p. 91.

62 Arnold, "The Function of Criticism," in *Poetry and Criticism of Matthew Arnold,* ed. A. Dwight Culler (Boston: Houghton Mifflin, 1961), p. 244.

63 Eliot, "What is a Classic?" in *On Poetry and Poets* (New York: Farrar, Straus, Giroux, 1961), p. 59.

64 The similarity has been noticed by other writers, viz., Stanley Mitchell, in Walter Benjamin, *Understanding Brecht,* trans. Anna Bostock (London: New Left Books, 1973), p. xvi, and Jameson, *Marxism and Form,* p. 72.

65 Wellek, "Walter Benjamin's Literary Criticism in His Marxist Phase," in *The Personality of the Critic,* ed. Joseph Strelka (University Park: Pennsylvania State Univ. Press, 1973), p. 172.

66 George Steiner feels that the Spenglerian moment is present in Benjamin's idea of the Baroque *Trauer* ("Introduction," in Benjamin, *Origin of German Tragic Drama,* p. 24).

67 See Shierry Weber, "Walter Benjamin: Commodity Fetishism, the Modern, and the Experience of History," in *The Unknown Dimension: European Marxism Since Lenin,* ed. Dick Howard and Karl E. Klare (New York: Basic Books, 1972), p. 265.

68 Hartman, *Criticism in the Wilderness,* p. 64.

69 This is in fact part of the history-oriented Habermas's critique of him. Habermas argues that "shock is not socioeconomically induced but universal" ("Consciousness-Raising or Redemptive Criticism," p. 67).

70 Igor S. Kon, "The Concept of Alienation in Modern Society," in *Marxism and Sociology: Views from Eastern Europe,* ed. Peter Berger (New York: Appleton-Century-Crofts, 1969), p. 146.

INDEX

Abrams, Meyer H., 128, 158
Addison, Joseph, 69, 78, 106, 117, 123
Adorno, Theodor Wiesengrund, 177, 185, 193, 194, 203
Aeschylus, 33; *Oresteia,* 39
allegory, 32, 33, 61, 139, 140, 184, 186, 205; in Benjamin, 180, 183, 192, 194, 203, 231 n. 28
Alter, Robert, 200
Aragon, Louis, 191–92
Arendt, Hannah, 180
Aristotle, 11–45 passim, 47, 50–51, 58, 111, 121, 136, 168; imitation in, 3, 13, 17, 20–21, 23–24, 39, 71, 209 n. 25; Mean in, 11, 44–45, 66, 80, 120, 171; influence of, 11, 65, 84, 87, 116, 125, 153; on kinship, 12, 14, 41, 43–44, 162–63, 171; on *pathos,* 12, 18–19, 25, 40, 42–43; *Nicomachean Ethics,* 13; language in, 14–15, 22; *Politics,* 14–15, 77, 187; *Metaphysics,* 16; form and substance in, 16–17, 20, 22, 24, 32, 53, 169; *Categories,* 17, 141; style of, 18, 199; *kosmos* in, 19, 38, 40, 44; catharsis in, 20, 25–26, 30, 60, 77, 192, 210 n. 35; *Rhetoric,* 22, 26, 42, 49, 76; form in, 23, 32–33, 38, 102; *hamartia* in, 28, 30, 198; *Physics,* 31; the irrational in, 33–35, 38, 43, 104; as a reader, 34, 38, 59, 85; era of, 63, 107. *See also* character; formalism; language; Longinus; recognition; unity
—*Poetics:* as recognition scene, 12; as semiotics, 14–16, 26; as physics, 17, 30; actuality in, 31; sincerity in, 54
Arnold, Matthew, 27, 40, 93; "Literature and Science," 164–67 passim; "The Function of Criticism," 200–01
Artaud, Antonin, 192
Auden, Wystan Hugh, 79
Auerbach, Erich, 34
Augustine of Hippo, Saint, 198

Bacon, Sir Francis, 126, 128–29, 136, 153
Bakhtin, Mikhael, 98

Bally, Charles, 174
Barbaro, Umberto, 7
Barthes, Roland, 114–15, 199
Baudelaire, Charles, 186, 203
Beardsley, Monroe, 188–89
Benjamin, Walter, 3, 87, 115, 177–86 passim, 191–200 passim, 202–05 passim; on distraction, 4, 171, 178, 192–93, 197, 199; aura vs. distraction in, 186, 191, 193–94, 196, 203. *See also* allegory; distraction; dualism; history
Berkeley, George, 132–33
Blackmore, Sir Richard, 99, 100, 110
Blackmur, Richard P., 84
Blake, William, 2, 138
Bloom, Harold, 68, 170–71, 200
Boileau-Despréaux, Nicolas, 50, 83, 88, 125
Brecht, Bertolt, 192, 193–94, 196, 203
Breton, André, 183
Bronowski, Jacob, 161–62
Burckhardt, Sigurd, 82
Burke, Edmund, 61, 65, **69**, 78, 84, 201
Burke, Kenneth, 26, 197, 198–99, 201
Bush, Douglas, 135
Butcher, Samuel Henry, 11, 18, 31
Byron, George Gordon, 6th Baron, 126, 128, 176

character, 27, 30, 51, 85, 189; in Aristotle, 13, 26–30, 36, 40, 50; in Dryden, 27, 108, 109, 118, 120; in Longinus, 50–52. *See also* Johnson, Samuel
Chaucer, Geoffrey, 88, 100, 102–03, 108–09, 114, 116, 122–23; Dryden's edition of, 97, 122; *Canterbury Tales,* 98, 104, 111, 113
Cicero, 77, 199
Coleridge, Samuel Taylor, 32, 125, 143, 150, 152, 164, 194, 197; on organic form, 11, 32, 153; *Biographia Literaria,* 70, 104, 128, 142
Collier, Jeremy, 89, 98, 115, 124
Cowley, Abraham, 96
criticism, 87, 110, 128, 166, 184, 196; history